EVERYTHING

YOU NEED TO KNOW ABOUT...

Spells and Charms

EVERYTHING

YOU NEED TO KNOW ABOUT...

Spells and Charms

TRISH MACGREGOR

D&C
David and Charles

A DAVID & CHARLES BOOK
David & Charles is a subsidiary of F+W (UK) Ltd.,
an F+W Publications Inc. company

First UK edition published in 2005
First published in the USA by Adams Media, an F+W Publications Inc. company,
as The Everything® Spells & Charms Book in 2001

A catalogue record for this book is available from the British Library.

ISBN 0 7153 2315 6

Printed in Great Britain by CPI Bath
for David & Charles
Brunel House   Newton Abbot   Devon

Visit our website at www.davidandcharles.co.uk

David & Charles books are available from all good bookshops;
alternatively you can contact our Orderline on 0870 9908222 or
write to us at FREEPOST EX2 110, D&C Direct, Newton Abbot, TQ12 4ZZ
(no stamp required UK mainland).

Everything You Need to Know About Spells and Charms is intended as a reference
book only. While author and publisher have made every attempt
to offer accurate and reliable information to the best of their
knowledge and belief, it is presented without any guarantee.
The author and publisher therefore disclaim any liability incurred
in connection with the information contained in this book.

Contents

Introduction

When I was eighteen, I met an Italian woman named Rosa who read tea leaves.

I was an undergraduate at university at the time, and I had mentioned to someone that I'd like to visit a psychic. One of my friends said she'd heard about this woman in town who read tea leaves, and why didn't we give her a try? Oddly, I don't have any clear recollection of my friend – neither her name nor her face. I know the two of us drove to the house on the hill, because I clearly recall pulling hard on the handbrake when I parked because the incline was so steep.

The house had a crooked roof and cracked stairs that led to a crooked stoop. The door was plain, I think, but Rosa's face was not. Expressive is the word that comes immediately to mind, but that doesn't quite describe it. Her dark, liquid eyes drew me in instantly.

It was only later that I noticed the rest of her, that she was short and plump, with a voice so calm, so soft, that most of the time I had to lean towards her to hear what she was saying. She exuded warmth and camaraderie. We chatted easily on our way through the labyrinthine rooms, to the heart of the house. It was as if we had known each other for years.

The room where she worked had a table with two chairs. A violet cloth covered the table. The table held a blue flowered teapot and two matching cups. We had tea, but it definitely wasn't Lipton's in a bag. This tea smelled strongly of a rainforest on a dark, mysterious continent. Leaves floated on the surface of my tea and when I finished drinking it, the leaves were stuck to the bottom and sides of my cup and formed patterns that she read.

Rosa didn't consider herself psychic, but that's exactly what she was. She peered into my teacup and studied the patterns for several moments and then began to talk. She gave details about my life that were specific enough to seize my attention and talked about the path I would follow as my life unfolded. Consciously, I don't remember any of her predictions. At some level, though, I must remember because much of what she said that day happened as she said that it would.

Now, many years later, I realize that prediction wasn't the point. I went there because I was hungry for something I couldn't even verbalize. I was seeking entry to a world whose shape I only sensed. Rosa invited me into that world, and my life has never been the same since.

I saw her many times after that. Sometimes she read cards for me, sometimes she studied my palm, and sometimes she simply looked at me and talked about what she saw. I learned about auras, the tarot, clairvoyance and palm reading. But most of all, I learned that we create the lives that we live. We do this through our deepest beliefs and passions, by tapping the power with which we are born. The challenge, of course, is to do this with conscious awareness and intent. Spells are one way to develop that awareness.

When you cast a spell, you ritualize your desire and galvanize the full force of your intentions and emotions. *You shift energy.* You feel it in your blood, your cells, your very bones. You become instinct. You become primal. Your brain stirs with dim memories of a time when men and women gathered in an ancient, wooded darkness and claimed their power.

Yes, there are other ways to focus and to shift energy: meditation, yoga, running, creative work, activities that awaken our right brain, any kind of spiritual practice. But to cast a spell is to enter into an intimate relationship with our personal mythology. It creates an immediate and direct connection between

our conscious and unconscious minds and awakens knowledge that has lain dormant in our very cells.

In casting a spell, we are taking what Carlos Castaneda called a leap into the void and are trusting that we will land on both feet.

Safety notes

· Never leave a burning candle unattended; set candles on a secure surface away from flammable items.
· Do not use essential oils directly onto the skin – always dilute with a carrier, or base, oil such as almond. Do not ingest essential oils because some can be toxic. Do not use essential oils if you are pregnant or are suffering from any serious medical complaint. If in doubt, seek medical advice first.
· When lighting and using a smudge stick (herb bundle) for ritual space-clearing, always hold a heat-resistant dish or other receptacle under the smouldering stick to catch any embers. If you burn incense, always set the incense on a secure surface away from flammable items, and do not leave it unattended.

Part I

Magic All Around Us

Chapter One
A Magical World

Fairy Tales and Myths

Snow White, Cinderella, The Wizard of Oz, Alice in Wonderland, Beauty and the Beast, Peter Pan, Star Wars. For most of us, these stories are where we first discovered spells and potions, wizards and witches, and the endless struggle between good and evil. Fairy tales showed us that the world is filled with magic – inanimate objects such as mirrors, stones, and gems have certain powers; animals talk, plants think; and, with a sprinkling of dust, kids can fly.

Then we, like Peter Pan, grew up and forgot about magic. Our lives became a little less rich, our imaginations started to shrivel, and for most of the time, we were mired in the mundane details of our daily lives. Once in a while, however, we recaptured some of that early magic through books and films such as *The Lord of the Rings* and *Harry Potter* series.

Did Arthur *really* pull the sword from the stone? Did Peter Pan *really* fly? Is Harry Potter *really* a wizard? Who knows? The point is that we recognize the magic in such stories. That recognition somehow transforms our perceptions, however briefly, of what might be possible if we, like Peter Pan, *believed*.

Belief, in fact, is the core of any spell. Without it, all you have are words and gestures, light and dust, nothing but bluster, rather like the wizard that Dorothy and her companions exposed to be just an ordinary man. But what, exactly is meant by belief? Go back to Oz. The lion sought courage. He *believed* that he was cowardly. That belief ruled his life until the wizard pointed out how courageous he actually was. The lion, as silly as it may sound, underwent a radical shift in his *beliefs* about himself and realized that he always had possessed what he desired most, but his belief that he *didn't* have courage had crippled him.

That's how most of us are. Maybe, for instance, you want abundance. To you, that means financial abundance, money in the bank, freedom from worrying whether the next cheque you write is going to bounce. But to your friends, your life appears to be incredibly abundant – you have a loving family, wonderful friends, a job you like.

Sometimes a shift in our deepest beliefs happens because someone whose opinion we respect or someone we love points out that the thing we desire is something we already have. And at other times, we reach the same conclusion on our own. In either case, the end result is the same: our beliefs shift and, ultimately, our reality changes.

Your Beliefs

In *Star Wars*, Luke Skywalker's training to be a Jedi knight involved learning how to use the light sabre that Darth Vader brandished with such finesse. But it wasn't enough to merely learn the mechanics – Skywalker had to learn to believe in his own intuitive perceptions so that he could feel The Force. He had to believe that he was capable of achieving his quest.

A belief is an acceptance of something as true. In the 1400s, for example, people *believed* the world was flat until Columbus proved otherwise. In the 1600s, men and women were burned at the stake because the people in power *believed* they were witches, demons who consorted with the devil.

On a more personal level, each of us is surrounded by the consequences of our personal beliefs. Your experiences, the people around you, your personal and professional environments – every facet of your existence, in fact – is a faithful reflection of a *belief*.

Some very common examples of ingrained and limiting beliefs are listed here:

- I'm not worthy (of love, wealth, a great job, whatever).
- I'm a victim.
- My relationships are terrible.
- I can't seem to do anything right.
- Happiness is what other people experience.
- People are out to get me.
- My health is bad.
- Money is the root of all evil.
- I can't do it (start a business, sell a book, whatever).
- I'm trapped.
- I can't attract the significant other who is right for me.
- I live in an unsafe world.

Lunar Magic

If you're in the doldrums, treat yourself to something special. Hire the film *The Wizard of Oz*. Start reading J.R.R. Tolkien's *The Lord of the Rings*. Open up a Harry Potter book and discover why adults and children alike rave about it. Go for a walk under the light of the full moon. Go dancing or horseriding, or do another thing that you love to do.

The point here is that you're treating yourself to something special. So make it special.

There are, of course, as many limiting beliefs as our imaginations can conjure. Many of these beliefs are laid down in childhood, when we adopt the beliefs of our parents, schools and other authority figures. Other beliefs are gleaned constantly from the cultures and societies in which we live.

If you don't like what's happening in your life, if you would like to change certain elements in your life, if you want to create a whole new you, then it's advantageous for you to know what you believe. You need to identify the beliefs that are holding you back, the beliefs that are beneficial to your goals, the beliefs that are *really you*, as opposed to beliefs you learned from someone else and unconsciously adopted as your own.

To discover what you believe, begin by taking inventory of your life in the exercise 'Brainstorming: Belief Inventory', shown on the opposite page.

The negative statements in the 'Brainstorming Belief Inventory' worksheet aren't facts about reality; they're *beliefs* about reality – and beliefs can be changed. Note which of the statements in the inventory you marked as a three or four. Now rewrite those statements as positive affirmations. Let's say that number 13 – *The world is unsafe* – merited a four in your answers. A possible positive affirmation for that belief might be: *I live in a safe universe.* By writing down the positive affirmation, saying it to yourself dozens of times during a given day and, most importantly, backing the affirmation with emotion, your unconscious eventually begins to believe it. Once your unconscious believes it, the process of change and transformation begins to show up in what you experience.

It can also be of great help to make a physical gesture that affirms your new belief; this deepens the new groove in your subconscious mind. In terms of number 11 on the list, for example, a physical gesture to affirm your new belief that your spouse does not expect you to do everything might be not to clean up after them. Visualize your partner doing some of the jobs you usually do in the home, then consciously give him or her an opportunity to share more domestic chores.

I have a friend who so deeply believes that she lives in a safe universe that she never locks her car or her house. *Never.* She has never

Brainstorming: Belief Inventory

You're the only person who sees this, so be honest. Check the category that applies to you. One applies in a blue moon, two applies occasionally, three applies often, four applies most of the time.

Statement	1	2	3	4
1. I can't seem to get ahead financially.				
2. My relationships are disastrous.				
3. My health isn't good.				
4. People are innately evil.				
5. I believe men are superior, women are inferior (or vice versa)				
6. What you see is what you get.				
7. Money is the root of all evil.				
8. I always screw up.				
9. I can't do anything right.				
10. My kids are monsters.				
11. My spouse expects me to do everything.				
12. I don't have enough time.				
13. The world is unsafe.				
14. I don't have any friends.				
15. I don't have time to do what I love.				
16. I need a regular salary.				
17. I'm not intuitive.				
18. You have to have a good education to make it in the world.				
19. Blondes have more fun.				
20. If I have too much, I'm depriving others.				
21. I'm fat.				
22. I'm ugly.				
23. I'm not deserving.				
24. Bad things happen to me.				

been robbed or victimized in any way. People who don't share her beliefs say that this is because she lives in a 'safe' neighbourhood, not in a 'rough' neighbourhood. My friend's response to this is that her belief in a safe universe is reflected in her outer life, not the other way around. The internal is made manifest: that's how beliefs work.

I'm not recommending that you stop locking your doors, if that's what you've been doing most of your life. Instead, simply begin to question yourself as to why you do certain things. It's the best way to start uncovering your invisible beliefs about yourself and about how life works.

Intent, Desire and Spells

The purpose of a spell is to manifest something that you need or desire. That need or desire (or both) comprise your intent. When you cast a spell, your intent is as vital to your success as your beliefs. What are you trying to accomplish? What's your goal? What outcome are you seeking? How badly do you want what you're trying to achieve or accomplish?

Defining your intent isn't difficult. Most of us do it all the time. On any given day, we make dozens of choices that manifest in any number of ways, and we manage to do it without the ritual of casting a spell. One afternoon, for instance, my friend Vicki was on her way to the supermarket to drop off a roll of film. The film developing section was at the front of the building. Even though she needed fruit, she was in a hurry and knew she didn't have time to run all the way to the back of the supermarket, where the greengrocery section was located.

On her way to the front door, she was thinking about peaches, about how much she would love to find some good peaches, the ones that are ripe and succulent and so delicious that your mouth waters just looking at them. The closer she got to the door, the more vividly she imagined those peaches. She could see their rich colour, could smell them, could almost feel them in her hands. By the time she reached the door, she was almost convinced that after she dropped off her film at the front counter, she should take a few minutes and hurry back to the greengrocery section.

The Eternal Spirit

'I do not think seventy years is the time of a man or woman, nor that seventy millions of years is the time of man or woman, nor that years will ever stop the existence of me, or anyone else.'

Walt Whitman
Leaves of Grass

Then she walked through the front door and stopped dead. There, in a huge bin on her right, was a display of fresh fruit from Chile, and most of it was peaches. In the many years that Vicki had been shopping at this store, she had never seen a display of fruit at the front. She had seen displays of beer and wine, and Halloween items such as pumpkins and novelty sweets – but never fruit.

She bought peaches, of course, and they tasted every bit as good as she'd imagined. That evening, she told a friend her 'peach manifestation' story, and the next morning her friend rushed over to the same store to see the display, but it was no longer there.

What's particularly fascinating about this story is that it aptly illustrates how our intent constantly creates magic in our lives. Yet despite our astonishment and delight when magic like this happens, we usually write it off as a magnificent coincidence and eventually forget about it altogether. But Vicki realized that something strange and marvellous had happened, and she now has a basis for understanding how powerful her intent and desire can be.

Most of us have what I call 'invisible beliefs'. These are deeply rooted beliefs that are largely unconscious and often so powerful that, despite our best intentions and conscious desires, we can't seem to make headway. The challenge is to bring these beliefs into conscious awareness and work to change them.

One of the best ways to identify these invisible beliefs is to take an honest look at the people and experiences in your personal life as though they were a mirror of the beliefs you hold. Does your boss continually overlook you when it comes to promotion? Do your colleagues ostracize you? Then perhaps you have an invisible belief that you're not worthy. If you continually attract relationships riddled with problems and drama or you attract abusive relationships, then perhaps the deeper belief also has to do with lack of self-worth.

Magic and Spells

We tend to think that magic comes in two distinct varieties – stage magic, such as what magician David Copperfield performs; or ancient magic, such as that attributed to Merlin. But the magic we're talking about is what you use to manifest what you desire.

> ### Change Your Invisible Beliefs
>
> The most common areas for invisible beliefs seem to be in relationships, finances and health. If you feel that invisible beliefs are preventing you from realizing your full potential, then by all means read *The Nature of Personal Reality* by Jane Roberts, *You Can Heal Your Life* by Louise Hay, and *Anatomy of the Spirit: the Seven Stages of Power and Healing* by Caroline Myss.

Consciousness and Your World

'Your world... is the result of a certain focus of consciousness, without which that world cannot be perceived. The range of consciousness involved is obviously physically oriented, yet within it there are great varieties of consciousness, each experiencing that seemingly objective world from a private perspective.'

Jane Roberts
The Unknown Reality

In the film *What Dreams May Come*, the character played by Robin Williams has died and wakes up in the afterlife. The place looks more or less like the so-called real world of the living; it smells and tastes and feels like the real world. But he quickly learns that in this place, whatever he thinks or desires is manifested instantly. *All of it is a construct of consciousness.*

In casting a spell, you use that same sort of magic. The manifestation may not be immediate – although it can be. If your belief and your intent are strong enough, if you bring passion to your spell, if you can focus your consciousness towards a specific goal, and, most importantly, if you don't seek to harm anyone or anything by casting the spell, then the chances are very good that you'll achieve what you want.

In fact, the creed of Wiccan practitioners probably says it best:

Bide the Wiccan law ye must
In perfect love, in perfect trust,
Eight words the Wiccan Rede fulfill:
An' ye harm none, do what ye will.
What ye send forth comes back to thee,
So ever mind the Rule of Three.
Follow this with mind and heart,
And merry ye meet, and merry ye part.

The Natural World

Despite appearances to the contrary, the 'natural world' isn't our average everyday world of computers and the Internet or offices sealed against the elements. It's the wind blowing through your hair as you take a walk by the light of a full moon. It's the birds that live by the lake nearby, the trees that your children climb, the flowers and the herb garden you plant during the summer. The natural world is just as natural as it ever was, except there's less of it than there was twenty-five years ago, and most of us don't take as much time as we should to enjoy it.

Recently, I got a an e-mail from a friend who lives in the country. She remarked that she'd spent the last few days outside, away from

Focusing

In spell work, as in life, you get what you focus on. If you're trying to create abundance or prosperity, you won't get it by concentrating on what you lack. If you want a meaningful romantic relationship, you won't attract it by concentrating on how lonely you are.

It may be difficult at first to focus on abundance when your desk is piled high with unpaid bills or to focus on attracting a relationship when you come home every night to a lonely, empty house. By engaging your imagination, making symbolic gestures and cultivating gratitude, you can overcome any difficulties.

Imagine your desk free of unpaid bills. Stack them neatly to one side of your desk or put them in a drawer, if that makes it easier to imagine. Imagine the pile dwindling, see it happening, conjure an uplifting emotion. As you pay off your bills, send them on their way with gratitude. Once a week or so, treat yourself to something special – make it your symbolic gesture toward a debt-free life.

If you're trying to attract a relationship, apply the same principles. Imagine yourself with someone who makes you feel good about yourself. Post a list of attributes that you're seeking in a significant other. Use photos, posters or anything visual that reminds you of what you're seeking. Don't keep photos or mementos that remind you of relationships that ended badly or that conjure up painful memories.

Believe that what you want is possible.

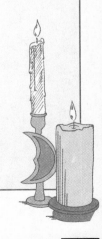

Books for Your Library

If you're interested in lunar information, especially if it is related to astrology, here are some recommendations for your own library:

Donna Cunningham: *Being a Lunar Type in a Solar World, Moon Signs*

Robert Hand: *Horoscope Symbols, Planets in Youth, Planets in Transit, Planets in Composite*

Haydn Paul: *The Astrological Moon*

Jan Spiller: *Spiritual Astrology, Astrology for the Soul*

Celeste Teal: *Predicting Events with Astrology*

her computer, rediscovering her natural rhythms and the flow of her inner life. If she doesn't do this periodically, she becomes burned out. Her body doesn't click along as it should. She feels out of sync with everything around her.

This is undoubtedly true for many of us. It's why we take holidays, long weekends and sick days. *We need time out to go within.*

In casting spells, these natural cycles that we seek when we take time out are vital to a spell's success. As the saying goes, timing is everything – and that timing is tied to the lunar calendar.

Lunar Cycles

Every month, the moon goes through eight distinct phases. For the first two weeks of a given month, from New Moon to Full Moon, the moon is waxing or increasing in size. This is a good time for casting spells dealing with manifestation and expansion. From the Full Moon to the next New Moon, a period of about two weeks, the moon is waning or shrinking in size. This is a good time for spells dealing with decrease.

Who, you ask, would want to do spells for decrease when most of us are seeking abundance? That would depend on your situation. If, for instance, you seek to decrease your responsibilities at work or at home, then you would cast a spell during the waning moon. Or maybe you want to streamline your life, decrease your debt, tie up the loose ends in a relationship that no longer satisfies you, or lose weight. In terms of spell-casting, all of the above would be done under the waning moon.

As any astrologer will tell you, the New Moon is when you plant symbolic seeds that represent whatever you're trying to create in your life. This is the time when you cast spells for launching a new business, starting a new relationship or if you're trying to get pregnant. Maybe you've got an idea for a book or an artistic project; the New Moon would be the time to start this and to cast spells for its successful conception. The New Moon is a good time to do divination.

In any given month when there are two New Moons, the second one is called the Black Moon. It is considerably more powerful than a regular New Moon, so any seeding spells you do under a Black Moon may manifest more quickly.

The Full Moon is generally considered the time of harvest. It's when you see the fruits of the seeds that you planted at the New Moon. It's the best time to concentrate on the culmination of the spells you did at the New Moon. If your intent and desire are strong enough, it's possible to see the results of your New Moon spells by the subsequent Full Moon, a period of about two weeks. Or you may not see results until several Full Moons later. But you *will* see results. Spells for healing and empowerment are best performed during a Full Moon.

The Blue Moon, the name given to the second Full Moon in a given month, is a particularly powerful time for focusing on spells you did at the New Moon.

The odd and wonderful thing about timing your spells according to the phases of the moon is that it makes you more aware of them. How many times have you gazed up at a slivered moon and wondered whether it was waxing or waning? Probably not very often, unless you're an astrologer or an astronomer. Once you begin casting spells, however, all that will change. There may even be subtle differences in your body rhythms, fluctuations in your menstrual periods, your libido levels, your hormones, or the level of your intuition.

The moon, after all, is our closest celestial neighbour. It influences ocean tides and blood tides. It is intimately connected to the ancient worship of goddesses, to the Druids' rituals, and to the Wiccan practices. In astrology, the moon represents the feminine, energy that is yin, the mother and nurturing, emotion and intuition. It is our most direct link to the collective unconscious. Once you find your lunar rhythms, you're able to tap your link to the divine.

Darkness

Some of us are larks, and some of us are owls. Unfortunately for the larks, darkness is the time to cast spells.

Forget the images you have of the three witches in *Macbeth*, stirring their cauldron and cackling under the light of a Cheshire cat moon. Darkness in the real world isn't like that at all. For many of

Morning Prayer to the Elements

'Air to inspire
Fire for desire
Water as my healer
Earth as my church.
I call upon you,
To bless this day anew.
So mote it be.'

Beliefs

If you're still unsure about your beliefs after doing the brainstorming activity on page 7, try the following. Draw a circle in the centre of a sheet of paper. Inside it, write one fact that you believe to be true about the nature of your life. Then, without thinking too much about it, go around the circle and jot a word or phrase connected to that belief.

The additional words and phrases you write down should give you insight into your core beliefs about the fact that you wrote in the centre of the circle.

us, the moment when the sun goes down marks the beginning of the time we spend with the people we love and doing the things we love. We help our children with their homework, make dinner, watch TV or listen to the radio, go to a film with friends, log on to the Internet... you get the idea. In the modern world, darkness usually means the end of the work day, the cessation of light, a winding down (or up, if it's Friday). Unless you work variable or graveyard shifts, darkness belongs to you.

In a deeper sense, however, darkness marks a perceptual change. Our imaginations spring to life; we hear and see things that the noise and light of the day swallows up; our intuition is sharper, more vivid. All of this adds to the mystery and wonder of all that is *possible* instead of confining us merely to what we think we know. If you're struggling with debt, if you can't make ends meet, darkness makes it easier to imagine yourself living in abundance. Portals open in your mind, your heart, in the very centre of your being. In darkness, your beliefs shift more easily and often shift in bold and dramatic ways.

This doesn't mean that spells cast during the daylight hours are so much gossamer in the wind. The universe, after all, doesn't care when you make your wish. It's just that in darkness, it's easier to imagine *what might be*, and the capacity to imagine is integral to the success of any spell.

Defining What You Want

This should be easy, but for many of us it's not. When you get right down to it, most of us know what we want *right this instant*, but don't have a clue about the bigger picture. We're mired in the trees and can't see the forest.

I have a friend who, after several bad relationships, decided to list the qualities she was seeking in a man. The act of writing the list prompted her to really think about it, to put *energy* and *intent* behind it. In a sense, that list became her spell. When she'd been working with the list for a couple of months, she met a man who seemed to fit the list. As time went on, however, she realized that the man – and the relationship – lacked one very important quality: her interest in the unseen, the psychic, the synchronistic, and the sublime. She had neglected to include this quality on her list.

So while you go through the exercise of 'Brainstorming: Life Outline' overleaf, be specific. Be honest. And take your time. The universe is never in a rush.

As you read through and cast the spells in this book, refer back to this brainstorming section periodically. The first hint you'll get about whether your beliefs are changing will be apparent in the quality of your experiences and relationships. Are strangers reacting to you differently? Is your life opening up in unexpected ways?

Gratitude

How do you react to a compliment? Do you feel suddenly conspicuous? Undeserving? Or do you accept the compliment with a gracious 'Thank you'?

One of the most valuable attributes you can develop, if you don't already have it, is the ability to give thanks for all the good things that come your way. An unexpected cheque for £10 arrives in the post. What do you do? Cash it and never think twice about it again? Instead, give thanks that the cheque arrived – and *then* deposit it in the bank. The next time someone compliments you, forget the *aw, shucks* routine; accept the compliment with a gracious 'Thank you' and realize this is the universe acknowledging your special individuality. Gratitude is intrinsic to any spell. Always end your spell with an expression of thanks.

Good Magic

You won't find any spells in this book that harm anyone or anything. There's a saying, in fact, that what you wish for comes back to you threefold; this also holds true for spells that seek to harm another.

With a spell, you're attempting to get the odds in your favour – or in another person's favour, if you're doing the spell for someone else. You're attempting to influence something in the future. We do this constantly, of course, through the power of our beliefs, but when you cast a spell, you bring your full conscious and creative

The Power of Positive Energy

'We now know that technology and science alone are not capable of solving our problems. Technology can be used for good or bad purposes. Only when used with enlightenment, wisdom and balance can technology truly help us. We must find the right balance. Love is the fulcrum of this balance.'

Brian Weiss
Messages from the Masters

Brainstorming: Life Outline

This exercise is rather like making an outline for a college course. What are the main ideas? What are the subsidiary points? How does Roman numeral I connect with Roman numeral II? How does IA connect with IIB?

For those of you who think in images, pick a favourite book you've read. What was the main plot line? What were the subplots? How did they connect? That's what you're doing in this activity: looking for connections. And remember that my friend who made her Significant Other list forgot to include a subplot in her outline.

First, select one of the following broad categories from the list:

- Love
- Creativity
- Money
- Family
- Spiritual Issues
- Home life
- Children
- Profession/career
- Education, travel
- Communication
- Health
- Entertainment (pets, fun)

On the next page, you'll find a worksheet for this activity. The broad category you selected goes next to Roman numeral I.

Under Roman numeral I is a capital A. Next to it, put something that is specifically related to your category.

Under A is the number 1; this is equivalent to the subplots in a novel. If needed, add more letters and numbers.

If, for instance, your broad category was Money, then your outline might look something like this:

I. Money
   A. Decreasing debt
      1. A raise in salary
      2. A new, better-paying job
      3. New contacts
   B. I deserve better
      1. Good organizational skills
      2. Gift of the gab (can talk to anyone about virtually anything)
      3. Great memory
   C. New beliefs to nurture
      1. I embrace abundance
      2. I have new opportunities
      3. I'm in the right place at the right time

Defining what we want is an organic process. It evolves, it's ongoing, and it's the vehicle through which we fulfil our potential. Without that definition, we are floundering about, looking for something without knowing what it is.

Worksheet for Brainstorming

I. _____

   A. _____

      1. _____

      2. _____

      3. _____

   B. _____

      1. _____

      2. _____

      3. _____

   C. _____

      1. _____

      2. _____

      3. _____

Your Lunar Journal

If time permits, keep track of the lunar phases for a single month, from New Moon to New Moon. Open a file on your computer or buy a notebook or journal, and write a couple of paragraphs each day about how you feel under each moon phase, what kinds of experiences you have, and any unusual events or contacts. If you're really ambitious, record any significant dreams or synchronicities you have and what kinds of spells you're doing and why.

By keeping a lunar journal, you not only become more aware of how the moon's phases affect you, but you create an ongoing record of your spells.

awareness to the process. So remember your mother's advice: be kind to others and be kind to yourself.

A Zen Prayer

This is actually the first spell you're going to cast. Even people who don't pray find this prayer acceptable. It's simple, powerful, and is at least 2,500 years old. It came to me from author Nancy Pickard, who advised me to write it out, post it where I could see it often and say it several times a day. It's a prayer said for someone in need. It's most effective when you say it without being attached to the outcome. In other words, by saying the prayer, you're acknowledging that a higher force is at work and that force or power knows what is best for the person for whom you're saying the prayer.

Nancy and I said this prayer for a month for a man who was an alcoholic. She also enlisted her mother's aid in saying the prayer for this man. In fact, the more people who say it for a particular person, the more powerful it is. Think of it as a boost to the spiritual immune system. We said the prayer for a month. By the end of that month, the man had stopped drinking. Did the prayer do it? Probably not. But the prayer increased the energy the man had available to him. Will he continue not to drink? That depends on *his* will.

When you write it out, jot the name of the person for whom you're saying the prayer at the top.

May S/He Be . . .
May s/he be filled with loving kindness.
May s/he be well.
May s/he be peaceful and at ease.
May s/he be happy.

Chapter Two
Ingredients and Tools for Spells

As any good cook will tell you, the key to great food lies in the ingredients chosen and how they are combined. The same thing is true for spells. The lists that follow are by no means comprehensive, but provide enough information so that you can eventually design your own spells. I don't recommend that you run out and buy everything on these lists; select a few staples that seem to fit the kinds of spells you want to do. As you become more proficient at casting spells, you'll compile your own lists of what works and what doesn't.

Scent

Think about it. A single scent can conjure virtually any memory and take you back through a lifetime of memories. That's how close our sense of smell is connected to memory. The whiff of a certain perfume, of sea air, of freshly baked apple pie and, presto, an entire panoply of memories unfolds about the man or woman who is or was the love of your life. So it isn't surprising that aromatic oils are used rather extensively in love spells.

Following is a list of essential oils. These oils aren't to be ingested. They are best used in aromatherapy burners. When anointing a candle with an oil, as some spells call for, add a few drops to a piece of soft cloth and rub upwards from the base towards the top of the candle. Do not use your fingers – essential oils are very powerful, and some can cause irritation if used undiluted on skin.

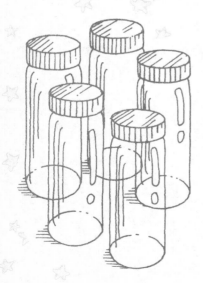

Essential Oils

Basil – promotes harmony
Cedar – instills courage; good for protection, money, prosperity
Clove – healing, for love spells, increasing sexual desire
Eucalyptus – healing
Frankincense (resin) – prosperity, protection, psychic awareness
Jasmine – love spells, meditation, to sweeten any situation
Lavender – healing, purification, love spells
Patchouli – love spells, protection, money spells

Other Uses of Essential Oils

1. To dispel household cooking odours, add a few drops of clove oil to a pan of simmering water.

2. For tired aching muscles or arthritis aches, mix one part cinnamon and sage oils to four parts sweet almond or other vegetable oil and use as a massage oil. Read the safety notes on p vi first.

3. To blend your own massage oil, add three drops of your favourite essential oil to 1 oz sweet almond or other skin-nourishing vegetable oil. Read the safety notes on p vi first.

4. Athlete's foot? Tea tree oil is great! Apply a drop of undiluted oil to the affected area using a cotton bud.

5. Apply undiluted lavender oil or tea tree oil directly to cuts, scrapes or scratches. One or two drops will promote healing.

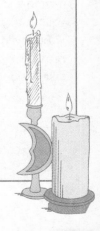

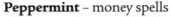

Magical Baths

Here are some traditional magical baths, for general interest, rather than practical application – particularly if you have sensitive skin or can't track down lotus root powder!

A maté tea bath supposedly cleanses the energy body. A clove bath is excellent for protection. If you want to fully end a relationship, bathe with walnuts in the water. A bath of lotus root powder and ground eggshells is for spiritual growth. Apple cider vinegar with a dash of salt in the bath water is to rid yourself of any negativity. If you want to increase your finances, mix nutmeg, parsley, cinnamon and brown sugar into your bath.

But even herbal baths can't help you if you don't take action in the real world!

Peppermint – money spells
Sage – cleansing, wisdom
Ylang-ylang – aphrodisiac, love spells; increases sexual desire

In addition to a stash of essential oils, you are likely to want to stock up on a selection of essential herbs as well. Herbs are to spells what CDs are to CD players.

Herbs and Their Magical Properties

It is not recommended that any of the following herbs be taken internally – the information below details their magical properties in ritual spells and charms.

Acacia – for meditation, to ward off evil, to attract money and love
Angelica – for temperance, to guard against evil
Anise – for protection: the seeds can be burned as a meditation incense; the scent of the fruit awakens energies needed in magical practices
Balm – soothes emotional pain, mitigates fears
Basil – balance, money, purification, divination
Bay – heals, purifies; good for divination, psychic development and awareness
Burdock – purifies and cleanses; protection, psychic awareness; wards off negativity; aphrodisiac
Catnip – insight, love, happiness
Chamomile – to bless a person, thing or place; for meditation, also a sleep aid; helps attract money
Cinnamon – good for love spells, purification
Cinquefoil – energy, memory stimulator, allows you to speak your mind, protection, eloquence in speech; also aids in divination, healing, psychic dreams
Clove – to get rid of negativity; cleansing
Clover – heightens psychic awareness; love spells, luck
Daisy – attracts good luck; love divinations
Elder – protection, healing rituals

Frankincense – meditation, power, psychic visions; used mainly as incense

Garlic – personal protection, healing, to lift depression

Ginger – love, assistance for quick manifestation

Hawthorne – success, happiness, fertility, protection

Jasmine – peace, harmony; to sweeten a situation or person, attract money, induce prophetic dreams

Laurel – for attaining success and victory

Lavender – healing, spiritual and psychic development, love spells

Marigold – love, healing, psychic awareness, marriage spells, success in legal matters

Marjoram – acceptance of major life changes

Mint – speeds up results in a spell; prosperity and healing, attracting money

Myrrh – usually burned with frankincense for protection, healing, consecration

Nettle – mitigates thorny situations such as gossip and envy

Parsley – protection, calming effect, eases money problems, good for health spells

Rosemary – protection, love, health; improves memory

Rue – strengthens willpower, good for health, speeds recovery from illness and surgery, expels negativity

Sage – excellent for cleansing a place of negative vibes; protection, wisdom, mental clarity; attracts money

Sandalwood – protection, spiritual communication, conjuring of good spirits, healing

Skullcap – relaxation before magical practices

Thyme – helps to focus energy and is used to prepare oneself for magical practice

Vervain – a favourite herb of the Druids; cleanses negative vibes; good for protection, general boost to the spirit; attracts riches; good for creativity, divination; used as an aphrodisiac

Willow – love, protection, conjuring of spirits, healing

Yarrow – divination, love, protection; enhances psychic ability

Colours and Candles

Unless you're colourblind, colour is intrinsic to your world. It's so intrinsic, in fact, that most of us take colours for granted unless we gaze on a particularly stunning sunset or sunrise, or a painting with vivid hues, or some other colourful person, place or thing that seizes our sight and imagination.

But science has proven that colours also have a particular vibration, a tone that touches us in a particular way. Blues, pale greens and pinks are tranquil; that's why you find them in hospitals, waiting rooms and dental surgeries. Red stimulates and energizes; that's why your favourite Chinese restaurant has predominantly red decorations. Yellow and golds buoy our spirits. On some days you feel better wearing something red, and on other days you need something more calming.

The colours you use in casting spells are a vital ingredient in the power of the spell. Even if you know nothing about colour or spells, you probably wouldn't use black to attract money because you intuitively know that green or gold fit much better.

Your choice of colours for a particular spell can be found in the hue of the cloth that covers your altar, of the quartz crystals, stones and gems you use, or, most frequently, in the colours of the candles you select. Just as green is a colour that symbolizes prosperity, money and abundance, pink is held to represent love and red almost invariably represents passion.

Candles are an essential ingredient in many spells. They release energy when they burn, they can be imbued with personal power, they provide a means for focusing attention and they offer protection. It's best to have candles in a variety of colours. The list below gives the basic meanings of colours used in spells. Remember, never leave a burning candle unattended or close to flammable objects.

Candle Colours

Amber – psychic sensitivity
Black – removing hexes, protection, spirit contact
      and communication

Blue – element of water, dreams, protection, intuition, health

Brown – element of earth, physical objects, perseverance

Gold – success, power, prosperity, healing energy, higher intuition

Green – element of earth, lady luck, healing, balance, money

Lavender – spiritual and psychic development, divination, mediumship

Orange – balance, clearing the mind, healing, attracting what you need or want

Pink – health, love, friends

Purple – spiritual power and development, business matters, spiritual wisdom

Red – element of fire, passion and sexuality, energy, courage, enthusiasm

Silver – psychic development, beginnings, intuition, meditation

Violet – psychic development and awareness, intuition

White – understanding, clarity, peace, protection, truth

Yellow – element of air, contracts, divination, mental clarity, creativity

If you're casting a circle and using coloured candles to light the four cardinal points, you would place a green or brown candle to the north, a white or lavender candle to the east, a red or orange candle to the south, and a blue or sea-green candle to the west.

Stones

Stones have a long history in the practice of magic and are generally used when you want or need to affect the deeper layers of reality. Just as is the case with herbs and colours, each stone has a different magical property.

Some people recommend keeping stones in a velvet or cloth bag, a wooden box or some special place, and they warn against other people touching them. This seems old-fashioned and superstitious to me – I keep my stones where they can be seen, touched and enjoyed. If I'm going to use them for a particular purpose, then I cleanse them with salt water and let them sit in the sunlight for a while, to charge them.

Fire Magic

Fire magic is about enthusiasm, initiative, passion and energy. Use fire magic when you're feeling lethargic or need to stir up passion or enthusiasm. If you lack initiative, fire magic will help you get started.

Candle magic falls into this category, and you can also use fire magic when you use an aromatherapy burner.

Just as a sculptor releases the form inherent in a stone, so does the magical practitioner release the power of a particular stone. With the proper attitude, a piece of jade will work as well as an emerald.

The relationship you have with your stones will be unique to you. Some will feel exactly right for whatever issue or purpose you have in mind, while others won't 'speak' to you at all.

For anyone working with stones, I recommend a book called *Gemisphere Luminary* by Michael Katz. In the introduction, Katz explains that the material was channelled through a woman who prefers to remain anonymous. Each chapter talks about a particular stone, as described by the 'guardian' of that stone, and covers its history and spiritual properties, and its role in the evolving consciousness of man. Entries on more than thirty stones are included, some of which are combinations of stones, and are sold through Katz's organizations mentioned in the book.

The guidelines provided below for stones and their magical properties are simply a place to begin. With time, you'll develop your own ideas about which stones to use for which spells.

Stones and Their Magical Properties

Amethyst – a spiritual stone. It can be used for meditation, for enhancing and remembering dreams, for the development of psychic ability, to attract success and prosperity. It ranges in colour from deep purple to rose. According to Michael Katz, amethyst was used in Atlantis and its purpose is to aid in the cultivation of wisdom.

Aquamarine – clarity and awareness. This stone is also good for healing, the creative process and for the awakening of spirituality and awareness of other levels of reality.

Bloodstone – healing, to connect more deeply with planetary energy.

Emerald – clairvoyance and divination, healing, growth. In *Gemisphere Luminary*, emerald is described as a green ray that 'disintegrates the disharmony that manifests as disease'.

Jade – for prosperity and to enhance beauty.

Jasper – red jasper is good for love spells, to stir up passions. Brown jasper is excellent for healing purposes. The stone also comes

---

Charging Aromatic Oils

Just as a crystal or a stone can be charged in the sunlight, so can the oils you use in spells. Place your bottle of oil in the windowsill where light will spill over it. You can request particular things from the oil or just say a general prayer. Let it charge for an hour, then use.

in yellow and green, but is most often found in the reddish hues and with mixed, swirling colours throughout its surface.

Katz mentions 'poppy jasper' and describes its effect as similar to that of adrenaline. Its energy '... helps to break up crusty patterns, physical impediments and blockages that prevent energy from entering certain areas of the body'. Jasper was used by the ancient Egyptians.

Lapis lazuli – opening psychic channels, dealing with children, to stimulate the upper chakras. The most coveted lapis has a deep blueish hue, with almost no white flecks in it.

In *Gemisphere Luminary*, lapis is described as a stone that was brought to earth during Atlantean times in exchange for something else. Its greatest strength was in ancient Egypt, when it 'charged' power meridians on the planet in much the same way that it charges energy meridians in the body.

Moldavite – energizes psychic talent, quickens spiritual evolution. I've never heard of moldavite being used in magical practices, but I've included it in this list because people I know who wear or work with it feel that it affects them in a positive manner, although intensely at times.

Moldavite is regarded as an extraterrestrial stone because it resulted from a meteor collision with the Earth nearly 15 million years ago. It fell over the Moldau River valley in the Czech Republic. Legend says that moldavite was the green stone in the Holy Grail.

I first learned about moldavite from a friend who used it in his psychic work to enhance psychic and intuitive ability and to open the upper chakras. If you find a piece that you can wear, make sure that it hangs about level with your heart. You may feel a sensation of heat when you first put it on.

Moonstone – to enhance the vividness of dreams and dream recall. Great for Cancerian individuals.

Onyx – for banishing and absorbing negative energy. Good for grounding during magical work. One of its primary functions, according to *Gemisphere Luminary*, is to help individuals break deeply ingrained habits, whether physical or emotional.

Shells as Power Objects

If you live near the sea or an ocean, you probably already collect shells. When you find shells that are whole and nearly perfect, they can be used as power objects and in water spells, to represent the ocean.

Shells can be charged just like crystals, by washing them in salt water and putting them out into the sun for a while. If the shells are coloured, they can also be used in spells that require certain colours.

If you collect other objects from the natural world, these can also be used in spells. Be imaginative!

Air Magic

Air magic involves expression and communication. The most powerful air magic you can perform is to find your magic word, the single word that resonates so deeply inside you that you can feel it racing through your cells, your bones. Once you find the word, you can use it to focus your personal power during magical practice or even to mitigate stress and anxiety anywhere, at any time. Incense is burned when you're doing air magic.

Rose quartz – for healing and balance, and to amplify psychic energy. In magical practices, quartz is often used in conjunction with other stones or orbs for a particular effect.

Ruby – stimulates the emotions, passion, love. Katz says that the ruby is about unconditional love: 'Ruby will open your heart and give you a taste of what divine love is'.

Tiger's eye – self-confidence, the freedom to follow your own path.

This is just a brief list of stones. Many others are used in magical work and, over time, you'll compile your personal list of stones and know which ones work best for particular spells.

Power Spots

Where you do your magic is as personal as the kind of magic you do. Some people prefer a specific spot that remains intact from the casting of one spell to the casting of the next. Other people have no such loyalties and move their spot around – the garden one night, the garage the next.

Find the spot that feels the most comfortable for you and that gives you some privacy if you live with other people and if you have pets. Cats are especially curious about anything new going on where they live – they may be witches' familiars, but the chances are that they'll sniff the incense or candles, too.

Interior Places

If you're going to be casting a circle for your spells, find a spot that's large enough to do that. Your goal here is to create an atmosphere that is calm and peaceful. Remove anything that might disturb your peace. The walls and the floor should also be peaceful colours; pastels work best. If the floor in your space is tiled or wooden, look for a throw rug or pillow that complements or matches the colours of the walls. You can also use it to sit on during your magical work.

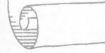

Some people prefer power spots with a minimum of furniture and *things*; others like having objects around that remind them of magic and enchantment. It's up to you. In addition to a throw rug, pillow or something else to sit on, you'll need a surface of some kind on which to work and to put things. This can be as casual as a wooden box or a board propped up by bricks or as ornate as an altar. Again, this is a matter of personal preference. If the surface is used for other purposes, smudge it before you use it. This entails burning sage and allowing the smoke to suffuse over it (see safety note on p viii).

The first spell I ever cast was in a garage, the only area that was large enough and private enough for drawing a circle. It wasn't a particularly peaceful place in terms of the colour of the walls or the surrounding objects. But it was private and quiet, and my need overcame the drawbacks. It didn't seem to have any effect on the spell, either, because within two days I got what I'd asked for. So even if you don't have a spot that's perfect, don't lose any sleep over it. Simply bring your intent, passion and belief to any spell you cast.

If you have a favourite object – a statue, a stone, a crystal, whatever it is – keep it in the area where you cast your spells. Consider it the guardian at the gates, a power object that will maintain the magical atmosphere even when you're not there. You may want an object small enough to be moved around or to take with you when you travel. This way, your magical atmosphere travels with you.

Outside Power Spots

To find a power spot in nature requires some time and intuition. Even if you decide to cast spells no further than your back garden, you still need to find a spot that feels right. You can do this by walking around the garden or the area you've chosen elsewhere and be alert for any unusual or intense body sensations: heat, cold, an unpleasant chill, a cozy warmth in the pit of your stomach. You'll know which spot is right for you.

Earth Magic

We are grounded by earth. We grow food in it, bury things in it. Through earth, we find security and stability. Earth magic is great for money and prosperity spells. Earth magic is also about nature. If you're in need of earth magic, go camping. Go trekking. Get out into the air and appreciate the beauty that surrounds you.

The bowl that represents earth magic is often filled with rice, but it can be filled with virtually any food that is grown.

Dowsing is another way to find the right spot. Dowsing was originally used to locate water. The idea is that the forked stick or whatever else you use is sensitive to the location of whatever you're looking for and dips down to pinpoint the best location. You can use the forked branch of a willow, if you can find one, or you can make a dowsing rod from wire hangers. For any dowsing tool to work, however, it should be infused with your intent and purpose. Request aloud that the dowsing rod locates the right spot for your spell-casting.

Whether your power spot is indoors or outside, you'll need a compass to determine the four cardinal points of your circle.

Casting the Circle

Think of Stonehenge, the ultimate circle of stone megaliths. Or think of the enormous ditch in Avebury, Wiltshire, that is 1,200 feet in diameter. Within its gigantic perimeter are the remaining stones of two smaller circles. Stonehenge would fit into either of them.

Since ancient times, circles have symbolized both power and protection. When you cast a circle, you're working on several levels simultaneously. On a physical level you're defining the boundaries for your work, and on a spiritual level you're imbuing the space with your personal power. In *The Spiral Dance*, Starhawk describes the circle as 'the creation of a sacred space.... Power, the subtle force that shapes reality, is raised through chanting or dancing and may be directed through a symbol or visualization. With the raising of the cone of power comes ecstasy, which may then lead to a trance state in which visions are seen and insights gained.'

The circle, then, is intended to contain the power you conjure. As in any magical work, you bring your beliefs with you into the circle. If you believe in demons or evil forces, then your circle also serves as a protective device, a wall between you and whatever you perceive to be evil. Try to get rid of that belief, if you can, before you cast any spell.

Some people use flour to cast the circle; others use sea salt. In the absence of either of these, earth, chalk, stones or brick, for example, will serve the same purpose. The substance you use to draw the circle is

Water Magic

When you need to sharpen your intuition or to boost your emotions, this is the magic to use. The sea is ideal for water magic if you're doing love spells. If you don't live near the sea or an ocean, then have objects that come from the sea — shells, stone, sand from a beach — and imagine yourself on a beach somewhere in the warm sun.

In casting spells, the cup represents water magic. It can be filled with water, wine or any other liquid that you can drink.

The Elements

Elements don't qualify as ingredients or tools of magic, but because they are intrinsic to casting a circle and to magic in general, they're included in this chapter.

The elements are powerful in magic. Think of them as conduits of your will. They have magical properties, however, just like anything else you use in spell-casting. The chart below provides a simplified guideline to those properties.

Elements and Their Correspondences

Element	Direction	Colour	Object	Quality
Air	East	White	Incense	Expression, communication
Fire	South	Red	Burner	Passion, initiative, energy
Water	West	Blue	Cup	Emotion, intuition
Earth	North	Black, green	Bowl	Grounding, stability, security

When you cast your circle, you can mark the cardinal points with any of the items listed in the 'object' column or with a candle of the appropriate colour. You can also use any other objects that are personally meaningful, which represent that element. A friend of mine has a miniature flute hanging from a key chain; she sometimes uses it to represent the element of air. Improvise. Have fun with it.

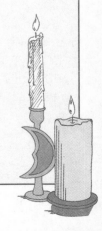

less important than the inner feelings and concentration you bring to the act. Remember: everything in spell casting is symbolic.

The circle should be large enough to accommodate the number of people who will be working inside it, any objects that will be in the circle and your work surface. It should be cast clockwise (or deosil), so that when it's completed you'll be inside it. Make sure you have your compass with you and something that represents each of the four elements (see 'The Elements' on the previous page). Use your compass to determine the four cardinal points.

As you cast the circle and reach each of the four cardinal points, place the object that represents the appropriate direction. Once your circle is closed (finished), face the east and focus on the object that represents that direction and that element. Then turn south, west and finally north and do the same thing.

When you've finished casting your spell, it's important to 'break the circle', a symbolic act that signals the completion of your magic. The circle is 'opened' and you can step back into the ordinary world.

Chapter Three

Spells, Oracles and Divination

An oracle is any type of divination tool that can be used for self-knowledge and insight, to depict psychological or behavioural patterns or to foretell the future. Oracles are useful in spell work. You can use them to explore your motives, needs and desires; to determine whether a particular spell is the right spell; or for any other question you might have.

The Ancient Search

It's likely that the human search for magical power began when we still lived in caves. Primitive art, depicting fertile women and reindeer, bison and horses, that decorates the walls of caves in France and northern Spain dates back 25,000 years or more, and there's no doubt that these images held magical significance. The animal figures may have been totems of some kind, drawn during initiation ceremonies where the participants identified with the powers and traits of the various creatures. Or perhaps the pictures were magical symbols intended to ensure the safety of hunters. If that's the case, then it's probable that the artists of these paintings were the first shamans.

Early humans probably believed they lived in a world filled with spirits. They may have believed that if they could live in communion with these spirits, if they could somehow appease them, life would be much easier and more fruitful.

As the centuries passed and rolled into ancient Greece, Egypt and Rome, the dependence on magic and divination grew in direct proportion to a belief in demons, ghosts and other things that went bump in the night. An ancient tablet from Sumeria, for instance, had a spell inscribed on it: 'Abrada Ke Dabra'. Sound familiar? *Abracadabra*. Perhaps this is the genesis of the belief that magicians must choose a magical name and a power word.

The idea that words possess magical power reached its height in ancient Egypt, particularly in the affairs of the dead. The Pyramid Texts, written in hieroglyphics on the inside of pyramids in Sakkara about 2500 BCE, is the equivalent of a witch's spell book, filled with spells and incantations to help a dead Pharaoh gain access to the Afterworld.

Magical incantations and rituals gave way to a fascination with divination and the future. In Mesopotamia, two of the most popular

**Divination
and Intuition**

'Divination is merely the voice of our intuition, clamouring to have its say. Listen to it.'

Anonymous

forms of divination were dream interpretation and hepatoscopy or liver reading. The Assyrians read entrails and, like the Babylonians, also read the stars. But horoscopes such as those we have today weren't readily available; astrologers and their art were reserved for royalty.

It seems that humans have always wanted to know what was going to happen tomorrow. This need reached a zenith in ancient Greece.

The Oracles at Delphi and Dedona

At the foot of the southern slope of Mount Parnassus, in the temple of Apollo, a woman named the pythoness (a priestess) sat on a gold three-legged chair called a tripod, above a chasm in the rocks. She chewed laurel leaves, which were sacred to Apollo, and inhaled the fumes that drifted upward and around her from the chasm. Intoxicated by the fumes, she muttered unintelligibly while a priest stood nearby and interpreted her mutterings. This was the famed Oracle of Apollo at Delphi. Maintaining the Delphi Oracle was expensive, and the common man didn't always have access to her. The Delphi Oracle really wasn't for the common man.

The oracle at Dedona, dedicated to Zeus instead of Apollo, was where commoners could get their questions answered. They wrote their 'yes or no' questions on strips of lead and the questions were put in a jar for the priestess to pick out and answer.

Perhaps the closest equivalents to the Delphi and Dedona oracles in the modern world are psychics who go into trances to obtain answers about the future. Although this kind of oracle is valuable for certain types of questions and under certain circumstances, the best oracles for spell work are the kind you do yourself.

Divination Systems Popular Today

The I Ching

This Chinese oracle is probably one of the most respected in the modern world. It dates back some 5,000 years, to the time of Confucius, and consists of sixty-four hexagrams that describe situations, events, people, and emotions in a lexicon that can be daunting to the Western mind. Even people who have studied the I Ching for years can be flummoxed by what the hexagrams mean. But the I Ching, unlike other oracles, is chatty, as one of my friends says. The Ching enters into a dialogue with you, and if you approach the hexagrams in a right-brain, holistic way, its advice is often astonishing.

The Richard Wilhelm translation, with an introduction by Carl Jung, is undoubtedly the most popular and widely read version of the I Ching. It is here that Jung first wrote about synchronicity, which forms the very basis of any oracle or system of divination. 'Synchronicity takes the coincidence of events in space and time as meaning something more than mere chance', wrote Jung.

When you toss the sticks or coins – or put down cards or runes or swing a pendulum – they form a pattern intrinsic to that moment. The resulting pattern is meaningful only if you're able to read and verify the interpretation through your knowledge of the objective and subjective situations, as well as the unfolding of events that subsequently follow. We seem to have some innate mechanism that recognizes synchronicities when they happen. We know when it res-onates. We experience an internal *Aha, that's it!*

As with any oracle, the questions you pose to the I Ching should be simple. *Should I take the job I was offered?* Or: *Is this spell the right one for this situation?* With practice, you'll refine the way you ask questions of the I Ching. In China, the person asking the questions tosses a handful of yarrow sticks; in the West, we use sticks or coins. In the Wilhelm system, the three coins are tossed together, which yields one line. The coins are tossed six times, for a total of six lines. Heads are yang and count for three. Tails are yin and count for two. If all three coins are yang, the sum is nine and is depicted as a straight line. If the three coins are all yin, you get six, shown as a broken line. A pair of yin lines and one yang are seven (solid) and two yang and one yin are eight (broken). Only lines six and nine are considered to be changing lines, which means they change into their opposite, in this way creating a second hexagram.

Confused yet?

Here's an example of how it works. In spring 1997, I was waiting to hear whether my fiction editor was going to buy my next thriller.

I posed my question and threw the coins. The first line I threw is the bottom line of the hexagram, the last line is at the top. I got hexagram 12, Standstill, changing to hexagram 35, Progress.

Hexagram 12	Hexagram 35
(7) ———	———
(9) ——— (changing)	—— —
(7) ———	———
(8) —— —	—— —
(8) —— —	—— —
(8) —— —	—— —

Hexagram 12 definitely pinpointed the situation at the time. Things had reached a standstill. My editor had received my proposal about a month earlier, I hadn't heard a word, and I was becoming worried. As soon as I saw that my changing line was in position five (second from the top), I felt relieved. That position is usually the best changing line to get in a hexagram. Then I read the interpretation:

> *'Nine in the fifth place means:*
> *Standstill is giving way.*
> *Good fortune for the great man.*
> *"What if it should fail, what if it should fail?"*
> *In this way he ties it to a cluster of mulberry shoots.'*

At the time, things didn't feel like the standstill was 'giving way'. But I felt encouraged that the I Ching said so. I was amused that the part about failure was precisely what I had been saying to myself.

The 'mulberry shoots' part of the interpretation is one of those lines in the I Ching that seemed so opaque to my Western mindset that I nearly slapped the book shut. Instead, I read a bit further: 'When a mulberry bush is cut down, a number of unusually strong shoots sprout from the roots. Hence the image of tying something to a cluster of mulberry shoots is used to symbolize the way of making success certain.'

Weird Divination

Divination by the forehead – called metoposcopy – uses the shape and lines on the forehead for divination. Its basis lies in astrology, with seven principal lines on the forehead governed by the original seven planets that the ancients used.

The interpretation goes on to quote Confucius, who cautions against feeling so secure that we forget danger, ruin or confusion. Sage advice, particularly in the publishing industry, where today's bestseller is in tomorrow's remainder bookshop.

In hexagram 35, Progress, what hexagram 12 was changing *to*, the interpretation was immensely encouraging: '... rapid, easy progress, which at the same time means ever widening expansion and clarity'.

Three more months passed before I got a contract for my next thriller. But the I Ching allowed me to sleep more easily at night.

You can ask the I Ching virtually anything. But if you ask the same question again and again, you'll get hexagrams that gently admonish you. As with any oracle, ask once, phrase your question simply and clearly, then release the question and the desire. If you don't like the answer you receive from an oracle, then remember that nothing is set in stone, nothing is predetermined. Any oracle is merely describing what exists in the moment that you ask the question – the situation as it stands now and the most probable way that it will unfold based on the present situation. *You* can change an outcome by exerting your free will – and that's where spells come into play.

Tarot

There are presently more than 300 tarot packs on the market, with artwork that depicts everything from angels to unicorns.

The tarot consists of seventy-eight cards that are divided into the major arcana – twenty-two cards – and the minor arcana – fifty-six cards. The majors are the most powerful cards because they depict archetypal energy, the situations and events that affect our lives in dynamic, important ways. The minors represent the details of our lives, the minutiae. They are divided into four suits – wands, cups, swords and pentacles – and correspond to the four elements, four personality types and four seasons. Each suit is numbered from one to ten and has four court cards.

The numbered cards symbolize patterns created by the archetypes in our lives and the court cards represent people, behavioural patterns or certain types of energy related to that pattern. Just as you throw coins or sticks to obtain hexagrams in the I Ching, you lay out tarot cards in spreads that are designed to give you specific answers to your particular questions.

Tarot, like many oracles, isn't particularly good with timing. With practice, you'll discover your own timing cards, however. The 3 of cups, for instance, often indicates the next major holiday. The High Priestess (II in the major arcana) can indicate something in twos involved – two days, two weeks, perhaps as long as two months. One way to get around the tricky issue of timing is to stipulate a time frame before you lay out a spread.

A basic Rider Waite deck costs around £10–15. This deck is the simplest to use, and many other decks are based on it. The investment is worth it, especially if you're going to be casting spells. You'll also need a book that provides the meanings of the cards and an assortment of spreads.

The spread you select to answer any question can be as simple or as complex as you want. If you're just starting out, you should probably use short, simple spreads that consist of one to seven cards. Two basic spreads are provided below.

Exploration Spread: Five Cards

This is a good spread for exploring your motives for casting a particular spell. Lay them out like this:

```
         ┌───┐
         │ 1 │
         └───┘
┌───┐┌───┐┌───┐
│ 2 ││ 5 ││ 4 │
└───┘└───┘└───┘
         ┌───┐
         │ 3 │
         └───┘
```

1. Represents the question or the spell
2. Something hidden that you need to know about your question or the spell
3. Your true motive for casting this spell
4. Possible repercussions of this spell
5. The final outcome of this spell

If a card turns up that you don't understand or that doesn't seem to make sense, draw another card for that position to clarify it. If the cards in position 3 or 5 are negative, consider refining the spell or using another one.

Ladle Spread: Six Cards

This spread is one of my all-time favourites. It can be found in *Power Tarot* by Trish MacGregor and Phyllis Vega and can be used for any kind of question.

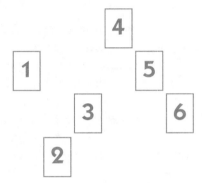

1. The issue
2. What is hidden
3. What is emerging
4. What is visible now
5. What you discard
6. Resolution

Astrology

Even though many astrologers prefer not to call astrology a divination system, it can certainly be used in that way. Many branches of astrology exist, and most of these are tied to your natal chart in some way or another.

Natal astrology takes your date, time and place of birth to produce a birth chart that indicates the blueprint of the talents, challenges and emotional, spiritual and intellectual characteristics with which you are born. It's the chart that in a way 'follows you' throughout your life.

For predictive purposes, transits, solar returns and progressed charts are the most popular. A transit chart indicates the passage of the planets through your birth chart on a given day. In terms of casting spells, the moon is the most important point to consider in transit charts. Its phase, sign and house position are all indicators about the inner you – your emotional and intuitive self.

A solar return is a chart drawn up on or around your birthday, which brings your sun back to its natal position. This chart is an overview of the year, from one birthday to the next. It's excellent for predicting broad patterns that will prevail in your life for that year, and can be read separately or with the natal chart. The solar return is also useful when used in conjunction with thirteen lunar returns for the year. A lunar return brings your moon back to its natal position, which it does at least once a month, and allows an astrologer to narrow predictions to particular months. This type of return can indicate the most auspicious times for casting certain spells.

Progressions also provide an excellent way to predict broad patterns for a year. In this type of astrology, your chart is moved forward a day for every year you've been alive. The progressed moon, as the most rapidly moving planet in this type of chart, holds vital clues about the inner you.

Horary astrology is another branch of predictive astrology. Instead of using your personal birth information, however, a chart is cast for the exact moment, date and place that you ask a question. In essence, it's a natal chart for your question. Horary charts can be incredibly accurate if the many rules and strictures are applied, but they require a fairly extensive knowledge of astrology.

Runes

This system of divination has been used since the first century, although its actual origins remain obscure. It was more recently popularized again when Ralph Blum's *The Book of Runes* was published several decades ago. Blum's book is still in print, and other rune books can be found in bookshops.

The runes consist of twenty-five symbols that are inscribed on squares that are usually made of ceramic or stone. Each symbol is actually a letter in the runic alphabet; the recent popularity of runes has led to ceramic amulets with a rune on them being available.

As with any divination system, the runes must be interpreted in terms of the question you ask. It helps to lay them out in a particular spread so that you have some sort of time frame and structure with which to work. You can use the spreads provided in the tarot section and use the following three-rune spread.

Past, Present, Future Rune Spread

1. The situation as it exists now
2. What's coming up
3. The resolution

You can assign your own meanings to the three positions to fit whatever question you're asking.

Dreams

All of us dream. The trick to using dreams as a divination tool, however, lies in remembering the dreams you do have, and compiling a personal dream dictionary. This usually requires suggestions before you fall asleep so that you will remember the most important dream of the night. A dream journal is indispensable for compiling your dictionary, and also serves as a record of what is going on in your life.

Dreams aren't always couched in symbols. Sometimes their message is very direct and concerns immediate problems, challenges and dilemmas in our lives. Dreams can also provide solutions, something a number of scientists have discovered over the centuries. Thomas Edison, Albert Einstein, Marie Curie and Nikolai Tesla found answers to problems through dreams.

Books on dreams and dreaming proliferate in the marketplace. Amazon.co.uk alone carries several hundred. Some of the most interesting are:

- *The Universal Dream Key: The 12 Most Common Dream Themes Around the World* and *Creative Dreaming: Plan and Control Your Dreams to Develop Creativity, Overcome Fears, Solve Problems, and Create a Better Self,* both by Patricia Garfield, PhD.
- *The Complete Dream Dictionary: A Practical Guide to Interpreting Dreams* by Pamela Ball
- *Writers Dreaming* by Naomi Epel

Pendulum

A pendulum is great for obtaining information quickly and can be used for virtually any kind of yes/no question. You may want to try it in terms of which spells in this book will work best for you.

Typically, a pendulum consists of a crystal or some other stone hung from a necklace or chain, or even a piece of string. You hold the chain at the top, so the stone or crystal hangs at the bottom, then open your hand, palm upwards, and let the stone dangle over it. Before you pose any questions, ask which direction the pendulum will move to indicate yes and which direction it will move to indicate no. The motion differs for everyone.

Once you establish the yes/no direction, pose your question. Keep it simple and direct. To build confidence in the process, you may want to keep a notebook of questions you ask, the date, the response, and what happens.

Crystal pendulums seem to be sensitive to the presence of other people. So if you're using one in a room filled with sceptics or the mood in a group is predominately negative, move off by yourself. Then later, at home, cleanse the pendulum by soaking it in salt water. The next day, hold it up in the sunlight, which 'charges' it.

Scrying

Scrying is a type of divination in which a reflective surface of some kind is used to heighten intuitive awareness. The surface used to

The Senoi Dreamers

The Senoi people of Malaysia live by a philosophy based on dreams and dream interpretation. Dreams, in fact, are central to their lives and are used for timing important events, for the development of mental and emotional stability, and for a host of other traits and talents.

Senoi children are taught, from a very young age, the techniques of dream control. These techniques, according to dream researcher and writer Patricia Garfield, focus on three principles: 'to confront and conquer danger, to advance toward pleasure, and to achieve a positive outcome'.

It would seem that we, in the Western world, might benefit from using some of these techniques!

induce this awareness was traditionally a crystal ball. But a mirror, the surface of a smooth stone or crystal, flames of a fire, even moonlit water serve the same purpose.

The most famous scryer was undoubtedly Nostradamus. He sat for hours at a time, staring into a bowl of water as visions of future times appeared before him. His quatrains, written about his visions, are believed to predict events that will extend well past the twenty-first century.

The best results for scrying are obtained during the Full Moon.

Other Divination Techniques

Animals as Oracles

Before you read this section, complete the brainstorming activity opposite. It will provide an overview of the role that animals play in your life – and thus the ways in which they may act as oracles for you.

Just about anything can be used for divination – and probably has been at some point in the distant past. Sticks, stones, shells, animal entrails, clouds, grains of sand, a bowl of water, a flame, fire, puddles, animals. *Whatever focuses your attention and to which you assign meaning can be used as a divination technique.*

One of my favourite divination tools involves animals. In a given day, for instance, what types of animals – besides family pets – do you come across? Did a dragonfly zip past your windscreen on your way to work the other day? Did a grass snake get into your garage? Is a particular kind of bird nesting in a tree in your garden? Do certain types of reptiles appear with regularity in your life? The idea here is that when an animal catches our attention, some kind of archetypal energy is being expressed through that creature.

Frogs are usually a good omen for me. When a frog appears in our house, we know something good is on the way. We note who sees the frog and in which room it appears; these details usually provide clues about the nature of what's coming and who in the family will be most affected. Over the years, the appearance of frogs has preceded royalty cheques, a prize, good news in general and unexpected visits from old friends, among other things.

Brainstorming: You and Animals

Circle the appropriate number that applies to your belief about each statement. One applies once in a blue moon, two applies occasionally, three applies often, four applies most of the time.

1. My pets are members of my family, not chattel.   1 2 3 4

2. Animals have an important place in my life.   1 2 3 4

3. Animals have emotions.   1 2 3 4

4. Animals are intelligent.   1 2 3 4

5. Animals act as healers.   1 2 3 4

6. I enjoy books and movies about animals.   1 2 3 4

7. Animals are psychic.   1 2 3 4

8. My pets sense my moods and feelings.   1 2 3 4

9. Animals teach me about myself.   1 2 3 4

10. Animals are messengers in my life.   1 2 3 4

Score:
36–40: Read on
30–35: Read with an open mind
25–29: You'd better explore your scepticism before reading on
20 and below: Skip the animal section

Instant Divination

When you have a pressing question and don't have access to any divination tools, tell yourself that the next voice you hear will provide your answer. It may be a voice on the radio, the TV or the voice of someone you live with. Or you can tell yourself that the next thing that seizes your attention will answer the question.

To get the answer we need, all we have to do is ask.

Insects often play the roles of messengers in my life. A dragonfly that flits past my car windscreen usually means good news soon – through the post, e-mail, or by phone. A dragonfly that got into our house recently was killed by one of our cats. I immediately thought, 'Oh-oh'. Sure enough, that afternoon our online service went down and for a week or so, we had no e-mail.

If you have an affinity for animals and have had any similar experience with animals, Ted Andrews's book, *Animal-Wise: The Spirit Language and Signs of Nature,* may provide essential clues about how animals act as oracles in your life. As Andrews writes, 'In understanding the language of animals... we must develop the mindset that *everything has significance...*'

Your Life as Oracle

If you scored twenty or below on the 'You and Animals' brainstorming exercise on the previous page, then you probably should skip this section as well. To the sceptic's mind, the idea that events in your life can act as oracles may be too much of a stretch. If you scored between twenty-one and twenty-five on the brainstorming activity, then you may find this part hard to swallow, but you'll probably read it anyway because you bought the book.

When events in your life act as oracles, you're experiencing synchronicity in a dramatic and very personal way. The events or objects can involve just about anything. Sometimes the connection to something in your life will be glaringly obvious; at other times, you may have to interpret the event or object as you might a dream.

Cars

If you live in an area where a car is a necessity, then some of the oracular events you experience may revolve around cars. Here are some fascinating true incidents:

A woman involved with a married man is on her way to their rendezvous, but her brakes fail and she can't keep their appointment. She realizes the failed brakes on her car means that she needs to 'apply the brakes' in the relationship.

A married couple are en route to their holiday destination when they have a flat tyre and discover they have no spare. They have to walk two miles to the nearest public phone box, and during the walk, begin to talk about their relationship. They both realize the relationship has 'gone flat' and they have no time to 'spare' in mending it – or ending it.

Some people seem to have car problems that happen over and over again. First the alternator goes, then the air conditioning or the radio, then the exhaust pipe falls off. So they trade in the old car for a new one and often find that the new car also has problems. *It's a nightmare* or *I got ripped off* are common laments in situations like this. But until the inner condition is rectified, the problems usually keep cropping up in one form or another. The inner self literally begs to be recognized.

Your Home

Our homes are our castles, our refuges and sanctuaries, the places where our public façades and masks drop away and we have the most freedom to be who we are. In consequence, a repetitive event in the home usually reflects the collective inner conditions of the people who live there. Quite often, these patterns portend a future event or situation. The challenge lies in the interpretation of the patterns to decipher the message.

Take the following example. In a single month, a family had four of their appliances go berserk. The fridge broke down. The tumble dryer and the TV died. They had to replace their garage door. The next month, one of the toilets in their house sprang a leak – a slow, innocuous leak that finally required the expertise of a plumber. Yeah, well, so what? It's just the normal wear and tear on a house, right?

That explanation is fine on one level. But by digging a bit deeper and looking at the function of the appliances and what went wrong with them, the pattern becomes apparent. The broken TV represented a breakdown in communication within the family. The broken garage door concerned the ease and difficulty with which the family released old relationships and situations and embraced new opportunities. Metaphor: that's the language of the inner self, and its voice is as loud or as soft as it has to be in order to be heard.

Travel

When we travel, certain habits and customs desert us. We are disconnected from the familiar, the prosaic. Sometimes, our frame of reference goes right out the window. As a result, travel to an unfamiliar place allows the inner self a uniquely rich atmosphere in which to weave its magic – and its confusion.

A young woman, a college student in Madrid for a year, got lost. She didn't know Spanish well enough to ask directions. She wandered along a city street, panic rising in her chest, and suddenly saw an American tourist in front of her wearing a T-shirt that read, *You aren't lost*. Two blocks later, she recognized an intersection and found her way back to her hotel.

A woman en route to the United States left from gate 33, sat in seat 33, and the flight number was 33. She realized that her mother, who was in a nursing home, stayed in room 33. Puzzled by the repetition of the number, she threw an I Ching about it and got hexagram 33, 'retreat'. She was in retreat from the situation with her mother.

A woman on a travel writer's tour of the Amazon was the only person in the group whose luggage was misplaced, who had passport problems and who became ill from the food. She recognized that her situation was a perfect reflection of her life at that time, and took steps to remedy it.

In addition to these three areas, oracular events also happen in the areas of work, health, finances and money and our relationships.

As you become aware of these phenomena, keep a journal of the events. In this way, you'll create a record of what has happened and how the events parallelled what was going on in your life.

Palmistry

This one smacks of fortune tellers at the fair. But palmistry has a long tradition. Supposedly, when Buddha was born, the sages recognized him by studying the symbols on his feet and his palms. The Hindus, Chinese, Japanese and the ancient Greeks and Romans were also said to practise this form of divination.

Chapter Four

Magic in Other Cultures

Santería

Santería is often referred to as a Cuban mystery religion. But what, exactly, does that mean? Is it really a religion, or is it more mystery than anything else?

Santería, which literally means the worship of saints, is actually a meld of Catholicism and Nigerian paganism that evolved centuries ago, when Yoruba slaves were taken from Nigeria to Cuba. It consists of a vast panoply of saints or *orishas*, which are a combination of Catholic saints and Yoruba gods and goddesses. Many of these *orishas* resemble mythological gods. Take Elegguá, who is a messenger of the *orishas*, the guardian at the gates; he sounds a lot like Mercury. Oshún, the *orisha* of love and marriage, is the equivalent of Venus. Changó, the patron saint of fire, thunder and lightning, could be compared to Zeus.

Over the centuries that Santería evolved, some of the *orishas* became associated with saints of the opposite gender, so they actually have two names. Changó is also known as St Barbara, the Virgin Mary of the Middle Ages. Obatalá, the patron saint of peace and purity, is also known as Our Lady of Mercy.

When an initiate to the religion becomes a santero (or santera, if she's female) he agrees to 'worship the saints, to observe their feasts, obey their commands and conduct their rituals', writes Migene Gonzalez-Wippler, author of *The Santería Experience*. 'In exchange for this absolute submission, he gains supernatural powers, protection against evil and the ability to foresee the future and even to shape the future according to his will.'

Included in a santero's work with clients is the casting of spells. As in traditional magical practices, there are spells for virtually anything and everything. But these spells are tailored to fit the belief system that Santería encompasses, so the rituals and many of the ingredients are vastly different.

A practising santero usually works in an area separate from his home, in a shed or room that is often on the same property. The work area is crowded with icons of the *orishas* and any other saints on whom the santero calls in his work. There's usually an altar that boasts freshly cut flowers, a bottle of Florida water, which is a type of cheap cologne used in many of the spells, a bowl of fresh water and other icons and statues of saints.

Nelly the Santera

In the early 1980s, shortly after half a million Cubans fled that island and arrived in South Florida, I was teaching English to Cuban refugees through a federally funded programme. My first exposure to Santería came through my Cuban boss, a woman who introduced me to Nelly, a santera. Even now, more than two decades later, I can easily conjure the moods and scents of the shed where she worked.

The inside of the shed was so jammed with religious icons, statues, candles and fresh flowers that there was barely space for the two of us. Initially, Nelly got me to stand in a shaft of light and asked me to turn slowly in place while she did a *limpieza*, or cleansing, of my energy field. She ran her hands through the air, several inches from my body, beginning at the crown of my head and going down one side and up the other. She repeated this with a bouquet of flowers, then threw the flowers out. The flowers, Nelly explained, had absorbed negative energy from my energy field, and by throwing them out, she was also ridding me forever of the negative energy. She lit a cigar and blew smoke around me, fanning the smoke with her hands so that it surrounded me. This, she said, cleansed my energy field.

Then we sat at a small wooden table and she flicked handfuls of Florida water at me, murmured an incantation and blew more cigar smoke around me. At this point, I was feeling claustrophobic and nauseated by the smoke, but I didn't want to offend her by hurrying her. She apparently sensed my impatience because she looked at me with her soft, dark eyes and stabbed the cigar in my direction.

'You are a very impatient *gringa*', she said.

'I just came for a reading', I replied.

'What kind of reading?'

'Cards.' My boss had told me that Nelly was incredible at reading with her cards.

Finding a Santero

Santeros are usually well known within Latin communities. If you have Hispanic friends or coworkers, ask for a recommendation or find a botánica in a Hispanic neighborhood and inquire about santeros. If you have objections to animal sacrifice, make sure that the santero you visit doesn't use animals in this way. One way to tell is if you see cages filled with doves or other birds in the area where the santero practices.

When looking for a santero, be sure to stipulate that you want a practitioner of good magic. There is a sect of practitioners known as *mayomberos* who practice black magic. Most of their spells are manipulative.

Mayomberos practice a form of black magic that originated at the same time Santería did. Mayomberos specialize in casting hexes, in binding spells, in causing harm to another.

'Ah', she murmured with a nod of her head, and popped open the lid of a small wooden box on the table. She removed a deck of cards, blew smoke at them, and then asked me to cut them into several piles.

I cut them, she picked them up, and began to lay them out. They weren't ordinary playing cards or tarot cards, or like any other deck I'd ever seen. When I asked what they were, she said they were *brisca* cards, which many santeros in Cuba used to foresee the future. She laid them out in no apparent order – four here, three there, six more, eight more; I couldn't discern a particular pattern. She puffed on her cigar and studied them. She puffed some more, her eyes glazed over and she started to talk.

'There's a man', she said. 'He is balding. He has two young children. He is divorced or widowed, I'm not sure which. You will hear soon that he has killed himself. There's another man, a man of words, like yourself. You will marry this man. You will produce books together and separately.'

At the time, I was single but going out with my future husband, who was a reporter. I couldn't place the balding man she mentioned who would kill himself. But I made note of it. Since that first time with Rosa years before, I always wrote down or recorded any reading that I had.

'Your first book will be published in several years. There will be many books. Some are stories, others are factual.'

She laid out another layer of cards. I suddenly felt that each layer of cards represented another layer of my life, some layers closer to actualization than others. When I said this to her, she just chuckled and shook her head, as if to say I was really quite naive.

'Our lives have many possible paths,' she said. 'Only some of them will materialize. Right now, your life is in flux, there is much that floats at the surface of your awareness. That is what I see, that's what I read, that's what the *orishas* tell me. If you marry this man, there will be at least one child.'

I pointed at the third layer of cards. 'What do those cards say?'

'That your life is about to go through tremendous upheaval, all for the better.'

Music to my ears. 'And that layer?' I pointed at the fourth layer.
'You have a sister. She will marry first.'

She went on at some length, laying out events blow by blow.
Then she instructed me to go to the local botánica when I left her
house, and to buy certain objects that would protect me during the
days ahead. And, with a sly wink, she added that if I loved the man
I was with, I should buy two statues. The first should be Elegguá,
the *orisha* who opened doorways; without his cooperation, nothing
could happen. The second statue should be of Oshún. I should
place both statues on an altar in my home and pay homage to
them. I should light red and yellow candles in honour of the *orishas*,
and I should also feed them.

'*Feed them?*' I goggled. She was talking about *statues*, not a pet.
'Feed them what?'

'Honey. Most of the *orishas* favour honey because it sweetens
their dispositions.'

Honey. I wrote it down in my notebook, and immediately
a million questions sprang into my head. Where was I supposed to
put this honey? What kind of honey did the *orishas* like best? Where
should the altar be? And how on earth was I supposed to explain this
to my flatmate?

The Aftermath

But I went to the botánica, a Hispanic religious goods shop. I saw
statues that ranged from several inches high to over five feet tall. I saw
a spectrum of cigars, bottles of Florida water and jars of concoctions
I couldn't even pronounce. I bought two small statues – Elegguá and
Oshún – and candles in every colour of the rainbow. When I left the
store, I felt rather foolish.

Three weeks later, a divorced man with two children with whom
I had been involved hanged himself. A year later, my sister got married. A year after that, Rob and I were married, and a year after that,
my first novel sold. About six years after my visit to the santera, we
had a child, a daughter. In the years since, Rob and I have written

several books together and, between us, have published about fifty books – both novels and non-fiction.

Did I create an altar?

Of sorts: no fresh flowers and no ritual; nothing but a few things that reminded me of other things. Yes, I put Elegguá and Oshún on the altar.

Did I feed the statues?

For a while. But I felt silly doing it and stopped.

Did my flatmate comment?

No. She moved out and my husband moved in.

Over the years, I've had sporadic contact with other santeros and have seen some astonishing phenomena for which I have no rational, left-brain explanation. One young man, Ruben, was able to walk barefoot on shattered glass and grind lit cigars into his arm without any visible injury to himself while in trance. He knew things about me that I had never shared with another human being. He also prescribed spells.

Did I do them?

No.

Because in the end, I rebel against religious structure. And Santería is definitely a religion, with rules and rituals that must be observed and followed. The beauty of it, though, is that despite the rules and the rituals, something wonderfully mysterious unfolds *in the process*. And that mystery, that unfolding, is linked directly to belief. If you believe a spell will work, then it will. If you believe that you need a structure of some kind to obtain what you desire, then find a structure and stick to it.

Sometimes we go through periods in life where everything unfolds like clockwork and we don't feel the need for any intervention. But at other times, life literally begs for some kind of intervention, and that's when spells – from whatever belief system with which you feel most comfortable – come in handy.

Wicca

This spiritual tradition honours the Goddess – feminine energy – and views the earth as a living, thriving entity, utterly sacred. Like Santería, it has numerous rituals and rules, but Wicca is more open-ended and

flexible. As Starhawk writes in her classic book on witchcraft, *The Spiral Dance: A Rebirth of the Ancient Religion of the Great Goddess*, 'The Old Religion, as we call it, is closer in spirit to Native American traditions.... It is not based on dogma or a set of beliefs, nor on scriptures or a sacred book revealed by a great man. Witchcraft takes its teachings from nature...'

You don't have to go through an extensive initiation period to practise the Craft, although many Wiccans do. You can join a coven, start your own coven or be a solitary practitioner. In the earliest days of witchcraft, practitioners were actually the village healers, teachers, storytellers and midwives. Their practice was simply part of their daily lives in the communities in which they lived.

Background

Although Christianity was prevalent in Europe in the early 1300s, witchcraft was still practised, and country priests often participated in the pagan festivals that honoured various gods and goddesses. But in the 1320s the Church declared the practice of witchcraft to be an heretical act, thus launching the persecution of witches.

By the late 1400s, the Inquisition was sweeping across Europe, and by some estimates, as many as nine million 'witches' were tortured and executed, most of them women and children. 'Misogyny, the hatred of women', writes Starhawk, 'had become a strong element in medieval Christianity.'

In the film *Messenger*, the latest Hollywood version of the life of Joan of Arc, the full horror and terror of the Inquisition is depicted in graphic and frightening detail. This occurs after Joan is captured by the English and a court of pompous priests and other church dignitaries convict her of being a witch. She is subsequently tortured in an attempt to get her to confess. The tortures span the full spectrum of horrors associated with the Inquisition – the rack, thumbscrews, beatings, sleep deprivation, and being deprived of food and water. Joan never confesses, and insists right up until the end that she is an emissary of God, not Satan.

The Inquisition lasted well into the seventeenth century and drove the practice of witchcraft so far underground that it didn't see

Magic and Scandal in the Middle Ages

Magic thrived in the courts of the Middle Ages. Officials and royalty alike often employed astrologers and magicians as advisers. A number of scandals grew out of this period.

In 1316, a sorceress accused the mother-in-law of Philip V of Spain of employing magic to reconcile the king with her daughter. In 1441 the Duchess of Gloucester was accused of using magic against Henry VI of England to increase her husband's power and stature, and perhaps to give him a chance of attaining the throne.

the light of day until centuries later. This emergence has been very gradual, but seems to be gaining momentum.

In the New Age section of most bookshops, both physical and online, you'll find a virtual explosion of books about witchcraft, magic and spells. Many of these books are intended for a mainstream audience: Phyllis Curott's *Book of Shadows*, for instance, describes the author's fascinating initiation into the spiritual traditions of Wicca, but becomes even more intriguing and palpable to mainstream audiences because Curott is a practising lawyer in New York – a hardheaded position if ever there was one.

Starhawk's Wisdom

To the Wicca creed of 'harming no one', Starhawk adds three other principles: immanence, interconnection and community. She explains that 'immanence means that the Goddess, the Gods, are embodied, that we are each a manifestation of the living being of the earth, that nature, culture, and life in all their diversity are sacred'. We are asked to live our spirituality, to incorporate it into our daily selves by living with integrity and responsibility.

Interconnection is the understanding that we are all connected – not only to each other, but to the planet. 'What affects one of us affects all.' Interconnection embodies compassion.

Community encompasses not only our personal worlds – families and loved ones – but also the larger world and everything in it. 'Its primary focus is not individual salvation or enlightenment or enrichment, but the growth and transformation that comes from intimate interactions and common struggles.'

One of the traditional practices of the Craft is divination through the tarot, astrology, runes, a pendulum or any kind of oracle. But prediction isn't the point of divination in the Wicca tradition; the idea underlying everything here is to use divination to deepen spiritual knowledge and understanding.

The casting of spells, of course, is intrinsic to Wicca. Yet there is a deeper meaning to each spell that is cast. 'Spells... go one step further than most forms of psychotherapy', writes Starhawk. 'They allow us not only to listen to and interpret the unconscious, but also to speak to it, in the language it understands.'

This language is largely symbolic, just as it is in Santería. An object that represents a person or a desire, a herb that represents a particular emotion, a candle of a certain colour that represents a desired outcome: these are all symbols. The symbols are imbued with power that flows from the person casting the spell. 'In one sense', Starhawk writes, 'magic works on the principle that "it is so because I say it is so".' But if the word of the person casting the spell is to have such tremendous power, the individual must have the utmost integrity. 'Unless I have enough personal power to keep commitments in my daily life, I will be unable to wield magical power. To work magic, I need a basic belief in my ability to do things and cause things to happen. That belief is generated and sustained by my daily actions.'

Once again, *belief* is the critical factor.

Hollywood's Take on Wicca

In the American film *The Craft*, a group of teenage girls begin to experiment with casting spells. It all starts innocently enough, with the outcast teens binding together and finding a unity within their little clique. Their belief in their power as a group is stronger than their belief in themselves and this is reflected in some of the feats they accomplish – levitation, telepathy and telekinesis.

Then one of the girls becomes intoxicated with her own power and begins to cast spells that hurt people who have hurt her. Events begin to spin out of control and in the end, two of the girls are pitted against each other in a showdown between good and evil. It's all done in typical Hollywood fashion, but the message behind the dramatic events fits one of the key principles of Wicca: 'If you hex or curse, you yourself are cursed,' writes Starhawk. 'What you send returns on you, three times over.'

So be careful what you ask for.

Other Belief Systems

Folk Magic

Folk magic, natural magic, earth magic: these mean basically the same thing. This type of magic is performed simply, without elaborate rituals, using whatever is at hand. Practitioners of natural magic 'needn't spend years collecting or fashioning intricately crafted swords, robes or even wands. Indeed, the most important tools of natural magic are free – the sky, the earth beneath our feet, beaches and deserts,' writes Scott Cunningham in *Earth, Air, Fire & Water*.

Natural magic is appealing precisely because of its simplicity. It has no strong connection to an established spiritual tradition, although its heart is inherently spiritual, in that the magic itself is approached with a reverence for all living things. This type of magic may appeal to you if your life is crowded with responsibilities and you simply don't have time for a lot of ritual. Or you may want to incorporate elements of natural magic into some other type of magic that you practise or into some other spiritual practice.

Natural magic spells also use visualization and affirmations, as with other types of spells, but there's nothing ritualized about them. Natural magic spells are included in this book, but the chances are that you're doing your own natural spells already and simply aren't aware of it. Do you have certain stones or crystals that you keep in sight when you're working? Are your house plants healthy and flourishing? Do you talk to your pets as though they understand every word that you're saying? Do you study the patterns that clouds make, and draw associations between these patterns and people and events in your own life? Do you use candles or incense to focus your attention?

If you answered yes to any of these questions, then you already use natural magic in your life. It's really as simple as that.

Voodoo

The word alone has enormous power over the human psyche. We immediately think of dolls stuck through with pins, of zombies, of hideous rituals carried out in darkness. But again, voodoo is simply a belief system. To some degree, Hollywood has capitalized on its darker aspects. Voodoo actually has some similarities to Santería, in that it was first brought to the New World by African slaves some time during the sixteenth century. In this case, the slaves were brought to Haiti, one of the poorest countries in the Western hemisphere. In the eighteenth century, voodoo emerged in Louisiana.

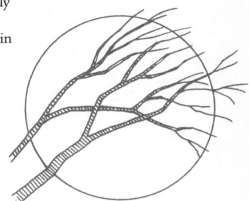

Like Santería, voodoo has a hierarchy of power. The spirit in charge is Legba, a mediator between man and the spirit world. Other *loa*, or high gods, include Damballah, a snake god imbued with virility, and Guede, goddess of love, and her darker sisters, jealousy and vengeance. There are also many lesser gods and innumerable spirits. All these spirits play a part in voodoo's elaborate rituals and spells.

In a traditional voodoo ceremony, worshippers work themselves into a frenzy through music, chanting and dancing, often with the use of various forms of drugs and alcohol. The goal seems to be an altered state of consciousness in which worshippers become possessed by one of the spirits. Possession is believed to have occurred when the worshippers collapse to the ground, writhing and speaking unintelligibly. Once possessed, a worshipper is able to bring about a cure, good fortune or some other human desire. During a typical ceremony, animal sacrifices are offered to the *loa* – to appease them and to win their favour. This practice is also found in the darker side of Santería – known as Mayomberia – and in other types of black magic.

It is only this dark side of voodoo, however, that has captured the collective imagination. This darker side smacks of everything that magic shouldn't be – control over others, ritual murders, cannibalism – the very essence of black magic. There are secret societies among voodoo practitioners, those who curse the recent dead and turn them into zombies – reanimated corpses who are slaves without wills of their own.

Voodoo in Literature

'Papa Doc' Duvalier, the dictator who ruled Haiti with an iron fist for many decades, is believed to have been a *houngan* – a voodoo priest – who capitalized on the local superstitions to maintain control over his little kingdom. He called his secret police the *tontons macoute*, which means itinerant magicians, and the licence plate on his car was said to consist of magical numbers.

Writer Graham Greene depicts life in Haiti under Papa Doc in his masterpiece *The Comedians*. In his autobiographical writings, Greene notes that *The Comedians* hit a raw nerve with Papa Doc, who attacked the novel and Greene in a newspaper he owned in Port-au-Prince. Five years after Greene's visit to Haiti, Papa Doc published an elegant glossy brochure addressing Greene's case. The brochure was distributed through Haitian embassies in Europe and called Greene 'a liar, a cretin, a stool-pigeon... unbalanced, sadistic, perverted'.

Years ago, in a hotel bar in Panama, I had a lengthy conversation with a Haitian about Greene's novel. This man had fled the island during Papa Doc's rule and said that the dictator was so enraged by Greene's depiction that he made it a crime to read *The Comedians*. I gave him my copy of the book, which he had never read, and the next day when I saw him, he said he'd stayed up most of the night reading it. As he handed it back, he said, 'This is exactly how it was.'

Chapter Five

Native American Magic: Shamanism

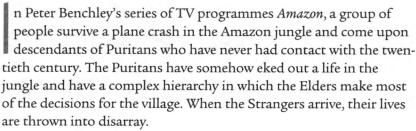

The Shamanic Library

Books on Shamanism are numerous. Here is a list of some of the best in the field.

- Taisha Abelar: *The Sorcerers' Crossing*
- Lynn Andrews: *Medicine Woman*
- Carlos Castaneda: *The Teachings of Don Juan; A Separate Reality; Journey to Ixtlan; Tales of Power; The Second Ring of Power; The Eagle's Gift*
- Florinda Donner: *Shabono; Being-in-Dreaming; The Witch's Dream*
- Nevill Drury: *Elements of Shamanism*
- Michael Harner: *The Way of the Shaman*
- Olga Kharitidi: *Entering the Circle*
- Terence McKenna: *True Hallucinations*
- Kenneth Meadows: *Earth Medicine*
- Petru Popescu: *Amazon Beaming*
- Alberto Villoldo: *The Four Winds*

In Peter Benchley's series of TV programmes *Amazon*, a group of people survive a plane crash in the Amazon jungle and come upon descendants of Puritans who have never had contact with the twentieth century. The Puritans have somehow eked out a life in the jungle and have a complex hierarchy in which the Elders make most of the decisions for the village. When the Strangers arrive, their lives are thrown into disarray.

One of the villagers, a woman, has been ousted from the community because the Elders believe she's a witch. She's actually a skilled herbalist and seer, and people often seek her help in secret. She cures one of the Strangers of leukaemia and is as powerful a shaman as the chief of the Spider People, a native tribe that is currently at war with the Puritans.

When the Spider People kidnap the youngest survivor of the plane crash, the chief recognizes that the boy will make a great medicine man and undertakes his training on the shamanic path. In short, Benchley has woven an ancient magical tradition through the series.

Early Shaman

One of the earliest depictions of a shaman was found in France, in the cave of Les Trois Freres. It's estimated to be at least 15,000 years old and shows a sorcerer disguised as a bison and armed with a bow. 'From early times, religion, art and magic seem to have been intertwined', writes Nevill Drury in *Elements of Shamanism*. 'The sorcerer was a master of wild animals – able to control their fate through his hunting magic, an adept at disguises and a practitioner of animal sacrifice... the Palaeolithic hunter–sorcerer was a precursor of the archetypal native shaman with his animal familiars, his clan totems and his belief that he could transform his consciousness into an animal form.'

The anthropologist Sir Edward Taylor termed this kind of belief system Animism, from the Latin word 'anima', which means soul. It fits the world of prehistoric man, where everything was believed to have a soul – not just humans, but animals, plants, stones, clothing, weapons, even the earth itself. In this belief system, the human spirit was as malleable as air, capable of entering other people, animals, even objects.

Contemporary Shamans
Carlos Castaneda and Don Juan

Shamanism gained popularity in the Western world during the 1960s, with the publication of *The Teachings of Don Juan: A Yaqui Way of Knowledge*, the first of many bestsellers by the elusive Carlos Castaneda. This book, like the others that followed, detailed Castaneda's apprenticeship and friendship with Don Juan Matus, a Yaqui Indian *brujo* – medicine man, sorcerer, healer.

Castaneda's apprenticeship with Don Juan lasted five years and took place first in Arizona, then in Sonora, Mexico, where Don Juan had moved. It included the use of three hallucinogenic plants: peyote, Jimson weed and the psilocybin mushroom. 'The importance of the plants was, for Don Juan, their capacity to produce stages of peculiar perception in a human being', wrote Castaneda in the first of his books.

Castaneda termed these peculiar perceptions 'states of non-ordinary reality', and they were intended to teach about the acquisition of power and of wisdom. They were also intended to aid Castaneda in finding a 'magical ally' who would enhance his powers and ultimately enable him to have complete control over his physical body. He would be able to project his consciousness into animals and plants and, eventually, to shapeshift to become an animal or a plant or any number of other forms.

The complexity of Don Juan's teachings and Castaneda's forays into these 'non-ordinary states of reality' became progressively stranger with each book and progressively more intriguing. This intrigue was compounded by the fact that Castaneda himself was so mysterious. According to some sources, his real name was Carlos Arana or Carlos Aranha, and he came from either Peru or Brazil. He took his authorial name when he became an American citizen in 1959. Beyond that, not much is really known about Castaneda. Even his death is veiled in mystery. Did he really die?

Even less is known about Don Juan. Did the sorcerer really exist? Did he really jump across a waterfall in *A Separate Reality*? Did he really leap into the void?

Does it matter?

Like Arthur pulling Excalibur from the stone, like Persephone being abducted to the underworld, some stories are meant to be mythic because their messages hold collective truths about the human condition.

This point became obvious to me a few years ago, when I was at a writers' conference in Kentucky. I made a remark about how writing is a bit like leaping into Castaneda's void – you never know where you're going to land, but you have to trust that you'll land on your feet. Throughout the crowd, heads nodded, smiles appeared. Everyone in that room had peered into that void with Castaneda. Most of them probably didn't know or care that he had critics. He had spoken to their hearts and opened their minds to the sublime.

Michael Harner

Harner is an anthropologist with impressive credentials. He has been a visiting professor at Columbia, Yale, and the University of California, and is presently the director of the Foundation for Shamanic Studies in Mill Valley, California. Through his foundation and its worldwide chapters, Harner teaches the fundamentals of shamanism to more than 5,000 people a year.

His apprenticeship in shamanism began in the late 1950s with the Jivaro Indians of Ecuador. In 1960, the American Museum of Natural History sent Harner back to the Amazon, this time to study the Conibo Indians in Peru. When he expressed an interest in learning about the Conibo's religious beliefs, he was told that he must first drink *ayahuasca*, the 'soul vine', a sacred drink of the shamans made from a hallucinogenic plant.

During his experience, giant reptilian creatures crawled out of Harner's spine and 'projected' a scene of Earth as it had existed before it contained any life at all. Then 'black specks' dropped from the sky, hundreds of them raining down over the barren planet. When Harner could see them more closely, he perceived them as

Knowledge Is Power

'Power rests on the kind of knowledge one holds.'

Don Juan,
as told by
Carlos Castaneda

'large, shiny black creatures with stubby pterodactyl-like wings and huge whale-like bodies'. He couldn't see their heads, but he didn't need to see their heads to hear them. Telepathically, these creatures explained they were running from their enemy in space and had come to earth to escape.

'The creatures then showed me how they had created life on the planet in order to hide within the multitudinous forms and thus disguise their presence,' he wrote. Hundreds of millions of years of evolution were condensed with a 'vividness impossible to describe'. Harner ultimately learned that these creatures were enfolded within all forms of life, even man.

When his experience was over, Harner – like Castaneda, like other anthropologists – began recording what had happened. He realized he wanted another perspective and walked over to a hut where an old blind man, a shaman, lived. He took his notebook with him and proceeded to tell this blind old man about his experiences.

But the old man, who had made many journeys into the spirit world, already knew what Harner had experienced. 'I was stunned. What I had experienced was already familiar to this barefoot, blind shaman. Known to him from his own explorations of the same hidden world into which I had ventured. From that moment on, I decided to learn everything I could about shamanism.'

Michael Talbot, author of *The Holographic Universe*, believes that experiences such as Harner's, through paths such as shamanism, may actually be 'sophisticated accounts of the cartography of subtler levels of reality'.

Terence McKenna

Shaman, visionary, crazy man, magician, genius: Terence McKenna embodies them all. Before his death from brain cancer in 2000, McKenna spent twenty-five years studying what he called 'the ethnopharmacology of spiritual transformation'. He was an expert on the ethnomedicine of the Amazon basin, the author of a number of books and an international spokesperson for the development of a global consciousness. But more than that, McKenna spent most of

Shamanism in the West

'In a sense, shamanism is being reinvented in the West precisely because it is needed.'

Michael Harner
The Way of the Shaman

his adult life trying to understand the lay of the land in these 'subtler levels of reality'.

In *True Hallucinations,* McKenna writes about an expedition that he and his brother, Dennis, and several other people took to the Amazon basin in 1971, in search of the mythic shamanistic hallucinogen of the Witoto. The experience led to McKenna's theory that psilocybin, the psychoactive ingredient in the *Stropharia cubensis* mushroom, is the missing link in the development of consciousness and language itself. 'The *Stropharia cubensis* mushroom is a memory bank of galactic history. Alien, but full of promise, it throws open a potential for understanding that will sweep away the petty concerns of a history-bound humanity', McKenna wrote.

McKenna in the Amazon

During his stay in La Chorrera in the Amazon, McKenna's experiences included a close encounter with a UFO that appeared about 200 feet above where he was sitting. He'd been sitting on the banks of a river all night, mulling over the many strange experiences he and the other members of his group had had since their arrival in the Amazon.

'All night long strange vistas and insights poured through me. I saw gigantic machineries and worlds of vegetable and mechanical forms on scales inconceivably vast. Time, agatized and glittering, seemed to pour by me like living superfluids inhabiting dream regions of terrible pressure and super cold. And I saw the plan, the mighty plan.... I was in ecstasy, an *ecstasis* that lasted hours and placed the seal of completion on all my previous life. At the end, I felt reborn, but as what I knew not.'

As the sky began to lighten towards a false dawn, McKenna got up and stretched and noticed that the line of fog in the distance seemed to have grown darker. As he watched, the clouds divided, darkened again and seemed to be reorganizing in some way. He also heard a high-pitched whine that seemed to come over the treetops and that was obviously emanating from the cloud formation he was watching.

Terror seized him. He wanted desperately to run back to the camp and wake the others so someone else could corroborate what he was seeing. But he couldn't move. Couldn't shout. Couldn't do anything except sit down again and shake. 'For the first time, I truly believed in all that had happened to us, and I knew that the flying concrescence was now about to take me. Its details seemed to solidify as it approached. Then it passed directly overhead...'

In the moments before it passed from sight, McKenna embraced the experience and noted the smallest details about the UFO – its lights, shape, the symmetrical indentations on the underside. Years later, when writing about it, he speculated that the UFO was 'a reflection of a future event that promises humanity's eventual mastery over time, space and matter'.

The Theory of Timewave

McKenna and a friend returned to La Chorrera some time after this first expedition for about two and a half months. He thought and wrote and slowly pulled together a new theory of time, based on the I Ching, which he terms the 'timewave'.

The I Ching – as a divination device, as a tool for self-discovery – can be difficult enough for the Western mind to absorb without tossing in McKenna's extraordinary insights of the I Ching as a kind of metaphysical calendar. 'What I am suggesting is a new metaphysics, a metaphysics with mathematical rigour; something that is not simply a new belief or new religious conviction. Rather, this insight takes the form of a formal proposition.'

McKenna's experience at La Chorrera became the central experience of his existence, the event from which the rest of his life and his work grew. He didn't simply follow a shamanic path; he *became* the path. He externalized his soul and connected with what he called 'the Logos of the planet'.

There would appear to be absolutely no correlation between shamanism and the World Wide Web. Yet, in reading through McKenna's website, it's obvious that he believed the Internet is a route to global consciousness, the very thing he writes about in *True Hallucinations*. In an April 1989 interview in *Magical Blend*, he said, '... from the time of the awareness of the soul until the resolution of the apocalyptic potential, there are roughly fifty thousand years. We are now, there can be no doubt, in the final historical seconds of that crisis – a crisis which involves the end of history, our departure from the planet and triumph over death. We are, in fact, closing distance with the most profound event a planetary ecology can encounter – the freeing of life from the dark chrysalis of matter.'

Olga Kharitidi

Olga Kharitidi was a young psychiatrist in a state hospital in the former Soviet Union, battling bureaucracy and an outdated medical system, when she joined a friend on a trip into Siberia's Altai Mountains. Here, Kharitidi became the apprentice of Umai, a mysterious Altai shaman, and unearthed a wealth of spiritual learning that had been hidden in Siberia for centuries. She entered the circle of a healing and magical tradition that not only shattered her view of reality, but brought her close to learning the secrets of Shambhala, a mythic civilization of highly evolved humans.

She began to apply what she'd learned in her medical work with schizophrenics. Among the natives of Altai, for instance, wax is believed to be able to absorb negative energies. A healer would walk around his patient with a pot of hot, melted wax, chanting spells intended to draw out the illness. When the healer had lured out the negative energy related to the illness, the hot wax was poured into cold water as the patient looked on. The wax would create strange shapes as it solidified, and the patient was supposed to interpret the nature of the illness that had been removed.

To avoid drawing attention to what she was doing, she told her patients and colleagues that she was trying out a new, experimental technique. They seemed to accept this without question, so she started introducing other methods that she had learned among the Altai and was able consequently to help a number of her schizophrenic patients.

Her apprenticeship, like that of Castaneda and Harner, involved journeying through the world of spirits in non-ordinary states of consciousness. Like the others, she learned that to find and keep personal power requires balance, dedication and commitment.

A Word of Caution

'Many people are looking for power, searching for new qualities to develop in themselves, seeking to open up their own inner magic. Some will learn how to contact this inner power, sometimes very successfully. But lacking the foundation to manage and control it, they will hold it too tightly and it will bite them. Its strength will overcome them, and instead of using it, they will become its servant.'

Olga Kharitidi
Entering the Circle

Alberto Villoldo

Alberto Villoldo travelled to the Peruvian Amazon in search of ayahuasca and the altered states of consciousness that the visionary vine supposedly produced. This journey in 1973 marked the beginning of a shamanic path that Villoldo finally wrote about sixteen years later in his book *The Four Winds*.

Like the books by Castaneda, Harner, Kharitidi and McKenna, Villoldo's *Four Winds* is a very personal story of its narrator's apprenticeship. It spans a period of about six years in which Villoldo experienced the Incan medicine wheel firsthand.

There are four directions on the Incan Medicine Wheel. In a sense, the medicine wheel is a blueprint to follow for spiritual awareness. In the South we learn what we are supposed to leave behind, to release. The power animal of the South is the serpent, and we are to shed the past in the way a serpent sheds its skin.

In the West, we discover what we must confront, the fear and violence that is inherent in our natures; we must overcome these so that we learn the way of peace. The power animal for this direction is the jaguar.

In the North lie the mystical teachings, the path we follow to become luminous beings, enlightened. The power animal for the North is the hummingbird.

The East, the most difficult direction of all, is where we bring what we learn into everyday life. The power animal for this direction is the eagle or the condor.

Since the early 1990s, Villoldo has been working closely with the Q'ero Indians, direct descendants of the Incas. Fewer than 600 Q'eros exist now, living in a group of isolated hamlets in the Andes, at between 15,000 and 18,000 feet. They chose to leave the Cuzco area some years ago so that their ancient teachings wouldn't be subsumed by the modern world. For decades, they have tended their packs of llamas and alpacas and kept their rich traditions alive.

But because of their isolation in such a harsh environment, they subsist primarily on potatoes, their herds are minimal and their nutritional deficiencies are extreme. The infant mortality

rate among the Q'eros is 45 per cent or greater, and their medical problems are serious. As a result, Villoldo set up the Four Winds Foundation, a non-profit organization intended to support the Q'eros by preserving their spiritual lineage and economic development.

A Q'ero Experience

The foundation's projects include a vast array of services, from medical teams to the preservation of the spiritual traditions of the tribe. In addition, Villoldo took it upon himself to bring the Q'ero Elders to the United States to pass on the Incan prophecies. They visited a number of American cities, where they spoke about the Incan prophecies and treated audiences to a native healing ritual.

My husband and I saw them at a Unitarian church in Palm Beach. There were perhaps a dozen of them, all in their native dress, with their drums and their medicine bundles, their coca leaves and their homemade brew. For nearly two hours, they concocted bundles, chanted, played music. Then, when the cleansing bundles – the *despachos* – were ready, the audience split into two groups and lined up in front of the two Q'ero medicine men.

Each medicine man used his bundle to cleanse the energy field of every person in the audience. Beforehand, Villoldo had explained that the cleansing was often felt as a rush of heat in the chakra where a person needed energy the most. I didn't really know what to expect, but certain parts of this ritual reminded me of my experience years earlier with the santera in Miami.

I reached the front of my line and faced a very short man with high cheekbones, dark, almost liquid eyes and thick dark hair. I could see the colourful threads in his clothes, the sweat that beaded on his forehead, the glazed, faraway look in his eyes. I extended my arms at my sides, and as he began to chant, he passed the bundle through the air several inches in front of my body, from head to toe. Then he moved the bundle along the sides of my body, several inches from it, in great sweeping motions. I didn't feel anything unusual.

He asked me to turn around, so my back was to him. This time, as he swept the bundle from my head to my toes, I felt an explosion of heat in my heart chakra. It was as if a hole had blown open in the centre of my chest and a hot summer wind was blowing through it.

Somewhere nearby a woman started to sob uncontrollably, and one of the Q'ero shamans took her aside. Other people were visibly affected as well. As Villoldo explained later, the energy of the ritual tends to affect the chakra that needs it most. Sometimes the energy is used all at once, and at other times it's used a bit at a time, as needed. I was facing problems with my elderly parents at the time, and the rush of energy into my heart helped me deal with it compassionately.

The Women in Castaneda's Circle

As an anthropologist and colleague of Carlos Castaneda, Florinda Donner provides a feminine perspective of an apprenticeship in sorcery. Her first contact with the world of the sorcerers occurred in July 1970, when she met a group of people in northern Mexico who followed a sorcerers' tradition that dated back to the Indians of pre-Columbian Mexico. Her teacher was Florinda Matus, from whom Donner took her name.

She wrote about this journey in *Being-in-Dreaming* and in *The Witch's Dream*. Like Castaneda's spiritual adventures, hers concerns piercing the barrier between ordinary and non-ordinary reality. Like Lynn Andrews (see right), she undergoes a series of bewildering experiences that ultimately shatter her concepts of time and reality. As her teacher says to her, 'When you joined the sorcerers' world you were made to understand that the designs of fate, no matter what they are, are merely challenges that a sorcerer must face without resentment or self-pity.'

Donner's *Being-in-Dreaming* was published in 1991. A year later, a woman named Taisha Abelar published *The Sorcerer's Crossing*. In the foreword, Castaneda refers to her as 'one of a group of three women who were deliberately trained by some sorcerers from Mexico, under the guidance of Don Juan Matus'. Everyone in this group had a tacit agreement not to talk about their experiences, and they upheld the agreement for twenty years. They didn't even speak of their experiences to each other.

Lynn Andrews

Thirty years ago, Lynn Andrews was an art dealer in Los Angeles. She was tracking down a Native American marriage basket she had seen in a photo, and the search led her to northern Manitoba, Canada. Here, she met Agnes Whistling Elk and Ruby Plenty Chiefs.

This meeting led to Lynn's initiation into the Sisterhood of the Shields, a group of forty-four women of power from indigenous cultures throughout the world.

When Lynn returned to Beverly Hills, she was so vastly changed that she no longer fit in. She flew back to Canada to see Agnes, to plead with the old woman to continue teaching her. But Agnes replied, 'Write a book and give away what you have learned. Then you may come back to me.'

So Lynn did exactly that. *Medicine Woman,* the first of nine books that detail Lynn's initiation, reads rather like a spiritual thriller.

Castaneda never really said why this agreement was eventually broken. 'Circumstances proper for our time and place have made it possible for Taisha Abelar to write about her training, which was the same as mine, and yet thoroughly different.'

Abelar's story, like the others, is very personal and involves numerous extraordinary experiences that can't be explained in terms of reality as we understand it. Her apprenticeship, however, didn't entail the use of mind-altering substances; instead, she used rigid mental and physical exercises that allowed her to enter into an alternative reality.

'The events I describe here', she writes in her preface, 'depict the initial stages of sorcery training. This phase involves the cleansing of one's habitual ways of thinking, behaving and feeling by means of a traditional sorcery undertaking, one which all neophytes need to perform, called "the recapitulation".' To facilitate and complement the recapitulation, Abelar says she was taught a series of 'sorcery passes' that entail moving and breathing in certain ways.

Some time after the publication of her book, a series of videos was released by Donner, Abelar and Carol Tiggs, the third woman in the group, called 'Tensegrity'. On Castaneda's official website, *www.castaneda.com*, the concept is explained as a modernized version of movements called 'magical passes' that were supposedly developed by Indian shamans in Mexico before the Spanish conquest.

This series of physical movements and breathing supposedly help an individual to transform energy into 'sensory data'. Ancient shamans considered this to be 'an act of pure magic: energy at large transformed... into a veritable, all-inclusive world in which human beings as organisms can live or die'.

It's unclear what is meant by this, exactly, but perhaps the meaning lies in the doing.

Power Animals

Power animals are also used for divination. In this process, the shaman journeys to the underworld through a special hole or entrance that symbolizes the opening between worlds. The entrances range from tree stumps to holes of burrowing animals to the *sipapu* of the Hopi Indians. Once the shaman goes into the tunnel, he usually

The Doctor Within

'The witch doctor succeeds for the same reason all the rest of us succeed. Each patient carries his own doctor inside him. They come to us not knowing this truth. We are at our best when we give the doctor who resides within each patient a chance to go to work.'

Albert Schweitzer

encounters his power animal not long afterwards. The shaman then poses his question. 'Most commonly', Harner writes, 'the power animal will provide its answer by moving its body before you in an unusual way. Other times it may lead you on a journey through portions of the Lowerworld, the experiences of the journey being in the nature of an answer to your question.'

This description bears an uncanny similarity to what santeros sometimes do in trance when they call their 'guardian spirits' to assist in the answering of questions from clients or in healing work. It also parallels what happens when a spiritualist seeks answers or attempts to heal a client. In this case, the spirits that are channelled are the souls of the deceased.

Power Objects

Harner, like Castaneda, talks about 'power objects', which are ordinary objects that can be used in a medicine bundle. Many of us, says Harner, collect power objects without realizing it – a special memento from a trip, a pretty feather found in a field, a smooth stone from a beach or river bed. 'If you have a visionary experience or sense power at a particular location, look about you and see if something distinctive is lying there for you to put into your bundle.' In a sense, a power object is a mnemonic tool for the shaman – when he handles it, he is able to recall his magical experiences.

The quartz crystal, writes Harner, is considered one of the most powerful objects among shamans of nearly every culture and in most geographic locations. Part of its appeal is that it appears the same in ordinary reality as it does in non-ordinary states. Since it is thought of as a living rock, some shamans 'feed' their crystals; again, this is reminiscent of how santeros 'feed' objects that represent the *orishas* (see page 53).

'When you start your own medicine bundle, it is desirable to acquire at least one quartz crystal to put into it', Harner advises. 'Such crystals are the centre of power in many shamans' medicine bundles or kits. Their power diffuses through the bundle and helps to energize and maintain the living aspect of the power objects.'

Shamans and Power Animals

One of the most important tasks that an apprentice must accomplish is to find his power animal. 'The connectedness between humans and the animal world is very basic in shamanism, with the shaman utilizing his knowledge and methods to participate in the power of that world', Harner writes in *The Way of the Shaman*. To move through this other world, the shaman needs a particular guardian spirit, what is referred to by native North Americans as a *power animal*.

Harner notes that the shaman's belief that he can metamorphose into the form of his power animal is widespread and the type of animal varies according to geography. The Lapp shamans in Scandinavia, for instance, take on the shapes of wolves, bears, reindeer and fish. The Arunto of Australia take on the form of eagle hawks.

Harner and Castaneda: A Comparison

Harner and Castaneda, despite the disparity in their backgrounds, followed shamanic paths that were strikingly similar: both used native hallucinogenic plants in their apprenticeship, entered non-ordinary states of consciousness and became fully committed to shamanic knowledge. The differences between the two are also striking: Harner teaches what he knows; Castaneda remained reclusive until the end of his life; additionally, Harner didn't confine himself to studying just one tribe, while Castaneda limited himself pretty much to the teachings of Don Juan and, later, to some of the female shamans who had studied under Don Juan.

Yet despite the differences in their shamanic paths, both men arrived at the same conclusions. The path of the shaman, through commitment, intent and discipline, is a worthy magical practice that produces tangible results in *this* reality.

Chapter Six
History's Magnificent Magicians

Merlin, Arthur and Camelot

A book about magic and spells doesn't seem complete without a discussion of Merlin, the most enigmatic figure in magical lore, and Camelot, the legendary kingdom of King Arthur.

As is the case with most legends, Camelot and the people who lived there are probably a colourful blend of fact and fiction. Few other legends, however, have captured our collective imaginations in quite the way this one has.

A search of the Internet, with nothing more than the words Merlin+King Arthur, yields hundreds of websites that cover everything from the historical perspective on King Arthur and Merlin to scholarly opinions to books and films. There's even a website about 'the truest account' of the Arthurian legends, which was allegedly culled by land developer Michael Miller, who regressed over a hundred people who recalled past lives in Camelot.

Merlin's Early Life

In the romantic version of Merlin's life, his mother was raped by an incubus and sequestered in a tower for the duration of her pregnancy, because in the fifth century adultery was a crime. When Merlin was born, he was covered completely in thick, black hair. His mother supposedly pleaded with the midwives to let him be baptized immediately and named for his maternal grandfather – Merlin (or Mellin). This baptism apparently negated the evil influence of his demon father, from whom he inherited his gift of prophecy and magical powers.

From the moment he drew his first breath, Merlin was precocious, a prodigy of unimagined talent. At the age of eighteen months, speaking in full sentences, he assured his mother that she wouldn't be burned at the stake because of him. When the judge at her trial condemned her for not naming Merlin's father, Merlin himself argued with the judge, claiming that he knew his father was an incubus. But God, he said, had granted safety to his mother by giving Merlin himself the ability to see the future.

His mother was subsequently released into the custody of her confessor and became a nun.

Merlin's Predictions

Merlin's association with Arthur began before Arthur's birth. After the Roman withdrawal from Britain, the throne was entrusted to Constantine, the legitimate heir. A nobleman named Vortigern instigated the assassination of Constantine's son, Constans, and then seized the throne. Constans' two brothers fled and prepared to proclaim their legitimate rights by raising an army to fight against Vortigern.

Vortigern, a lustful, ambitious man, invited a pair of Saxon mercenaries to Britain. This invitation ultimately allowed the Saxons to gain leverage in Britain and they set out to conquer it for themselves. Vortigern escaped to the recesses of Snowdonia in Wales, where he decided to build a mountain fortress at Dinas Emrys that would be impregnable against the invading Saxons.

The walls of the fortress, however, kept collapsing and Vortigern had to call in his magicians to find out what could be done to reverse the situation. They advised him that a human sacrifice of a fatherless child would remedy the problem. Vortigern dispatched his envoys to find such a person – who was, of course, Merlin.

The sacrifice never took place because Merlin, using his visionary prowess, challenged the house magicians to reveal what lay under the soil where the fortress's foundations had been laid. He ascribed the problem to a subterranean pool inhabited by a red and a white dragon. The red dragon, Merlin said, represented the Britons and the white dragon the Saxons. The dragons would fight and, ultimately, the red dragon would drive the white dragon back. The meaning of the prophecy was clear: Vortigern would be killed, and Ambrosius Aurelianus would be crowned king, followed by his brother, Uther Pendragon, and then by Arthur, the greatest leader of them all.

Merlin's predictions came true.

Shortly after Uther had ascended the throne, at a feast in London, Uther fell in love with Igerna, or Ygraine, wife of the Duke of Cornwall, Gorlois. His passion for the woman was so blatant and unrestrained that Gorlois whisked his wife away to a castle high on a cliff at Tintagel. Merlin's powers transformed Uther into an image of Gorlois, and he gained access to the castle – and to Ygraine. She became pregnant with Arthur. Gorlois was subsequently killed by Uther's troops, and Uther later married Ygraine.

Merlin and Arthur

After Arthur was born, Merlin became his tutor. He, of course, arranged for the sword-in-the-stone contest and Arthur won, thus confirming his noble bloodline. Merlin later convinced the mystical Lady of the Lake to present King Arthur with Excalibur, the legendary magical sword.

In the romantic version of Arthur's life, Merlin created the Round Table and advised Arthur throughout his reign in Camelot. As Joseph Campbell writes in *Transformations of Myth Through Time*, 'Merlin was the great "guru" of the Arthurian world. He had the whole programme in mind.' And part of this programme involved the quest for the Holy Grail. The Grail is supposedly the cup Christ used at the Last Supper and the cup that held his blood when his body was taken off the cross and his wounds were washed. According to legend and myth, it holds the gift of eternal life.

In the final scenes of *Indiana Jones and the Last Crusade*, Indy finds the cave where the Templar Knights have been guarding the Grail since it was hidden after Christ's death. Indy's quest, in fact, was to find the Grail and when he finally did, magical things happened. He was able to cross a chasm by walking on an invisible bridge, his father was healed when he drank from the Grail, and the evil antagonist was prevented from getting his hands on the Grail.

Joseph Campbell mentions the quest in terms of King Arthur and his knights. In the dining hall where Arthur is seated with his knights, '... the Grail appears, carried by angelic messengers and covered with a veil. Everyone sits there in rapture, then the Grail is withdrawn. This is the call to adventure, and Gawain... the nephew of King Arthur, stands up and says, "I propose a quest. I propose that we now should go in quest of that Grail, each to behold it unveiled."'

The knights never did find the Grail. But their quest was what mattered. In much the same way, what difference does it make if the story of Merlin, Arthur and Camelot is just legend? The story has had no less of an impact on human consciousness because of it. If anything, these stories transport us into the realm of true magic.

Mysterious Deaths

Even the deaths of Merlin and Arthur are shrouded in mystery and wonder. When Arthur was wounded in his last battle at Camlann, a location still unknown, Merlin accompanied him to the Isle of Avalon, so that he could be healed of his wounds. Arthur supposedly told Sir Bedivere to throw away Excalibur, and when the knight tossed it into a lake, a hand reached out and grabbed it. This scene has been beautifully depicted again and again, but is it *true?* Where was this lake? And where is Avalon?

Some people believe the lake, now dry, lies under the Pomparles Bridge near Glastonbury, and that Glastonbury is the legendary Avalon. In 1191, local monks claimed to have found the remains of Arthur and Guinevere. It appeared that the grave was discovered on the abbey grounds after a Welsh bard revealed the secret to King Henry II. When the monks excavated the grave, they found a stone slab and lead cross about seven feet down inscribed with words that translated as: *Here lies buried the renowned King Arthur in the Isle of Avalon.*

The Legend Continues

Today the ruins in Glastonbury draw all sorts of tourists. Some are lured by the Arthurian legends; others are seduced by the mystery surrounding the Holy Grail, where legends say the Grail was hidden. Specifically, the Grail is said to lie at the bottom of an old well at the foot of the hill, or tor, in the ruins of Glastonbury Abbey. The spring waters run red from the iron oxide, hence the well's name – Blood Spring. It's also known as Chalice Well: according to legend, the shaft of the well was built by the Druids and Christ's chalice is supposedly there as well.

The final resting place of the chalice is no less mysterious than the end of Merlin's life. The magician supposedly fell so deeply in love with the Lady of the Lake that he taught her all his magic. She became so powerful that Merlin was no match for her, and in the end she imprisoned him in a crystal cave so that she wouldn't become enslaved by him.

Sacred Sites

Glastonbury is just one of many sacred sites worldwide. Other sites are Machu Picchu, the Mayan ruins, the Hopi reservation in Arizona, Canyon de Chelly in Arizona, the Nazca lines in Peru, and Easter Island. Around the town of Sedona, Arizona, are a cluster of vortices, or power centres, that are also said to be sacred.

Another version recounts that Merlin had supposedly prophesied his own death in three distinct ways: that he would be stoned and clubbed to death, that he would be stabbed by a sharp stake, and that he would drown. All three supposedly happened. On the day that he was beaten and stoned by shepherds, he slipped down a river bank and was impaled on a stake stuck in the river bed and simultaneously drowned as his head slipped under the water.

Where was he buried? No one seems to know, a fitting end to the life of such a legendary figure. In England, one popular belief about Merlin is that he never died – that he is, in fact, alive and well and living in the forest of Broceliande. In this version of things, Merlin looks like a young man because he knows the secret of the elixir of life. He lives with the beautiful fairy Vivien, the legendary Lady of the Lake. Supposedly, the enchanted forest of Broceliande still exists, but is visible only to those who believe in magic.

Alchemy and Magic

OK, so the Merlin of legend was a magician. But what kind of magic, exactly, did he do? We can safely assume that it wasn't stage magic – no Harry Houdini tricks, no David Copperfield antics. Merlin's magic was the *real thing*. But what exactly does that mean?

Perhaps the answer lies somewhere in alchemy. In a nutshell, alchemy is the process by which ordinary metal is transmuted into gold. Some of the greatest minds in history have studied it – Paracelsus, Roger Bacon, Sir Isaac Newton and Carl Jung. Of these, Jung did the most to relate alchemy to modern man, and he did it through his study of the unconscious and mythology.

Learning from Films and Books

In *Psychology and Alchemy*, Jung writes, 'The fact is that the alchemists had little or nothing to divulge in the way of chemistry, least of all the secret of goldmaking.' Alchemists, says Jung, 'projected what I would call the process of individuation into the phenomena of chemical change'. In other words, by going within, by delving into his own

unconscious to discover its inherent powers and uniqueness, the alchemist became a true master.

Know thyself. Perhaps that's the real battle cry of alchemy.

The Jungian concept of alchemy pervades some of our favourite films and books. In *Star Wars*, Luke Skywalker must learn the ways of the Jedi Knights to defend himself against Darth Vader – and save the universe. He must become a Jedi Knight, able to direct his will and passion in a focused way so that he *alters matter and his relationship to it.*

When he is learning to use the Jedi sword, he makes mistakes because he hasn't learned how to tap into the Force. He doesn't understand how his *will* directs the Force and that the better he knows himself, the stronger his will is. In every magical tradition, will is our most powerful ally, and it increases in direct proportion to our knowledge of ourselves.

Look at Harry Potter. In his schooling at Hogwarts, he certainly has to learn the mundane things – the spells and incantations, the ingredients, the entire topography of becoming a wizard. He has to learn the rock face work. But until he goes deeper, until he learns *how to direct his will*, he's just going through the motions.

Young Harry and wise Luke Skywalker have certain things in common. They are both initiates into greater knowledge, the domain of Jung's collective unconscious. Harry has his Jedi knights and Skywalker has his Hogwarts. Both are heading for the same goal. Both strive to become the highest of what they might be: wizards, alchemists, magicians.

So when you're preparing yourself and your space to cast a spell, think of Harry Potter, of Luke Skywalker, of Carl Jung, of Merlin and Camelot. Think myth. Think collective unconscious. Think, *I can do this.* And feel, *I am a magician.*

In the film *What Dreams May Come*, Robin Williams plays a family man who is killed in a car accident. When he comes to, he is dead – but still conscious. He finds himself in a world where his every thought and desire is immediately translated into reality. That's how Merlin did his magic, how Luke Skywalker learned to master the Force, and how Harry Potter will become a wizard.

The Art of Alchemy

'Not for nothing did alchemy style itself an "art", feeling – and rightly so – that it was concerned with creative processes that can be truly grasped only by experience.... Experience, not books, is what leads to understanding.'

Carl Jung
Psychology and Alchemy

J.R.R. Tolkien, in his masterpiece, *The Lord of the Rings*, created a magician named Gandalf. Some scholars have speculated that Gandalf was actually built on the legend of Merlin. John Fowles, in his novel *The Magus*, supposedly fashioned his magician character on the personality of Aleister Crowley. Good and evil, light and dark – in the end, that's always what it comes down to in great novels, great films and in life.

Back to Reality

The problem with life, of course, is that good and evil are rarely as well-defined as in novels and films. There are too many grey areas. Boundaries blur, issues blur, conscience blurs. We want something and we want it now, and if a spell looks like a way to go for it, we indulge ourselves.

You're offered the dream job. You're on top of the world. And two days later, the offer falls through and you're in the pits. What happened? Well, maybe you didn't want it enough, maybe you didn't use the full power of your will, maybe it really wasn't the dream job and a higher, less obvious part of yourself knew that.

Remember: know thyself.

The point is that we aren't simply our conscious minds. We aren't one-dimensional. Given a bit of practice, we're all Harry Potters. We are all alchemists and magicians. We simply need a little guidance. We need an Obi-Wan Kenobi, a Merlin, a Jung, to point us in the right direction. And in the absence of a teacher like this, we need to trust our inner magician.

Magic, Magicians and Secret Societies

Secret societies have been around for centuries, and most have certain things in common: shared beliefs, myth and ritual, passwords and signs, an exclusivity of membership. The irony of secret societies, however, is that they aren't always totally secret.

Members of the Freemasons are often open about their affiliation. The goals and objectives of the Rosicrucians are today public

Magic and You

The creed: know thyself.

Who are you in the darkest hours of the darkest night? A raving maniac? A panicked human being? A corpse who lies very still, hoping the angst will pass? Or do you rise to the challenge and do what has to be done? *Do you commit to a course of action?* Can you commit to inner exploration? Can you commit to the journey that will take you into the heart of true magic?

Take the Magical Mystery Tour Quiz that follows and find out for yourself.

Magical Mystery Tour Quiz

Circle the number that applies to you: 1 = rarely; 2 = sometimes; 3 = often;
4 = nearly always.

1.	I'm aware of an underlying pattern in my life.	1	2	3	4
2.	I may not always understand this pattern, but it intrigues me.	1	2	3	4
3.	I try to see the positive side of all my experiences.	1	2	3	4
4.	My friends consider me an upbeat person.	1	2	3	4
5.	I approach life with a sense of wonder.	1	2	3	4
6.	I look for deeper meanings to my experiences.	1	2	3	4
7.	I believe that I create my experiences through my deepest beliefs.	1	2	3	4
8.	I enjoy time to reflect.	1	2	3	4
9.	I experience synchronicity in my life.	1	2	3	4
10.	I appreciate myself.	1	2	3	4
11.	I'm intuitive.	1	2	3	4
12.	I try to live creatively.	1	2	3	4

Score: Give yourself four points for every number 4 that you circled, three points for every number 3, two for 2, one for 1.

36–48: You live magically.

30–35: You're on your way to living magically.

24–29: There's hope. Loosen up, learn to go with the flow.

18–23: You're resistant. Ask yourself why.

Below 18: Hire the film *Merlin* or read *The Forever King* (Molly Cochran and Warren Murphy), *The Crystal Cave* (Mary Stewart) or *The Eight* (Katherine Neville).

knowledge. The teachings of the Sufis are known to be rooted in mysticism and involve complex initiation rituals.

In secret societies that use what we would call magic, ritual plays an important role – but spells may not. Magic is considered to be the result of power that rises from self-knowledge: in other words, the more self-aware an individual is, the greater his or her ability to influence reality.

The Rosicrucians

The origin of the Rosicrucians dates back to around 1614, when three short books were published anonymously in Kassel, Germany. The first book, *Fama*, related the story of Christian Rosenkreuz, a mythical young man who is supposed to have travelled for many years in the Near East, studying occult knowledge and seeking illumination. Upon his return to Germany, he selected seven disciples, and they compiled a massive library of arcane knowledge. Afterwards, five of the seven disciples went out into the world to look for successors and to heal the sick.

Rosenkreuz supposedly came from a noble German family who had sent him to a monastery to study Greek and Latin. When he was sixteen, he set out for the Holy Land accompanied by a monk. En route, the monk died and Rosenkreuz allegedly travelled alone, studying with holy men in Arabia and Egypt. He eventually returned to Germany, where he died at an advanced age – some accounts place his age at 120, others at 150, but most accounts agree that he died because he wanted to and not because he was ill.

Fama, the first volume in the trilogy, glorified alchemy as the transmutation of the soul rather than the transmutation of base metal into gold. The first edition sold out, and the reading public of the era clamoured to sign up with the brotherhood. The problem here was that no one knew where the brotherhood was located and/or whom to contact.

The second book in the series, *Confessio Fraternitatis*, provided the purpose and intention of the brotherhood. It claimed that the Pope was the antiChrist and that he could be overthrown if people cooperated with the brotherhood to bring about a spiritual awakening. The author said that the appearance of new stars in the constellations of Serpentarius and Cygnus portended this spiritual revolution.

The third book, *The Chemical Marriage of Christian Rosenkreutz*, is the most well-known and probably the most important of the three books in terms of occult knowledge and its influence later on the Society of the Golden Dawn. The story is a hermetical romance in which death, spiritual rebirth and the perfection of man are the central themes.

Rosicrucians made impressive claims – that they never experienced hunger or thirst, that they could summon spirits and render themselves invisible. They claimed they could heal the sick and attract riches to themselves. Around 1620, fascination with the Rosicrucians began to wane and the movement went underground for some years.

In 1619, the French philosopher René Descartes was in Germany and tried to track down at least one person who was a member of the Rosicrucians. He couldn't find any. The English mystic Robert Fludd, however, became a loyal supporter of the Rosicrucians; he believed they were practically divine. William Lilly, an astrologer whose works are still studied today, and several other celebrated thinkers of the 1600s became members of a Rosicruician society that was formed in London. Their objective was to elevate mankind through spiritual means – the alchemy of the soul. Their objective today remains the same.

> **The Power of Seeing**
>
> 'It is looking at things for a long time that ripens you and gives you a deeper understanding.'
>
> Vincent van Gogh

Freemasonry

Freemasonry doesn't seem to have much to do with magic, but it has a great deal to do with secrecy, ritual and allegedly arcane knowledge available only to members. This element dates back to the early 1700s, to the Grand Lodge of England, when the Grand Master was the Duke of Montague.

The first Masonic circles in the United States appeared in 1733, and by the time the American Revolution rolled around, there were 150 lodges scattered through the colonies. Masons, who believe in tolerance and political liberty, were participants in the Revolution. But because it was a secret society, it was denounced by the clerical groups that ruled in the colonies, and in 1739, Pope Clement condemned the brotherhood through a papal bull – an official declaration from the Vatican. By 1832, the anti-Mason movement had grown strong enough for them to nominate a candidate for the presidency – William Wirt, an attorney. He was defeated by Andrew Jackson, who was a Freemason.

A number of American presidents, industrialists, bankers and other people with political and financial clout throughout the Western world have been Freemasons, a fact that has made the organization a target for conspiracy theorists.

The Golden Dawn

Its full name was the Hermetic Order of the Golden Dawn, and it was founded in 1887 by three British Freemasons who were also members of the Rosicrucian Society of England: William Wescott, a coroner; S.L. MacGregor Mathers, a translator of occult writings; and William Woodman, a physician.

The order's principles and doctrines were heavily influenced, of course, by the beliefs and doctrines of Freemasons and Rosicrucians. Its founders, however, claimed that their order was based on cipher manuscripts that had been found in a bookshop in London. The manuscripts were deciphered and apparently contained magical theories based on the cabala, alchemy, astrology and the work of Eliphas Lévi. Apparently included were notes on the rituals that were incorporated into the order. The actual rituals for the order were written by MacGregor Mathers and the poet William Butler Yeats, who was one of the Golden Dawn's most prominent members.

In its heyday, which lasted about fifteen years, the Golden Dawn was favoured by sophisticated occultists interested in magic. Three types of magic were taught within the order, all of them based on Mathers' translations of cabalistic texts. Mathers used the cabala's Tree of Life as a metaphor for the spiritual quest. 'Mathers' vision for the Golden Dawn was that the magicians in his order could follow the mythic pathways on the Tree of Life and grow in spiritual awareness as they ascended through each life', writes Nevill Drury in *The History of Magic in the Modern Age*.

Part of the magician's training involved enhancing the senses through a variety of rituals, incantations and practices that represented a particular purpose. Sight, for instance, might be enhanced by looking at certain colours that represent the magician's purpose and trigger what Jung called 'the active imagination'. The sense of hearing might be enhanced through incantations of a sacred name or word. Quite often the sacred name was the magician's own magical name, which was intended to trigger archetypal forces that helped him communicate with his higher self – often referred to as the Holy Guardian Angel.

The various symbols that magicians of the Golden Dawn used in their practices are similar to those used in other magical practices: the circle, the cross, the triangle, the square, the crescent and bells. In addition, they used scents from oils and trances, and Tattva symbols, which come from Hindu mythology and represent the four elements plus a fifth element called spirit.

The Tattva symbols were a red equilateral triangle (called Tajas) that represented fire; a silver crescent (Apas) that symbolized water; a blue circle (Vayu) that represented air; a yellow square (Prithivi) that was earth; and a violet egg (Akasha) that represented spirit. These symbols were often used in meditation, as portals to other states of consciousness.

The magicians of the Golden Dawn also used the Major Arcana of the tarot (twenty-two cards) in conjunction with the Tree of Life to indicate the stages of personal transformation that any practitioner of magic must go through to arrive at illumination. Members of the society also studied scrying, astrology, geomancy, astral travel and the theory of alchemy.

The most infamous member of the Golden Dawn was Aleister Crowley, who was expelled in 1905 and established his own order, which was based on sexual magic.

In Colin Wilson's masterpiece, *Mysteries: An Investigation into the Occult, the Paranormal and the Supernatural*, he writes, 'What is perhaps most difficult for the Western mind to grasp is the notion that magic could be a purely *natural* phenomenon, like botany or the game of chess.'

Time Magic

On 10 August 1901, Anne Moberly and Eleanor Jourdain, Oxford professors, went for a walk in the garden of the Petit Trianon at Versailles. A kind of shimmering effect passed through the garden, and immediately they realized the landscape had changed dramatically. Men and women in eighteenth-century costumes had appeared. An ugly man with pockmarks on his face urged them to change direction. They did so, following the man into a garden where a woman was painting and music drifted through the air.

Then the vision gradually dissipated. The experience was so vivid that the women conducted extensive research and finally determined they had walked back in time and that the woman in the garden was Marie Antoinette.

The women wrote a book about their experience, but the question remains: did they really walk back in time?

William Butler Yeats

Most of us know Yeats as a poet. But he figured prominently in many magical societies and is an integral part of the history of magic. He was a member of the Golden Dawn, a Theosophist and probably quite a psychic himself.

Yeats underwent a series of magical experiments with MacGregor Mathers and had numerous visions that compelled him to study magic for most of his life. As Colin Wilson writes, 'Yeats recognized the connection between magic and Magic: that is, between moods of deep and intense delight and the ability to summon "paranormal" powers.'

Theosophy

This mystical religion was founded by Helena Petrovna Blavatsky, an enigmatic woman whose followers included, among others, Thomas Edison, William Butler Yeats, and Alfred, Lord Tennyson. Even Mahatma Gandhi visited Blavatsky. The religion was based on material that Blavatsky supposedly channelled from Indian teachers and masters.

Many of the details about Blavatsky's life are simply conjecture because she was a number of times exposed as being an egregious liar. What is known, however, is that she was born in 1831 to Russian parents and when she was sixteen she married a Russian general. She abandoned him eventually and took off for Constantinople. After this, the story gets hazy. Blavatsky supposedly travelled extensively and had a variety of unusual jobs. In 1873, however, she landed in New York City, one of a wave of immigrants.

She quickly found opportunities in the land of opportunity, and in 1874 she and Henry Steel Olcott, a colonel and a student of the occult, founded the Brotherhood of Luxor. In 1875 this became the Theosophical Society. Blavatsky had no shortage of devotees. Her ideas, especially those put forth in her hefty tome, *Isis Unveiled*, were allegedly given to her by her spirit guides. But critics pointed out that she'd borrowed from numerous spiritual disciplines – Buddhism, the cabala, Hinduism and Taoism, and even from Pythagoras. This didn't deter her followers or Blavatsky herself.

In the late 1870s, she moved her society to India, the spiritual home of her guides and spirit masters. The Theosophical Society flourished, and at its peak had somewhere between 50,000 and 100,000 followers worldwide. One of the central themes of Blavatsky's belief system was that mankind's history dates back millions of years, to the legendary Atlantis and Lemuria. She believed that seven types of humans would evolve over the course of mankind's history and that currently five of those types have appeared. The great races, as she called them, are separated from each other by cataclysms – volcanic eruptions, earthquakes, ice ages – which are controlled by non-human intelligences.

Sounds a bit like *The X-Files*, doesn't it?

Even though the London Society for Psychical Research came to the conclusion that Blavatsky was basically a fraud, there's no denying the woman's dedication and influence.

Magicians

Carl Jung and Magic

One of the principles of magic is the use of what Carl Jung called 'active imagination'. His discovery of how to use active imagination occurred in 1913, when he experienced relentless visions of a coming war. The visions disturbed him so deeply that he finally decided to tackle them head-on.

In his autobiography, *Memories, Dreams and Reflections*, he explains: 'In order to grasp the fantasies that were stirring in me "underground", I knew that I had to let myself plummet down into them.' So on 12 December he was sitting at his desk, mulling over his fears, when the following situation occurred (in Jung's own words): 'I let myself drop. Suddenly it was as though the ground literally gave way beneath my feet and I plunged down into dark depths. But then, abruptly, at not too great a depth, I landed on my feet in a soft, sticky mess.'

A waking dream ensued in which Jung experienced highly symbolic images that confirmed his earlier visions about an approaching war. What's more important, though, is that Jung developed his 'conscious dreaming' and called it 'active imagination'.

He believed that active imagination was a way to access the collective unconscious, a kind of primordial soup that holds dreams and symbols from the entire history of man. In working with his patients and with the stuff of his own unconscious, Jung identified certain symbols and images as archetypes. '... there are archaic psychic components which have entered the individual psyche without any direct line of tradition', he wrote.

In other words, regardless of our race or religion, where we live or what we experience, certain images and symbols unite us all. 'In recognizing the archetypes of the collective unconscious', writes Colin Wilson, 'Jung had rediscovered the basic principle of magic.'

The Paradox as Truth

'Only the paradox comes anywhere near to comprehending the fullness of life. Non-ambiguity and non-contradiction are one-sided and thus unsuited to express the incomprehensible.'

Carl Jung

Jung's Stone Fortress

Toward the end of his life, Carl Jung built a fortress of stone at the edge of Lake Zurich in the town of Bollingen. As Laura van der Post writes in her biography of Jung, "at Bollingen, he could just *be*. This quality of sheer being in the fullest measure was his own preparation for the end to come and what might be beyond."

After reading Jung's autobiography, I was in Europe and went to Bollingen, just to see this fortress. A young man was standing near the fence.

"Is this Carl Jung's home?" I asked.

He nodded. "Vastly changed. We have electricity now." He spoke in a heavily accented English.

"Who owns the castle now?" I asked.

"My mother," he replied.

"Your mother? Who are you?"

He smiled briefly, with an almost sad humility. "Jung's grandson."

In essence, when a feat of magic is performed, the adept is able to summon forth the power of a particular archetype and direct it according to his or her will. This is also the basis of visualizations, affirmations, the casting of spells – and every other component of magic, come to that.

Eliphas Lévi and Magic

Born in 1810 as Alphonse Louis Constant, Lévi was the son of a shoemaker. His name invariably appears in connection with magic, thanks in large part to several books that he published on the subject. *The Dogma and Ritual of High Magic*, published in 1850, reflected his study of the occult yet seemed to be more concerned with the mechanics of magic than with its soul. His works were never considered as scholarly as those of Cornelius Agrippa and Dr John Dee, the famous magician-astrologer to Queen Elizabeth I, yet his theories were studied in the Golden Dawn Society.

Lévi's central belief about magic was that it was essentially a power of the mind, an untapped and unexplored resource that we all have. He believed that the purpose of ritual magic was to learn to direct our will towards achieving what we desire. This echoes the very essence of spell-casting and of magical practices in nearly every culture. Lévi notes, too, that most people don't want anything badly enough to summon their 'true will' – in other words, without desire, without passion, the will is powerless.

Colin Wilson classifies Lévi and Crowley as 'the most important representatives of the modern magical tradition'. And yet Lévi apparently tried magic only once, when he attempted to raise the ghost of Apollonius of Tyana, a famed magician of the ancient world, and evidently succeeded. He described the figure as 'wrapped from head to foot in a species of shroud which seemed more grey than white'. Lévi was apparently so terrified at seeing the figure that he couldn't bring himself to ask anything.

By most accounts, Lévi was a plump, lonely man with a rich imagination. Raised a Catholic, he eventually turned away from the religion of his youth when he decided not to become a priest because he knew he couldn't live as a celibate. He married a sixteen-year-old girl, who subsequently left him for the Marquis de Montferrier, the owner of several radical journals for which Lévi wrote.

As a result of Lévi's association with the Marquis, he met a Polish nobleman, Joseph Maria Hoene-Wronski, a student of the Jewish cabala. Lévi became Wronski's initiate in hermetic magic and when Wronski died, Lévi studied the nobleman's manuscripts and changed his name from Constant to Lévi. It was then he wrote his books on magic, which subsequently influenced the founders of the Golden Dawn.

Lévi didn't make much money from his writings while he was alive. But after his death, the books gained popularity and were studied by followers of ritualized magic. One of those students was Aleister Crowley, who believed he was the reincarnation of Lévi.

Count Saint-Germaine

No figure in the history of magical practice is more enigmatic than that of Count Saint-Germaine. By some accounts, his mother was the widow of Charles II of Spain, and according to other versions, he was the son of the prince of Transylvania. Either variation has it that he was born around 1690.

He was supposedly skilled in alchemy, was a talented painter and violinist, and also had a way with stones. He boasted that he knew how to make pearls grow in size and that he could take several small diamonds and make them into one very large diamond. As if to support this claim, he wore clothing with gems sewn into it.

At various times, history places the Count in Versailles and Paris, where he was a confidential adviser of Louis XV; in Russia, where the Count claimed he participated in a plot to put Catherine the Great on the throne; in Germany, where he studied alchemy with Prince Charles of Hesse-Kassel. He was so well versed in the ins and outs of secret societies, and was such a smooth talker, that he led people to believe he'd been present at ceremonies that had happened a century earlier. This is probably how the rumours began that the Count was 500 years old, a tradition that has persisted to the present day.

According to Freemason documents, the count supposedly represented the Freemasons at a meeting in 1785. Theosophist Annie

Besant claimed she met Count Saint-Germaine in 1896. As recently as 1972, a Frenchman came forward who claimed to be the count.

Dion Fortune

It sounds like a glamorous name, a Marilyn Monroe versus Norma Jean Baker sort of name, theatrical, ripe for fame. It actually was the magical name of Violet Mary Firth, who figured prominently in the Golden Dawn and the Theosophical movement. Her full magical name was Deo Non Fortuna – by God and not by luck.

In the earlier part of her life, she was heavily influenced by Freud, Adler and Jung, but she felt a special affinity for Jung's theory of archetypes and his investigation into mythic images and symbols. She wrote several books, of which *Applied Magic*, *The Esoteric Philosophy of Love and Marriage* and *Psychic Self-Defence* are the best known. The first book was recently reprinted; the second book led to her eventual expulsion from the order founded by MacGregor Mathers's wife; and the third grew out of her belief that Moina Mathers was attacking her magically.

She also wrote two novels that expressed her exploration of feminine archetypes, a marked departure from the male-dominated archetypes of the Golden Dawn. Fortuna went on to establish her own society, which eventually became known as the Fraternity of Inner Light, and died in 1946.

Aleister Crowley

In most of his photographs, Crowley's mesmerizing eyes dominate the picture. Like the eyes of Rasputin, they seize you, pull you in, seem to speak to you. By most accounts, Crowley's hypnotic hold over people he encountered was practically legendary.

He has been billed as the greatest occult magician of the twentieth century, but it's questionable whether Crowley ever actually performed any feat of magic. He excelled at publicity, however, and was a relentless self-promoter. He quickly discovered that to grab headlines, he had to shock the public. He was thrown out of three countries, and at the pinnacle of his career, was branded 'the wickedest man in the world'.

The phrases used to describe Crowley stem largely from his practice of sexual magic. This is a type of magic that involves sexual depravity as a means of destroying the conscious, moral self, thus exposing the psyche to possession by primitive and powerful forces.

In *The Book of Law*, which Crowley wrote during his extensive nomadic wanderings, he makes it clear that he believed the path to enlightenment lay in orgiastic abandon: 'Do what thou wilt shall be the whole of the Law.'

In the course of his lifetime, he was connected to several secret societies. In 1898 he was initiated into the Hermetic Order of the Golden Dawn. In 1900 he tried to take control of the order and was ousted. He subsequently formed his own secret society, Astrum Argentinum, or Silver Star, which practised sexual magic. In 1901 he became a Freemason. In 1914 he joined the Order of the Templars of the Orient, a German secret society.

Crowley was married for a time to a woman named Rose who had mediumistic abilities and was involved in his magical practices. They had a daughter, but were divorced in 1909. Crowley's bisexuality found a vehicle in his sexual magic, and for a number of years he was involved with Victor Neuberg, one of the early members of Crowley's organization, Silver Star.

In 1920, after inheriting a modest sum of money, Crowley consulted the I Ching about where he should go to carry on his magical activities. The I Ching seemed to favour Cefalù, a port in northern Sicily. Crowley travelled to Italy with a French woman and her son, and eventually Leah Hirsig, with whom he'd had a daughter, joined them. Here, Crowley rented a villa surrounded by olive groves and converted it into a sanctuary where he could explore all the nuances of sexual magic. According to a story in the *Sunday Express*, life at Crowley's sanctuary focused on 'unspeakable orgies, impossible of description... suffice it to say that they are horrible beyond the misgivings of decent people.'

The sanctuary, however, enjoyed a steady stream of visitors eager to study under the legendary Crowley. There were many rules at the sanctuary. Men had to shave their heads, leaving a phallic forelock. Women had to dye their hair red or gold to symbolize the energy of

Mind and Matter

'I believe that the mind has the power to affect groups of atoms and even tamper with the odds of atomic behaviour, and that even the course of the world is not predetermined by physical laws but may be altered by the uncaused volition of human beings.'

Sir Arthur Eddington

Horus. No one but Crowley was allowed to use the word 'I', a deliberate attempt to kill the ego. If a follower slipped up and said the word, he had to slash his body with a cut-throat razor.

One of Crowley's followers, Raoul Loveday, may have developed a blood infection from the numerous slashes on his body, and when he subsequently died, his wife returned to England and gave an interview to the *Sunday Express*. This resulted in the beginning of adverse publicity against Crowley; it was during this time that he was dubbed 'the wickedest man in the world'. When word of the depravity on Cefalú reached Benito Mussolini, he deported Crowley and his followers from Italy.

Crowley's Legacy

Despite all this, Crowley's mythic persona endures. Somerset Maugham, whom he'd met in Paris in 1902, based a character on Crowley in his book *The Magician*. Science fiction writer James Blish did the same in his classic *Black Easter*. Crowley's photograph was on the cover of the Beatles' *Sergeant Pepper's Lonely Hearts Club Band* album, and his life inspired Led Zeppelin's guitarist Jimmy Page, who bought Crowley's home in Scotland.

Nevill Drury, author of *The History of Magic*, believes that Crowley's continued popularity has more to do with his defence of personal freedom than anything else. 'Crowley was invariably provocative in thumbing his nose at the status quo... he always emphasized that every person has it within themselves to change their circumstances and to wrestle with their own destiny.'

Huxley on Experience

'Experience is not what happens to a man. It is what a man does with what happens to him.'

Aldous Huxley

Part II

Practical Magic and Casting Spells

Chapter Seven

Your Code and Common Questions

Every magical tradition, from the Druids to Wicca to Santería, has a code of some kind – principles that guide the practitioner, boundaries that he or she won't cross, a core of beliefs that permeates everything he or she does. These core beliefs define the parameters of the magical practice.

In Wicca, for instance, the primary principle is to harm nothing and no one; in Santería, it's to honour the saints, or *orishas*. Practitioners of 'green witchcraft' revere the earth and see it as a living entity. What's your code? Have you defined it?

What Makes Us Unique

Cultural differences, of course, sculpt a particular code. To some santeros, the sacrifice of an animal is simply a way of honouring an *orisha;* a practitioner of Wicca finds animal sacrifice abhorrent. And yet there are santeros who refuse to sacrifice an animal, individuals who develop moral principles apart from or beyond the dictates of their culture and define their own parameters. In the end, it's what each of us must do as we evolve from children raised in the belief systems of our parents to adults who decide for ourselves what we believe.

Childhood conditioning about beliefs can be immensely powerful. Inside the man or woman who lacks the sense of self-worth lurks a small child who may believe she's a sinner or untrustworthy or not good enough. But we don't have to remain victims of childhood conditioning or anything else. With will, intent and passionate desire, we can define for ourselves what we believe or don't believe, what we desire and don't desire. We can define our own parameters.

This is not to say that any of us is omnipotent, that any of us has all the answers or even a good chunk of them. We're all seekers, and we all have a need for some sort of belief system. Joan of Arc believed that God whispered in her ear, and that belief helped her to win victories for her country. But consensus belief branded her a witch, and she was burned at the stake.

A child who didn't speak until he was four was written off by his teachers as a hopeless student. But Einstein went on to give us the Theory of Relativity.

Core Beliefs

A core belief is often invisible to our conscious minds. It may be a belief that is 'accepted' in childhood as a belief about reality. Core beliefs are probably the most difficult to change unless we strive to become aware of them. Recommended reading: *The Nature of Personal Reality* by Jane Roberts; *Beyond the Winning Streak* by Lynda Dahl; *The Invisible Path to Success* by Robert Scheinfeld; *The Education of Oversoul Seven* by Jane Roberts; and *Excuse Me, Your Life Is Waiting* by Lynn Grabhorn.

A woman was diagnosed as having vaginal cancer and her doctors wanted to perform immediate surgery. She realized that the disease was a metaphor for the physical, sexual and mental abuse she suffered as a child, so she said she couldn't afford the operation and went to work on herself, on her beliefs, on forgiving the people who hurt her. Six months later, the medical establishment said she was in remission. Louise Hay went on to write *You Can Heal Your Life* and the book has been published in twenty-five languages in thirty-three countries, and has sold millions of copies. Hay then went on to establish her own publishing house. She is now in her seventies and her cancer has never recurred.

In each instance, consensus reality was a wall the individual had to break through, a wall he or she had to move beyond to define personal beliefs. And that's how it is for all of us.

Your Belief System

If you're not sure about your belief system, the time to define it is before you begin casting spells – not after you've started. Once you know what you believe, it's easier to define your parameters, your boundaries and the lengths you will go to attain something – and what you won't do, your bottom line.

A belief system usually evolves over time. It's something that we grow into it, as our needs and goals evolve and change. Think, for instance, about how you felt when you discovered there was no Father Christmas. Were you disappointed? Annoyed? Relieved? Whatever you felt, the discovery and the emotions you experienced probably changed something intrinsic to the belief system you held at the time, a belief that undoubtedly included magic. As one belief system began to dissolve, a new one began to form and you started to make the transition from childhood to adolescence.

This is a simple example of a process that continues throughout our lives. Even when we find a system of beliefs that works for us, we hone and fine-tune it, working our way deeper and deeper into its essential truth. Everything we experience, every thought that we have, every desire, need, action and reaction, everything we perceive with our senses goes into our personal databank

> **Brainstorming: Describing Your Beliefs**
>
> This activity is intended to be fun, stimulating and revealing. In 200 words or fewer, describe your beliefs, your code. If you're not sure about your belief system, simply list what you think you believe.

The Wicca Creed

As Starhawk writes in *The Spiral Dance,* 'Love for life in all its forms is the basic ethic of Witchcraft. Witches are bound to honour and respect all living things, and to serve the life force.' This code includes:

1. Preserving the environment.
2. Honouring yourself and others.
3. Seeing sexuality as 'numinous and sacred'.
4. Understanding 'What you send returns on you, three times over'.
5. Knowing that we have the right to control our bodies.
6. Honouring the Goddess. 'The Goddess has infinite aspects and thousands of names — She is the reality behind many metaphors. She is reality, the manifest deity, omnipresent in all life, in each of us.'

and helps create the belief system that we hold in this instant. If your parents were divorced when you were five, that's somewhere in the databank. If you were hospitalized at the age of ten, that's there in the databank, too. You get the idea here; nothing is ever lost or forgotten in our lives.

Your belief system may include an adherence to an organized religion or to some other spiritual discipline, or it may not include any sort of spiritual ideas at all. But at the heart of any belief system lies a code by which you live your life, and it may not have any connection whatsoever to other people's concept of good and bad. After all, even thieves have codes.

Do you believe in an afterlife? In a supreme being? In good and evil? Do you believe that reality is exactly as it appears, that what you see is what you get? Do you believe people can't be trusted, that all Dobermans are vicious, that it's every man for himself, that you're a victim and there's nothing you can do about it? Then your experiences will confirm those beliefs.

If, on the other hand, you believe that nothing is fated, that your free will and your innermost beliefs form your reality, then your experiences will confirm that, too. In fact, because you have picked up a book on magic and spells, you probably already believe that you can shape your own destiny and are looking for practical information on how to do it more efficiently and pragmatically.

Magic is one route. But there are hundreds of ways to get to where you want to be.

I recently read a book called *The Invisible Path to Success: Seven Steps to Understanding and Managing the Unseen Forces in Your Life* by Robert Scheinfeld. The seven steps the author presents aren't news to anyone who is looking for practical results with metaphysical concepts. But the way the author presents the steps and his *practical application of ideas* are unique because he speaks to you from *his* experience, in terms anyone can understand. *He knows what he believes*, he states it, and he shares it. He also says that what works for him may not work for you. And really, that's the bottom line of any exploration: you have to define what you believe and what works for *you*.

Common Questions

Do spells work?

Yes, sometimes. And when they don't work, this is usually due to several things:

1. You can't force another person to do something that isn't in alignment with his or her highest good. Tom can curse Sue, hex her and cast spells for her to fall in love with him until he's blue in the face. But if loving Tom doesn't align with Sue's highest good, nothing is going to happen – not for Tom, anyway.
2. Your intent isn't strong and clear enough.
3. Your emotions aren't behind the spell 100 per cent.
4. What you want isn't in *your* highest good.

Who or what determines what is in my highest good?

The answer to this one goes by different names: the higher self, the soul, the grander self, All That Is, the Goddess, God.... The central idea here is that when you look in the mirror, the reflected image is a fraction of the whole picture. Somewhere in each of us is something, some type of energy, that grasps the whole picture.

What whole picture?

You can't see the forest for the trees. For years, that adage really bothered me. It seemed, well, so obvious. Of course you can't see the whole forest if you're in it. You see the bark on the trees, the leaves, their colours and shapes. You see the ground around the trees, the rocks scattered around the trunks. You see the moss, the insects, the anthills. You're mired in the details. Lost in the details. Much of the time, our lives are like that.

According to esoteric thought, each of us has a blueprint of our lives, a kind of master plan, that we designed before we were born. We set up certain events and encounters that would provide the types of experiences that would help us evolve. Whether we keep these appointments with destiny is up to us, which is where free will comes in.

Can I design my own spells?

Absolutely. Once you have a grasp of the basics, you can design spells for any situation. Remember, though – the most important elements in a spell are your intent and passion, not the words or the ritual.

What remedial measures can I take when I don't get results from a particular spell?

If you've applied the four criteria in the first question in this section and your spell isn't working, then perhaps you're asking for too many things. You should determine what's most important to you, then ask for just that item. Sometimes, just rearranging the wording of a spell fixes the problem.

Another possibility is that you haven't given the spell enough time to work. How much time is enough? This is a sticky point. A spell that is in alignment with your highest good, backed by intent, clarity and passion, can work immediately. For a complex spell that involves several people, the spell may take longer. Give it at least a month if it's complicated and a couple of weeks if it's not. Alternatively, break the complex spell down into its components and simplify it.

Another possible reason that a spell may not work is that you may be investing too much energy in the outcome. Once you cast your spell, forget about it. Release it. Let the process unfold. Trust that you'll get what you want.

Remember that casting spells is meant to be fun. If your spells don't seem to be working, take a closer look at your mood. Are you approaching it too seriously? If so, then lighten up.

When I'm doing spells for prosperity, am I taking away someone else's prosperity?

Not at all. Prosperity and abundance don't have limits. You may have trouble, however, if you're casting spells to win the lottery or at gambling, or if you're attempting to swindle someone out of money.

My spouse (or partner, parent, children, boss, whoever) says that by casting spells, I'm aligning myself with evil. How do I deal with that?

You're not going to change anyone else's opinion about spells or anything else. Your best bet is to simply follow your practice in private. You

---

Have a Hunch?

'Whether we call them hunches, gut feelings, senses, or dreams, they're all the same thing – intuition, speaking to us, giving us insight and knowledge to help us make sound decisions about any number of actions we take. Intuition occurs when we directly perceive facts outside the range of the usual five senses and independently of any reasoning process.'

Mona Lisa Schulz, MD
Awakening Intuition

may even want to cast a spell to help the person in question to become more open-minded.

When you encounter someone who is opposed to what you're doing, arguing about it is probably the worst thing you can do. If possible, step back from the situation and ask yourself what in you has attracted the opposition. Try to look at the other person as a teacher. What is the lesson to be learned from the opposition?

Is a complicated spell better than a simple spell?

One isn't better or worse than the other. The complexity or simplicity of a spell should fit the situation and the end result that you want. If your life is busy and you're already pressed to make free time for yourself, simple spells may suit your lifestyle better than complicated rituals.

Do I absolutely need an altar to do spell work?

No. This is a matter of personal preference. If the presence of an altar troubles the people you live with, then either put the altar in your personal area or outside, if weather permits, or simply don't have one.

Does it matter if I don't cast a circle each time I do a spell?

You do what feels comfortable to you. Some people enjoy the ritual of casting a circle or have a belief that urges them to cast a circle. If you don't like ritual and your beliefs say it's fine to do a spell without casting a circle, then do so. In some magical traditions, however, the casting of the circle is such an integral part of a spell that to not cast a circle is the equivalent of, well, heresy!

How often should I do a particular spell?

Always give you first spell a reasonable amount of time to work – several days to a month. If nothing is happening, revise the spell or your intent. If nothing happens then, just release your desire. Quite often, the act of releasing something brings what you want.

More on Spells That Don't Seem to Be Working

Invariably, when you begin to practise visualization of any kind, there are times when nothing seems to be working, when the energy isn't

Creating Your Own Spells

You can cast a spell for virtually anything. This can be ritualized or without ritual, formal or informal. It can be done with a group, as in a coven, or with a few people or when you're alone. You may or may not want an altar. There are no hard and fast rules.

In creating your own spells, however, it's best to adhere to the magical properties of the items you use. For instance, you probably wouldn't use frankincense to smudge a room; sage is the herb to use for smudging. Use the lists in this book as your preliminary guideline and add to it as you become more practised at casting spells.

shifting. Give your spell a reasonable amount of time to work, and if nothing happens, then do some fine-tuning.

First, re-evaluate your goal. Since you first did the spell, has your goal changed? If so, then revise your spell to reflect your needs and desires now.

One woman had done a love spell intended to deepen her lover's commitment to her. Six weeks later, however, his life had gone through some major changes – a new job, a death in his family and a move – and the woman realized she didn't want to marry him right away. Even though she still loved him, she wasn't prepared to move across the country. She revised her spell to reflect her new needs.

If your goal has remained the same, then perhaps you should do the spell again, but with renewed passion and greater clarity about what you want. The more passion and emotion you put behind a spell, the greater the chances are that it will work quickly. The other element about spells that we sometimes overlook is that they should be done in a spirit of fun and adventure.

When casting any spell, it's always wise to open with a prayer for protection for yourself and others. This prayer can be from a traditional religion or one that you create yourself. Make such a prayer your opening ritual.

The Mysterious Mind

'We know very little about the nature of our minds. They are the basis of all our experiences, all our mental and social life, but we do not know what they are. Nor do we know their extent.'

Rupert Sheldrake
Seven Experiments That Could Change the World

Chapter Eight

Prosperity and Abundance Spells

Brainstorming: My Prosperity and Abundance

The idea here is to bypass your rational left brain and allow your intuitive right brain to express itself. Don't think about it, just allow your intuitive self to speak.

1. I am happiest when I
   _____ .
2. My wildest dream is to
   _____ .
3. Given the chance, I would spend most of my time_____ .
4. I thoroughly enjoy
   _____ .
5. I would love to _____ .
6. I now spend my free time _____ .
7. I feel a sense of accomplishment when I
   _____ .
8. My greatest passion is _____ .
9. _____
   makes me feel terrific!
10. One of my favourite hobbies is _____ .

Do you define prosperity as an amount of money – a cool million pounds, for instance – or as an abstract concept such as happiness or good health? Does abundance mean having more of everything or having enough of everything? These distinctions may seem trivial, but before you work with spells involving prosperity and abundance, it's prudent to have some idea about what the concepts mean to you.

What Do Prosperity and Abundance Mean to You?

Some years ago, I conducted a very informal survey among friends and acquaintances and asked each person what prosperity and abundance meant to him or her. The responses covered a wide spectrum: to have enough or more money; to be in a better job; to have a happy marriage or relationship; to write a bestselling novel or screenplay; to own a horse; to be self-employed; to be rich; to own a home. If I were to ask these same people today what prosperity and abundance meant to them, it's likely that, in most cases, the answers would be different.

Our lives, after all, are in a constant state of flux. Once the horse is owned or the novel hits the bestseller lists or the ideal relationship is found, our ideas about prosperity and abundance change accordingly. So in the brainstorming activity 'My Prosperity and Abundance' on the left, you're going to define what prosperity and abundance mean to you *today, right now, in this moment*.

In the exercise, you identified ten items that make you feel happy and prosperous. Now find an object that represents each entry on your list. Select these objects with care; they're going on your altar and will be used in spells.

Let's say that your wildest dream is to get your pilot's licence. Any number of objects might be selected to represent that dream: a model aeroplane, a photograph of the type of plane you would like to fly, even a child's plastic toy plane. The point is to choose something that immediately connects you to the *feeling*.

Once you've selected your symbolic objects, you're ready to prepare your altar.

Altars

Earlier we discussed your power spot. Your altar, if you choose to have one, goes in your power space, unless your spot is outside – then you may have to create something a bit more portable.

An altar is merely a special place you create that contains objects that symbolize who you are and what you desire. Nothing more, nothing less. It doesn't need religious connotations or dogmas attached to it. In fact, if the word feels uncomfortable, then call it something else.

This place is *yours*. You can put whatever you want on it – fresh flowers, sticks of incense, candles, photographs, statues, figurines, a bowl of fresh water.... The objects you place on your altar should also include the ten objects you selected to represent the things and experiences that make you feel prosperous and abundant.

Candles are great objects to have on an altar. They represent illumination and tell your conscious mind that something is beginning. Lighting a stick of your favourite incense or setting out fresh flowers triggers your sense of smell (remember, though, not to leave any burning item unattended). Water aids in focusing intuition. The idea is to ritualize this time you are setting aside for yourself. Try to have each of the four cardinal points represented on your altar.

If you decide to set up your altar permanently in your power spot, then the consistency of the place signals your deeper self that you mean business. The physical location can be virtually anywhere you want it to be, but preferably in a spot where you won't be disturbed. A garden will do as well as a corner of a room. However, depending on the weather where you live, you may not want to leave your various altar objects outside. In this case, you can simply take your things with you and set them up when you use your altar. There aren't any hard and fast rules.

For years, my husband has kept a ceramic bowl at his desk that is filled with various rocks, crystals, totems and other objects that mean something to him. Recently, he added a small fountain that sits on a shelf behind his desk and contains other stones and objects over which the fountain water runs. I doubt that he would call this an altar, but that's precisely what it is. When he works, meditates, reads, researches and focuses, he does it at his desk,

surrounded by the objects on his altar. So your altar can be as casual as that or as formal as you like to make it.

In Wicca, an altar is the heart of the circle that's cast for doing spells. In this chapter, however, none of the spells require you to cast a circle. So at the beginning, keep your altar simple.

The Colour of Money

One afternoon I was queuing up in a shop. The woman in front of me was annoyed because the line was so long, and she became quite vocal about it, muttering snide remarks that everyone around her could hear. By the time she got to the counter, her agitation was so extreme that I braced myself for some kind of confrontation.

The woman had a number of coupons for the items in her basket, so it took the assistant a while to ring up everything. The assistant gave her the total and the woman snapped, 'That can't be right. You've made a mistake somewhere. Check the coupons again.'

The assistant, whose patience and courtesy were admirable, did what the woman asked. No mistakes. The woman fumbled in her purse for notes, counted them out, didn't have enough to cover the total. She handed the assistant her credit card, but the card didn't go through. She demanded to see the manager. The assistant had to call the manager. By then, the line was much longer and the assistant had to ring for help. Most of us moved to another counter. While the new assistant was ringing up my order, the woman, now behind me, ranted and raved at the manager. The manager listened to her diatribe, then calmly said, 'Madam, we take cash, credit cards and cheques. If you don't have any of those things, there's nothing I can do about it.'

The woman left in a huff without any of the items in her basket.

As I left, I kept asking myself, *What's wrong with this picture?*

At the time, income tax day was just around the corner. My husband and I are both writers, self-employed. That year, we had underpaid and I knew we were going to be faced with a large tax bill. We were owed money on contracts and I was afraid the money wasn't going to arrive in time for us to pay our taxes. My prosperity consciousness was, well, scraping the barrel.

Buddha Says

'All that we are is the result of what we have thought.'

As I thought this, I suddenly realized the woman who had made such a scene was merely a reflection of my own lack of prosperity consciousness. In terms of spells, we'd both forgotten that the colour of money is green. In other words, if you don't have prosperity consciousness – the belief that you are deserving – then you need to develop it before you attempt a spell for prosperity.

Louise Hay, writing in *You Can Heal Your Life*, devotes a chapter to prosperity. She provides a list of negative money beliefs and then shows you how to change any of these beliefs that you may hold. For prosperity, she writes, it's necessary to:

· Feel deserving
· Make room for the new
· Be happy for other people's prosperity
· Be grateful

To these she adds, 'Love your bills'. The first time I read this, everything inside me rebelled. *What? Love my grocery bill? My electric bill? My mortgage payment? This woman's crazy.* But the more I thought about it, the less I rebelled. After all, a bill is simply an acknowledgment that the company trusts that I can and will pay, a sort of cosmic honour system. Why should I resent it? Money and prosperity are expressions that we live in a universe that is infinitely abundant. All of us can tap into that abundance without depriving someone else. It boils down, once again, to belief.

While you're building your new belief in prosperity, make symbolic gestures, as mentioned in Chapter 1. Drop your loose change into the Salvation Army collecting bucket at Christmas. Buy yourself something special. Treat yourself to dinner at your favourite restaurant. Buy a hardback book that you really want. Create your own affirmation about prosperity – make sure you always phrase it in the present tense – and either write or say it at least a dozen times a day for as long as it takes for your unconscious to get the message. *Back that affirmation with emotion.*

And copy and put up this quote from Louise Hay's book in a spot where you'll see it frequently: 'True prosperity begins with feeling good about yourself.... It is never an amount of money; it is a state of mind. Prosperity or lack of it is an outer expression of the ideas in your head.'

Prosperity and Abundance Spells

Creating New Beliefs

Tools: 14 green scented candles
            1 empty glass container
When: On the New Moon

While you're still in the process of writing your affirmation, buy fourteen scented green candles. Little candles are good for this, the kind that are sold for aromatherapy burners. On the night of the next New Moon, light one of the candles at your altar or special place. While it's burning, say your affirmation aloud and feel its truth. After five minutes blow the candle out and rub your hands in the smoke. Wave the smoke towards your face, your body, your clothes.

Remember that fragrance, associate it with abundance, prosperity and your new belief. Set the candle aside where you can see it.

Repeat this for the next fourteen days, using a new candle each time, until the next Full Moon. Set each spent candle next to its predecessor. On the night of the Full Moon, after you have burned the fourteenth candle, light all fourteen and let them burn down. Then pour the wax into a glass container.

This new candle symbolizes your new belief about prosperity. Once the wax has solidified, throw it out, thus sending that belief out into the universe.

Each time you do this spell, remember to give thanks.

Your Desire

Tools: 1 green scented candle
An object that represents your desire (choose from your list)
When: During the waxing moon

At night, under the waxing phase of the moon, light a green candle at your special place. State your need or intention. Place or focus on something on your altar that represents this need or intention, and repeat your affirmation. Visualize the manifestation of whatever it is you need. Don't worry about how it will manifest; simply trust that your wish will be fulfilled. Blow out the candle and leave it and your symbolic objects on the altar, and be grateful for all that you *do* have.

Repeat as often as you feel is necessary during the waxing moon. When you trust that what you need is forthcoming (and yes, this does take trust), clear your altar and let the candle burn all the way down. Then throw it out, release it.

To Increase Your Income

Tools: Green and white candles
A pack of tarot cards
An object that represents your desire (consult your list again!)
A pen with green ink and a piece of paper
When: During the waxing moon

The colour green is obviously important in money spells. White, however, can also be useful because it represents understanding.

Put your candles at opposite ends of your altar. Then between them, place an object that represents your desire to increase your income. This can be an object that symbolizes something on your list or anything else – a coin, a banknote, a sacred stone, whatever you want.

From your pack of tarot cards, remove the suit of pentacles or coins, which represent money, and the Star and the 9 of cups. In front of the white candle, place the ace of coins; this symbolizes new financial undertakings and opportunities. In front of the green candle, put

Believe, Believe

In *The Wizard of Oz*, Dorothy got back to Kansas because she believed the wizard when he told her all she had to do was close her eyes and click her heels three times. Dorothy got back because she believed in magic. Belief: that's what it always boils down to.

the 10 of coins; it's called the 'Bank of England' card and symbolizes a financial windfall. In the middle of the two candles, place the 9 of cups – the wish card – and the Star, which symbolizes, among other things, success.

Now light the candles and say:

> *The money I spend*
> *or the money I lend*
> *comes back to me*
> *in multiples of three.*

Visualize the figure you have in mind. Jot it down on the piece of paper. Imagine what you can do with an increase in your income. The more vivid you can make your visualization, backed with intense emotion, the faster it will manifest. This ritual can be as short or as long as you want. The point is to do it with full conscious awareness and intent, backed with emotion. End the spell by blowing out the candle and giving thanks, then throw away the candle.

On the next night, repeat the ritual, but with certain changes. First, remove the 2 and 5 of pentacles from your deck. You don't want these two cards on your altar. The 2 of coins means you're robbing Peter to pay Paul; the 5 means poverty and heavy debt.

Light your candles. Say the poem. Then take the remaining cards and place them between the ace and 10 of coins and the wish card and the Star. Say the poem, visualize, affirm, then blow out the candles and throw them away. Keep everything else on the altar as it is overnight.

On the third night, light the candles and give thanks for everything you have, repeat the poem and feel the reality of your increase in income taking form around you. Blow out the candles and throw them away.

Keep saying the poem as long as you need to, as often as you like, even after the increase begins to manifest.

Purple Ribbons

If your money seems to be going out faster than it comes in, try this quick fix. Buy a roll of purple, violet or lavender ribbon, available in the gift-wrap area of most department stores and supermarkets. Tie a piece of ribbon around every tap in your home and as you do so, say: 'As water flows, my finances grow.'

Good-bye Debt

Tools: 1 red candle
           Paper and pen
           Empty heatproof bowl
When: During the waning moon

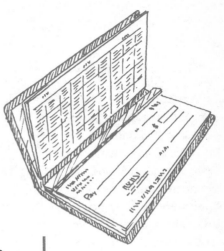

Remember that even quick and easy spells must be done with vivid intent and visualization. Also, for safety reasons, perform this spell outside in a garden or yard, or inside in a sink. Set the candle on a non-flammable surface.

First, write down the amount of your debt on a small piece of thin paper. Light the red candle. Red represents energy, and what you're doing here is drawing on energy to cancel your debt. Say the following words:

> *Debt begone*
> *lickety split,*
> *debt begone*
> *before I spit.*

Then take the piece of paper and drop it into the candle flames until it catches fire. Let it burn to ashes in the empty bowl. Extinguish the candle's flame, then throw out the candle. On the next New Moon, bury the ashes far from your home.

Be Careful What You Wish For

At some point in your spell casting, something invariably happens that brings home the truth of the adage, 'Be careful what you wish for. You may just get it.'

This adage is actually addressing the power of intent. If, for instance, you ask for abundance or financial freedom, have you really thought about the repercussions of that wish? How will that abundance or financial freedom affect your family? Your relationship with your friends? Your job and living situation?

Attracting Money

To attract money – or anything else, for that matter – pour a pint of mineral oil into a clear litre bottle. Add seven magnetite stones (found at most New Age bookshops) and a pinch or two of iron filings. Charge your concoction in sunlight, preferably the light of the rising sun, for seven days. Then transfer your oil to smaller bottles with dark glass, label them and put them in the dark.

To bring in money, rub some oil on your thumb and forefinger, then rub your fingertips on money before you spend it. The idea here is that the charged, magnetic oil will attract money into your life.

One woman asked that she be allowed to pursue her interest in Wicca. She got her wish, but at a cost that she didn't anticipate when she made the wish. Her husband of thirty-two years left her for a much younger woman, her life fell apart, and for a while she was so depressed she had to take medication to get through the day. But she now had the freedom to pursue her interest in Wicca and today is the high priestess of her own coven. Her advice? Think carefully about what you wish for.

Creating Prosperity

Tools: Sprig of sage
           1 green candle
           Empty bowl
           Pinch of cinnamon

When: During the New Moon

This spell can be for any kind of prosperity, but works best for the prosperity of inner peace, the source of all true prosperity. Sage is a good herb for getting rid of negativity, and cinnamon is excellent for boosting your energy and creativity.

On the night of the New Moon, put the green candle in the empty bowl with the sage. Light them both. As you sprinkle cinnamon into the flame, say: 'I embrace prosperity and inner peace.'

Repeat these words and keep sprinkling cinnamon into the flame until the cinnamon is gone. Let the candle and the sage burn down, then bury them in your garden or yard. If you do this during the winter, you can bury the remains in the earth of an indoor plant.

Attracting Financial Opportunities

Before you do this spell, read the section in Chapter 9 on the correspondences between astrological planets and days of the week, and glance through Chapter 2 to refresh your memory about the importance of the cardinal points in casting spells.

Tools: 1 gold candle
          Your favourite scented oil
          Clear quartz crystal
          Pen and paper
When: On a Thursday during the New Moon

Thursday is Jupiter's day, the planet in astrology that represents expansion, and expansion is what you're attempting to do with this spell. Place the gold candle at the northern end of your altar, the direction that represents, among other things, fertility.

On the piece of paper, write: I embrace all opportunities for expanding my financial base. Place the piece of paper in front of the candle and put the quartz crystal on top of it. The crystal acts as a magnifier of your thoughts.

Light the candle, and visualize new financial opportunities flowing into your life. Read aloud what you have written down. Then burn the paper, releasing the desire. Let the candle burn down and throw it out.

As always, give thanks for the prosperity you already have.

To Increase Your Cash and Prosperity Flow

Tools: 12 plants with purple blooms
When: Whenever you feel the need

In feng shui, purple, violet and lavender are associated with wealth and prosperity. Standing at your front door, locate the furthest left-hand corner of your home. This is your prosperity area. Put your plants in that room, if it has enough light. If it doesn't, place the plants as close as possible to that room.

Prosperity for Busy People

One of the most frequent complaints people have about casting spells is that they take so much time. So here's a sixty-second spell to increase your general prosperity.

Gratitude and Prosperity

'Be sure you are not rejecting prosperity now. If a friend invites you to lunch or dinner, accept with joy and pleasure.... If you get a gift, accept it graciously. If you can't use the gift, pass it on to someone else. Keep the flow of things moving through your life.'

Louise Hay
You Can Heal Your Life

Tools: Any purple, violet or lavender object
        Piece of paper and a pen
When: Whenever you feel the need, but most powerful on New
        Moon

Jot down the specific things you're trying to create in terms of prosperity. Tuck the list under the purple object and say, 'Make it so.'

Affirmations and Prosperity

The power of affirmations can't be emphasized too strongly, particularly in the area of prosperity and abundance. Even if you don't believe in the power of words, if you say something enough times, your unconscious mind begins to believe it and your reality begins to shift.

It can work for things both simple and grand. Are you waiting for a cheque that hasn't arrived? Then fifty times a day, repeat, 'My cheque is here' or 'My cheque arrives'. Or perhaps you need extra money this month for repairs to your home. In this instance, you might say, 'I have enough money to do the repairs'.

Try not to concern yourself with *how* you're going to get that extra money. Simply be aware that opportunities will begin to present themselves to you if you continue to say the affirmation. Be alert for patterns of coincidence, which can serve as signposts to new opportunities. And *always* phrase your affirmation in the present tense!

The Power of Three

In magical traditions, there is a saying that what you do comes back to you by the power of three. Applied to prosperity and abundance, it works the same way. Every time you buy something and money exchanges hands, say to yourself:

*This money comes
back to me
by the power of three.
So mote it be.*

Chapter Nine

Love Spells

Defining What You Want

Spells for love are numerous and varied, and before you do any such spells, it's important to define exactly what you want. Are you trying to attract someone to you? Looking for your soulmate? Hoping to enhance a relationship? Seeking to seduce someone? The more specific you can be, the greater your chances of success.

But keep in mind that the purpose of a love spell isn't to *make* someone fall in love with you. The purpose is to enhance and empower your own energy so you attract the individual who is the best for you. Fairy tales and Shakespeare aside, we all have free will and nothing can violate that will, not even magic or spells.

In 'Brainstorming: Your Love Life' opposite, you're going to take inventory of your love life. The questions apply whether you're single or committed and should give you a fairly clear idea about the *patterns* that run throughout your intimate relationships. Once you identify the patterns, it's easier to change them.

Loving Yourself

The first prerequisite for casting any love spell is that you have to love yourself. This sounds simple enough, but so many of us have grown up believing that we aren't worthy, aren't attractive or intelligent enough, aren't this or that. So before you try any love spell, spend a little time uncovering your beliefs about yourself.

If you find that you hold negative beliefs about your worth as an individual, try one of author Louise Hay's most powerful affirmations: *I love and approve of myself.* Say it out loud, write it out and post it on your mirrors, your fridge, wherever you're going to see it frequently. Yes, you probably will feel a bit foolish at first, but that just means that the affirmation is working. When you repeat something often enough and back it with positive, uplifting emotion, your unconscious mind gets the message.

Brainstorming: Your Love Life

1. Describe your ideal intimate relationship.
2. Describe the worst intimate relationship you ever had.
3. How would you rate your present sex life?
4. If you're involved, is your partner romantic?
5. Are you romantic?
6. If you're involved, is your present relationship emotionally satisfying?
7. What, if anything, would you change about this relationship?
8. If you're not involved, list five things you're seeking in an intimate relationship:

   a. _____
   b. _____
   c. _____
   d. _____
   e. _____

9. Describe the most satisfying relationship you have now. This can be with anyone —
   a partner, a child, a parent, even a pet.
10. Do your love relationships have a spiritual component? If so, in what way?

11. List five things you would like to change about yourself:

    a. _____
    b. _____
    c. _____
    d. _____
    e. _____

12. List five things you love about yourself:

    a. _____
    b. _____
    c. _____
    d. _____
    e. _____

13. List five things you love about the person you love most:

    a. _____
    b. _____
    c. _____
    d. _____
    e. _____

14. List five things that make you feel good:

    a. _____
    b. _____
    c. _____
    d. _____
    e. _____

Power Days

In astrology, the days of the week are governed by particular planets and the planets have particular meanings. In order to tip the odds in your favour, try to align the type of spell to the most propitious day of the week.

DAYS AND THEIR RULERS		
Day	**Ruler**	**Meaning**
Sunday	Sun	Success, healing, happiness
Monday	Moon	Intuition, women, mother figure, creativity
Tuesday	Mars	Energy, passion, sexuality, aggression
Wednesday	Mercury	Communication, messages, the mind, the intellect, siblings
Thursday	Jupiter	Expansion, luck, success, higher education, the law
Friday	Venus	Love, art, beauty, money, women
Saturday	Saturn	Responsibility, structure, duties

Since these are love spells, they should be done on Venus's night, Friday, unless stated otherwise.

Astrology and Love Spells

Another way to tip the scales in your favour when doing love spells is to use something that represents the other person's sun sign and element. If, for example, the other person is a Taurus, which is an earth sign, then you may want to enhance the earth element in your spell. Since water represents emotions and intuition, you can also enhance the water element.

Love Spells

To Attract a Lover

Tools: Aromatherapy burner
1 pink tealight candle
Ylang-ylang essential oil
Sandalwood essential oil
Lavender or your favourite essential oil
List of qualities

When: Friday, preferably around the New Moon, definitely
during a waxing moon

The list of qualities you're going to create requires some forethought. What are you looking for in a lover? Certain physical characteristics? Certain personality attributes? Be specific, but brief. Write your list in pink ink.

On or around the New Moon – or, at the very least, during the waxing moon and definitely on a Friday night – light your pink candle. Place your list next to the candle. Add several drops of sandalwood oil, lavender oil or your favourite oil to the water bowl in your burner and light the candle inside it. If the burner's candle is also pink, so much the better.

As the water warms and the scent of the heated oil is released into the air, vividly imagine your lover. How does he or she look, act, dress? Be as detailed as possible. What kind of car does this person drive? What type of work does he or she do? What are his or her passions? At the bottom of the list, draw the symbol for Venus: ♀

Continue the visualization for as long as you need to make the mental images as vivid as possible. Inhale the scent of oils from the burner. Extinguish the candle's flames. At least twice between when you do the spell and the next Full Moon, make your oil mix and light the pink candle and the candle in the burner. As the scent permeates the air you breathe, *feel* the presence of your lover. As always, express thanks.

On the Full Moon, release your wish by throwing away both of the candles.

Signs and Elements

Sign	Dates	Element
Aries	March 21–April 20	fire
Taurus	April 21–May 21	earth
Gemini	May 22–June 22	air
Cancer	June 23–July 23	water
Leo	July 24–August 23	fire
Virgo	August 24–September 23	earth
Libra	September 24–October 23	air
Scorpio	October 24–November 22	water
Sagittarius	November 23–December 21	fire
Capricorn	December 22–January 20	earth
Aquarius	January 21–February 19	air
Pisces	February 20–March 20	water

Love Incense

This is a fun and effective way not only to empower yourself, but to attract the person you desire. It requires three types of herbs: lavender, marigold and rosemary. The herbs should be charged under the light of the full moon before they are ground. Several hours of exposure to the light of the full moon should be sufficient.

Once the herbs are charged, they should be ground and sprinkled over incense coal. This type of coal is available in most New Age bookshops and is commonly used for wands made of sage. Before the person arrives, light the sprinkled incense on a safe, heatproof surface, and watch it as it smoulders.

An Instant Boost

Tools: Ylang-ylang oil
When: Whenever you need a spiritual or emotional boost

This spell is actually to bolster your self-confidence when you're going to be with the person you care about. You can do it anywhere, at any time. Set aside a few minutes where you won't be interrupted. Add a couple of drops of ylang-ylang oil to a teaspoon of almond oil and dab it behind your ears and on the inside of your arms. Vividly image what is going to happen when you're with the person you're going to see. Hold the images in your mind as long as possible, maintaining the vividness and detail. Then release the images with the certainty that everything will come to pass as you have imagined.

To Find Your Soulmate

Tools: 1 fresh rose
Geranium essential oil
Sandalwood essential oil
1 pink candle
1 red candle
Empty glass container
When: On the New Moon, preferably on a Friday

The red rose, which symbolizes the love you're looking for, should be placed in a vase of water on your altar. Put several drops of geranium oil and sandalwood oil in your burner. Place the pink and red candles in a shallow ceramic or glass bowl. Light the candle in your oil burner. As you light the pink and red candles, say:

Winds of love, come to me,
Bring my soulmate, I decree.
This I wish, so mote it be.

Imagine yourself with your soulmate. Be as detailed and vivid as possible in your imagining. Pour emotion into this visualization. Feel the potentiality of attracting this person forming in the air around you. Let the candles burn all the way down, so the pink and red wax flows together in the shallow bowl. While the wax is still warm, shape it with your fingers so the pink and red are fully commingled. Run cold water into the bowl so the wax doesn't stick, remove the pink and red wax, now newly shaped, and place near the door of your home.

On the night of the Full Moon, throw the wax out, releasing it, and also throw out the now dried rose.

Tarot Love Spell

Tools: Aromatherapy burner and candle
Pack of tarot cards
Orange or lemon essential oil
Pink, red or orange candle

When: Waxing moon, preferably on a Friday when you're with the one you love

This spell is designed to draw the one you love closer to you. The candle colour is your choice of the three above and depends on what you're trying to accomplish. Pink represents love, red represents passion, and orange represents balance. The choice in oils depends on which scent you like best. Either one will do the job.

During the waxing moon, before you're going to be with the one you love, put several drops of the oil you selected into the water bowl of your burner. Now anoint the candle using a small piece of soft cloth (do not use your fingers – essential oils are very powerful and can cause a sensitive reaction). From your pack of tarot cards, remove the suit of cups, which represent affairs of the heart. Select the king, queen and 9 of cups (the wish card). Place the three cards on your altar, between the candle and the burner.

Light the burner and your candle and state your wish. Be specific. Imagine it happening. Blow the candles out when you've finished, anoint them again with the oil, and place them in the area where you and your lover will be spending time together. When you're together in that room, make sure these candles are burning.

On the night of the Full Moon, light the candles again, state your wish once more, then extinguish the flames. Throw away the candles when you've finished, and give thanks.

Tarot and the Elements

One variation of the tarot love spell is to select significators that represent you and the person you love. This method pegs the suits of the court cards to the elements. If you're a Gemini, for instance, and the one you love is a Sagittarius, then you would select a king or queen of swords to symbolize yourself and a king or queen of rods to represent the other person.

If you're doing a love spell that involves younger people, you would use the pages of the appropriate suits. If you're doing a spell that involves a pet, use a knight of any suit that feels right to you. If you know your pet's sun sign, use the appropriate suit.

Results

How quickly you get results from a spell depends, of course, on the clarity of your intent and your beliefs. If, in your heart of hearts, you really think this is just so much mumbo-jumbo, then it's unlikely that you'll see results, and your time would be better spent working on changing that belief. On the other hand, if you're sceptical but open and receptive to the possibility that you live in a magical universe and have the power to manifest what you need and desire, then you'll see results.

Sometimes when you do a spell, the situation seems to get worse before it gets better. This is possible with any kind of visualization exercise. Part of the reason is that when you consciously work with your beliefs and your intent, you're polarizing power within yourself, which helps rid you of negative beliefs. Once you have become free of the negative beliefs, the situation can improve.

To Enhance Your Relationship

Tools: 1 red candle
1 pink candle
Sprig of rosemary
Sprig of sage
Object that represents the enhancement or expansion of
the relationship, such as a ring

When: A Thursday night during the waxing moon

You're doing this spell on Thursday because it belongs to Jupiter, the planet in astrology that signifies expansion, success and luck. Before you begin your spell, light a sprig of sage and smudge the room where you'll be working. This simply means you move the burning sage around the room so that its smoke passes over the walls and windows, the doorway and your altar, purifying and cleansing the air. As you do this, hold a saucer or small bowl under the smouldering sage to catch the embers.

With the sage still smoking, place the pink and red candles at opposite ends of your altar, with the object that represents the expansion in the middle. Next to the object, place a sprig of rosemary. Now light the candles and the rosemary. Inhale the mixture of scents, shut your eyes and imagine your relationship expanding in the way you want. Be detailed and make your visualization vivid.

Give thanks, watch the candles burn down and throw them away.

Spell for Personal Empowerment

This spell is particularly good when you're in a new relationship and are feeling somewhat uncertain or unsettled about where the relationship is headed. It's also good for any situation or time when you need to feel personally empowered.

Tools: 2 gold-coloured candles
Frankincense resin
Sprig of sage
Deck of tarot cards
Pen and paper

When: The Full Moon

Compatibility Factors and the Stars

With whom are you most compatible? In theory, the best match is someone whose moon sign is in your sun sign, or vice versa. This would give you an instinctive understanding of each other. Another good match occurs when there are connections between sun, moon and rising signs. The most passionate relationships often occur when the sign of your Venus matches another person's sun or moon sign.

If at all possible, do this spell where the light of the Full Moon spills across your working area. Begin by lighting a sprig of sage to smudge the area where you'll be working and to increase your mental clarity. Next, remove the kings and queens from each of the four suits in your tarot pack.

If you're doing this spell for personal empowerment, simply select a king or a queen that represents the element of your astrological sign. (See the sidebar on the left for element correspondences.) If, for instance, you're an Aries, Leo or Sagittarian female, then you would choose the queen of wands. If you're doing a spell that involves another person, then select a king or queen of the suit that represents the element of that person's astrological sign. If you don't know the person's sign, allow your intuition to guide you in your selection of a card.

On the sheet of paper, write out your intent. Keep it simple and specific. Place the paper on your altar, with the card or cards on top of it. Put one of the gold candles to the west, the other to the south. Light the candles and the frankincense. Shut your eyes and visualize what you desire. Then say:

> *Spirits of the west,*
> *Clarify my love,*
> *Spirits of the south,*
> *Empower me.*
> *So mote it be.*

Give thanks, let the candles burn down, then throw them away the next day.

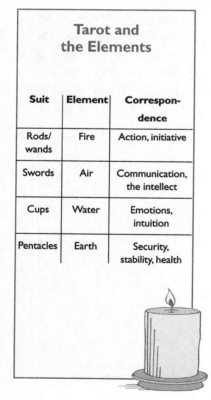

Tarot and the Elements

Suit	Element	Correspondence
Rods/wands	Fire	Action, initiative
Swords	Air	Communication, the intellect
Cups	Water	Emotions, intuition
Pentacles	Earth	Security, stability, health

A Spell to Enhance Your Sex Life

Do you or your partner work so much overtime that you never have time for each other? Does your home always seem to be filled with other people? Are your schedules so frantic that you and your partner seem to be moving constantly in opposite directions? Then this spell might be just the ticket to rectify the situation.

Tools: Ylang-ylang essential oil
           Jasmine essential oil
           4 red candles
           Sea salt
           Your favourite music
When: Full Moon or on a Tuesday, which is ruled by Mars

A Full Moon on a Tuesday is the absolute best for this spell, but if nature doesn't fit that time schedule, a Full Moon on any day of the week is fine. It can also be done with good results on any night when you're in the mood. First, draw a bath and sprinkle sea salt into the water. Sea salt is an excellent psychic and spiritual cleanser. Soak as long as it takes to really relax – not just your muscles, but down to your very cells.

When you're completely relaxed, dry yourself and put on loose and comfortable cotton clothing. If you have set up an altar, add several drops of both oils into the filled water bowl of an aromatherapy burner. Light the candle beneath it. As soon as the fragrance begins to permeate the air, place a candle in each of the four directions, beginning in the north and moving clockwise. As you light each candle, say:

> *Goddesses of the north and south, the east and west,*
> *Bestow your blessings, your power best,*
> *On me and him (her) to make us one*
> *It will be done.*

When you're finished, put the candles, still lit, into the bedroom or wherever you and your partner will be. Watch them as they burn down. Wipe out the oil container and add fresh drops of the ylang-ylang and jasmine oil. The candle under the container should be lit when you and your partner are together, so that the fragrance suffuses the room where you make love.

Tarot Decks

When selecting your first tarot deck, it's wise to stick with the Rider Waite pack or one of its clones, simply because most books are written to that pack and it's easier to learn. If possible, handle the pack that interests you — see how the cards feel in your hands.

Once you've got the meanings down pat, become adventurous in your selection of a second pack. Check out the round packs — Motherpeace and Tarot of the Cloisters. The Voyager Tarot is one of the most exquisite packs, appropriate for the twenty-first century. Some other fascinating packs are the Unicorn Tarot, Tarot of the Witches and the miniature Albano Waite deck. Whatever pack you choose, be sure that the art speaks to your intuition.

Love Divination

Love divination is like any form of divination, except that you're tailoring your questions specifically to romance. Love divination is a useful tool for gauging the progress of your spell, to find out how well it's working or why it isn't working. It provides information and insight you may need to fine-tune your love spells.

For the types of love divination we're going to do here, you'll need a deck of tarot cards or a set of rune stones, about ten sheets of white paper and a box of coloured pencils.

Divination Using the Tarot or Runes

Question 1: Is my spell working as I had hoped?

As you repeat the question to yourself, shuffle your cards or shake your runes, then fan them out face down in front of you. Select seven cards or runes and lay them out from left to right, as shown below.

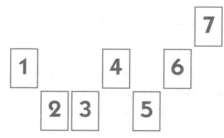

1. The first position represents your question. If the meaning doesn't seem to have anything at all to do with your question, it may be indicating there are facets to the situation that you don't see or that you weren't focusing on your questions when you drew the cards.

2-3. These two positions represent unrealized potential about your question. If both cards/runes are negative, you may want to redesign your spell. If only one card/rune is negative, then just a bit of fine-tuning is required. If both cards/runes are positive, trust the process and believe that things are unfolding the way you hoped.

4. The fourth position represents what is visible now.

5. This position tells you a great deal about what is hidden from you, what you don't know about the situation.

6. This position tells you what is emerging in the next few days or weeks. If you don't like what it says, then by all means redesign your spell.

7. This is the final outcome.

Question 2: What is this relationship about?

Shuffle, fan out and select eight cards or runes. Lay them out as indicated below.

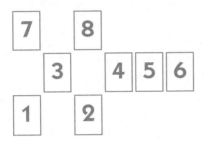

1. This position describes the general tone of the relationship as it exists in the moment you do the reading.

2. Here you find your blind spot – what you don't see about the relationship that you need to know.

3. This position describes how the other person perceives the relationship.

4. The fourth position describes how you perceive the relationship.

5. In this position lie potential challenges that may arise in the next few weeks.

6. Here are the strengths of the relationship that will help you overcome the challenges.

7–8. These tell you the ultimate resolution about the relationship.

Question 4: What am I looking for in a soulmate?

Shuffle, fan out and select six cards. Lay them out as indicated.

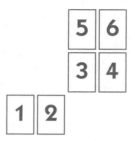

1. The qualities you think you're looking for
2. The qualities your higher self is seeking in a soulmate
3. The qualities you must develop or nurture to find your soulmate
4. Your strengths
5. How your soulmate enters your life
6. How the two of you mesh

Colour Divination

For this next type of divination, cut your paper into ten squares. With your coloured pencils, write one of the following colours on each of the ten squares: red, blue, yellow, pink, white, green, brown, orange, black, silver. The meanings of the colours are:

Red: Energy, sexual passion
Blue: Tranquillity, fidelity
Yellow: Happiness
Pink: Romance, 'in the pink'
White: Spiritual understanding
Green: Abundance, growth, fertility
Brown: Prosperity, sensuality
Orange: Balance
Black: Unknown, hidden
Silver: New beginnings

Question 4: What is going on in my relationship?

Shuffle the squares as you think of your question, then lay them out as shown below:

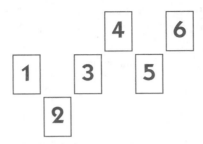

1. The general nature of your question
2. What you don't see
3. What is coming up soon
4. What you see
5. What you find
6. The resolution

With any of these spreads, you can change the questions to fit your particular situation and needs.

A Sample Reading

Marcia had recently met a man her age (thirty-three), who seemed to have all the qualities she was looking for in a mate. But she had certain reservations she couldn't explain. Her question was: what does he think about our relationship? She drew the following colours:

1. **Red.** With red in the first position, it was apparent that he felt the relationship was filled with sexual passion. That was Marcia's take on it, too. Since the card resonated for it, a sure indication that the cards reflected her question, she continued the reading.
2. **Black.** There's something she doesn't see in this relationship, something unknown and hidden.
3. **Yellow.** Happy events and experiences are coming up soon in the relationship.

Brainstorming: Your Love Divination Reading

Using the format below as a guide, you can record your own reading, using tarot cards, runes or the squares that you made.

Type of divination:

_____

_____

_____

Your question:

_____

_____

_____

The layout:

_____

_____

_____

Your interpretation:

_____

_____

_____

4. **Silver.** What she sees in this relationship is a new beginning.
5. **White.** She ultimately finds that the relationship is spiritually based – or needs to be.
6. **Blue.** Ultimately, the basis of this relationship is about fidelity and tranquillity.

The reading turned out to be accurate.

Astrology and Love Divination

This type of divination combines astrology with the tarot. To derive the maximum benefit from the spread, you should know the sun sign of the person about whom you're inquiring. First, separate the kings and queens from the pack and set the rest of the cards aside. Then, using the earlier lists of correspondences (see pages 121 and 126), select the two cards that represent you and the other person.

If, for instance, you're an Aries woman, then the card that represents you – your significator – is the queen of rods. If you're a Pisces man, your significator is the king of cups. If you're asking about a child, you would use a page of the suit related to the element of the child's sun sign. Once you've chosen the two significators, place them side by side. Leave the rest of the court cards in a separate pile and shuffle the rest of the deck. Draw seven cards and place them as below.

Significator 1 (you)	Significator 2 (the other person)
1	2
3	4
5	6
	7

Sun Sign Compatibility

Aries: You're most compatible with another fire sign – Sagittarius or Leo – or with an air sign – Gemini, Libra, Aquarius.

Taurus: You're most compatible with other earth signs – Virgo and Capricorn. You should probably stay away from other Tauruses in romantic relationships; it would always be a contest of wills. You also get along with water signs – Cancer, Scorpio, Pisces.

Gemini: Fellow air signs, Aquarius and Libra, would work for you. You also get along well with fire signs, especially Sagittarius, who is your polar opposite on the zodiac wheel.

Cancer: You're compatible with other water signs – Scorpio and Pisces – but should probably stay away from other Cancers; you would drive each other crazy. Earth signs work well for you – Taurus, Virgo, Capricorn.

Leo: Despite popular opinion, another fire sign may not work for you. You're best with an air sign and, for some Leo temperaments, another fixed sign – Scorpio, Aquarius, Taurus.

Virgo: Taurus or Capricorn would be compatible, although Capricorn's ambition may annoy you. You're also good with water signs or with two of the other mutable signs – Gemini and Sagittarius.

Libra: Another air sign works well. So does a fire sign. You may also be compatible with other cardinal signs – Capricorn, Cancer, Aries.

Scorpio: Cancer and Pisces are both a good bet, but both may have drawbacks, too. Earth signs probably are most compatible – Taurus, Virgo, Capricorn.

Sagittarius: Other fire signs are good for you. But air signs may be best; they feed your energy and interests: Gemini, Libra, Aquarius.

Capricorn: You're most compatible with fellow earth signs – Taurus, Virgo – and with water signs – Cancer, Scorpio, Pisces. The latter, however, may be too impractical for your pragmatic nature.

Aquarius: Other air signs or fire signs. A Gemini or Libra understands your intellect. You feel a natural magnetism for Aries, Leo and Sagittarius.

Pisces: The best signs for you are Cancer or an earth sign. Forget Scorpio; even though the element is like yours, the energy is too intense.

The first and second positions represent how you each perceive the relationship as a whole. The third and fourth positions describe how the relationship is evolving at the present time for each of you. The fifth and sixth positions describe your individual expectations about where the relationship may be headed in the future. Depending on the cards you draw for the previous two positions, the seventh card can represent one of two things: the most likely outcome of the relationship, or the event that ultimately unites you – or separates you.

This spread can be adapted in various ways to ask about any kind of relationship in your life – with a child, a parent or grandparent, a friend, a lover, a spouse, even with a pet. By using significators pegged to the element of each person's sun sign, you personalize the energy.

If three people are involved in the question, you would simply choose a third significator and draw nine cards in all, placing them from left to right. The maximum for this spread is four people. Any more than that and the spread becomes difficult to read.

Spell for Fidelity

Many spells dealing with fidelity and bringing home a wayward lover are manipulative in that they attempt to influence the other person. While these spells often work very well, they can also backfire. So this spell focuses on you rather than on the other individual.

Before you cast a spell concerning fidelity, be sure of your motives. Do you suspect that your significant other is being unfaithful? If so, do you really want to remain with that person?

Tools: 4 candles of the appropriate colours for the four cardinal points
Object that represents your lover
Object that represents you
When: The full moon

Magical Properties of the Sun Signs

The magical properties of sun signs can come in handy during spell-casting that involves attracting love in general or a particular person.

Aries: Ruled by Mars, the god of war, you're a cardinal fire sign, whose colour is red.

Taurus: Ruled by Venus, goddess of love and romance, you're a fixed earth sign. Your colour is pale blue. However, some astrologers question Venus's rulership; they feel that Taurus is actually ruled by the Earth. So shades of brown will work with your sign, too.

Gemini: Ruled by Mercury, the messenger. As a mutable air sign, your colours lie in the pastels.

Cancer: Ruled by the Moon, you're a cardinal water sign. Your colour is the hue of the ocean or the pale luminosity of the Moon.

Leo: Ruled by the Sun, you're a fixed fire sign. Your colour is definitely yellow.

Virgo: Ruled by Mercury, you're a mutable earth sign. Your colour lies in earth tones.

Libra: Ruled by Venus, you're a cardinal water sign. Your colours lie in the pastels.

Scorpio: Ruled by Pluto, the god of the underworld, you're a fixed water sign. Your magical colours are the deeper tones – navy blue, magenta, olive green.

Sagittarius: Ruled by Jupiter, you're a mutable fire sign. Your magical colours are hot and luminous – hot pink, burning yellows.

Capricorn: Ruled by Saturn, you're a cardinal earth sign. Your colours are earth tones.

Aquarius: Ruled by Uranus, you're a fixed air sign. Your colours fall in the pastels, like those of Gemini and Libra.

Pisces: Ruled by Neptune, god of the sea, you're a mutable water sign. Your colours fall in the vast spectrum of blues.

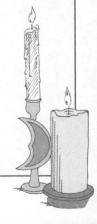

Before you cast your circle, make sure you have the objects you've selected on your working surface. Use sea salt to cast your circle. As you light each candle moving clockwise from the east, visualize the element of each direction. Make the visualization specific.

As you face east (air), for example, you might breathe deeply and evenly and imagine your intellect as lucid, crystalline, capable of making the necessary decisions. For south (fire), you might imagine you and your lover passionately embracing. When you have finished lighting the candles, stand facing the east and say:

Winds of the east,
Goddess of the feast,
Keep (name of person) with me
So mote it be.

As your face south, say:

Fires of passion
Keep (name) close to me
So mote it be.

As you face west, say:

Waters of our hearts
Never do part
So mote it be.

As you face north, say:

Goddess of the earth
Keep (your name and other person's)
Together for now and ever more.
So mote it be.

Break your circle. Let the candles burn out naturally (but don't leave them unattended), then bury them together in your garden.

Chapter Ten
Spells for Personal Power

S ome years ago at the Miami Book Fair, my husband and I were having lunch with some editors and writers on the terrace of a Miami Beach café in Florida. It was a warm, humid day for November and no one was particularly comfortable out there on the porch, but the tables inside were taken. Suddenly, a hush fell over the crowd and all eyes turned towards the front steps.

Writer Isabel Allende stood there, eyes sweeping across the terrace in search of a table. She looked regal, beautiful, utterly untouched by the heat. But most of all, her personal presence radiated such power and charisma that for a few moments that hush hovered over the noonday crowd.

Then Allende was ushered into the building and we all resumed our lunches and conversations. In retrospect, I realized that even though we were reacting to her as Allende the writer, the presence she radiated had nothing to do with Allende the writer. The presence came from Allende the woman, the person – it came from something internal, not external.

At the same book fair several years later, my daughter and I were hurrying along the pavement towards the university campus where the fair was held. We were supposed to meet friends and were late. I noticed a black limo parked at the curb. A very tall man stood next to it, listening to a woman who seemed to be doing most of the talking.

'Mum', my daughter whispered, jerking on my hand. 'That's Stephen King!'

I stopped, she stopped, and we stared. King was dressed completely in black, and stood about six foot six or seven. He looked like a friendly giant – but with an air of unmistakable dignity. The woman was obviously a fan, chatting non-stop, her hands darting through the air, and I almost expected her to thrust a manuscript at him.

Despite the heat and humidity of Miami in November and despite the fact that King had just spoken for an hour and signed books afterwards, he stood there listening attentively to the woman. He had the same commanding presence that Allende did – and he would have had it even if he weren't Stephen King the writer, because it *came from within*.

This isn't to imply that to have *presence* you have to be a writer, politician, celebrity or someone in the public eye. In fact, your job or

Energy Fields

'There isn't any delusion. It is absolutely clear that this body energy is a genuine phenomenon of some kind.'

Michael Crichton
Travels

career really has nothing to do with it. I've met children who have *it*. I've met elderly people who have *it*. I've met people from all walks of life who have *it*, and quite often, they don't realize what they have. In some instances, a person may be born with presence, but usually it's something that must be cultivated, nurtured, explored. Usually, it's an ineffable quality that manifests over a period of time, with the development of self-knowledge.

There it is again. That adage. *Know thyself.*

To know yourself and to use what you learn requires an act of will. The dictionary definition of 'will' describes it as 'choice, determination, volition'. But what does any of that really mean?

Will

Your will is the crux of every visualization, manifestation and spell. It's the act of galvanizing yourself at the deepest levels to achieve something that you desire. You don't simply say the words. You don't just go through the motions. You plunge into yourself, you delve, to discover your true motives, needs and desires. You work to bring that self-knowledge to full consciousness, into your daily awareness. And then you commit to the path and trust the process that unfolds.

When you develop this sort of awareness, synchronicities tend to proliferate in your life, and they often occur in clusters. More and more frequently, you may find that external events precisely mirror inner conditions, as described in Chapter 3, under the heading of 'Your Life as Oracle'. At the same time, you may find that your dreams are especially vivid and that they cluster around one or two themes.

Recently, for instance, a series of seemingly innocuous and irritating events in my life clustered around the word 'key'. I couldn't find a book I needed on fiction writing called *Story*, by Robert **McKee**; I had misplaced a car **key**, and I had a vivid dream in which **key** played a part.

In the dream, my husband, daughter and I were on an island and had missed the boat back to Key West, Florida. It was nearly dusk. I could see the lights of Key West in the distance. My agent's son-in-law (also an agent) was waiting on the pier with us. He had missed

---

Power Inventory

To increase your personal power, you should first pinpoint which area of your life lacks power. Is it your professional life? Your love life? Your spiritual life? Your family life? Your creative life?

Once you've determined which area you want to work on, redesign the Spell for Personal Empowerment so that it fits your needs. Use the material from Chapter 2, on ingredients, to decide what to use in your spell. It is best to do this one during a Full Moon.

the ferry, too. We were going to rent a smaller boat, and for some reason I didn't think the lights of Key West would be visible then and I was worried about crossing open waters at night.

When I asked the native boy on the dock about how we were going to navigate in this small boat at night, he answered, 'We'll use a compass and navigate by the stars.'

I have a group of friends with whom I share dreams and weird experiences, and I got four or five different opinions from them about what the dream might mean. All of the opinions could fit, but I didn't understand the theme until the other 'key' factors entered the picture. I broke down the components:

McKee: his book, *Story*, is about what constitutes a great story in screenwriting and in novels. That might refer to my fiction writing.

Lost key to the car: a car gets me where I'm going. Without the key, I can't move forward. So what does the **key** represent?

Missing the boat: I may miss – or I may have already missed – an opportunity of one sort or another.

Navigating using a compass and the stars: to successfully navigate the open **ocean** in the **darkness** (the unconscious, instinct, intuition), I must summon my will to select the right direction and use my knowledge of astrology to get where I'm going. I was making some feng shui adjustments to our home at the time, so the compass and the direction west (Key **West**) may also be significant. West, in feng shui, is the direction of creativity and children. It represents autumn, its number is seven, and its colour is white.

Agent's son-in-law: represents my books, the person who sells them.

Native boy: intuition, instincts.

Key: the key to the synchronicities, the deeper significance.

Because this dream occurred in the early morning, when I seem to have most of my precognitive dreams, I think the dream refers to something that is coming up in the autumn. It relates to creativity, possibly to fiction, and if I don't follow my instincts and intuition, I may miss an opportunity. I need to 'navigate' this experience by using my astrological knowledge, perhaps for pegging propitious times to undertake a project.

There's another possible meaning to these 'key' events, a more straightforward interpretation that I stumbled over accidentally. I was

Magic and Visions

'Magic has often been thought of as the art of making dreams come true; the art of realizing visions. Yet before we can bring birth to the vision... we have to see it.'

Starhawk

playing around with some horary charts using a book by Anthony Louis called *Horary Astrology, Plain and Simple*, and decided to cast a chart for the lost car key.

The rules and strictures of horary have always daunted my enthusiasm for this type of astrology. It took me quite a while to figure out the details about the rulers, houses and planets that pertained to my question, but Louis' easy explanations made the process simpler than it had been in the past. I finally determined that the sixth house of the chart would describe where the key was. 'In a container or pocket, inside something', Louis writes about the sixth house in horary astrology. 'In a place where one works or does chores... near a pet or small animal... west northwest.'

I clearly remembered coming into the house through the garage, which leads into our washroom. The washroom lies in the western part of the house. The northwest corner or wall holds a laundry shelf that contained, among other things, four Frisbees, stacked on top of each other, that our dog plays with. I found the key resting in the bottom Frisbee. Only later did I make the connection to my dream—

Key West... compass... navigating by the stars...

It still doesn't explain some of the other elements in the dream. But I learned that sometimes the simplest explanation is the one that gets the most immediate and practical results – if you pay attention!

The spells that follow are intended to expand self-awareness and to enhance your will power.

Spells for Personal Power
To Expand Self-Awareness

    Tools: Frankincense resin
                Myrrh resin
                1 amber-coloured candle
                Object that represents personal power
                Quartz crystal
    When: Preferably on a Thursday night during a Full Moon

Power Tools: Amulets

A power tool is anything that connects you to the deepest core of yourself. It may be a stone, a piece of jewellery, a saying typed on a slip of paper, an animal totem – *anything at all*. But for the object to qualify as an amulet, a tool of power, it should elicit a strong, instinctive reaction in you when you see or touch it.

If, for instance, you need an amulet for spiritual power, a purple object that feels right for you would be in order. Follow the chakra colours on page 146.

Thursday is Jupiter's day, and Jupiter symbolizes expansion. If you can't do it on a Thursday, then definitely do this during a Full Moon, on any day except Tuesday (Mars) or Saturday (Saturn).

The object that represents your personal power should be something solid and three-dimensional – a stone, for instance, not a photograph. Select the object with care. The crystal you're using can be any colour, but should be clear. It will amplify your desire.

Pick a spot where you won't be disturbed. This spell works nicely outside, under the light of the Full Moon. Put a little of the frankincense and myrrh resin in a heatproof receptacle and place it on your left. Put the amber-coloured candle on your right. The object that represents your personal power and the crystal should go directly in front of you.

Light the candles and resin, then throw open your arms to the moon. Vividly imagine its light suffusing you and say:

> *This light is presence,*
> *This light is power.*
> *It fills me*
> *Until I am presence,*
> *Until I am power.*

Allow the aroma of the oils to permeate the air, then extinguish the flames. Place your power object in a safe place. You may want to let your crystal soak in salt water overnight to cleanse it; or you can leave it outside, where the light of the Full Moon will charge it.

Spell for Sexual Charisma

Tools: Rue, the herb
          Sage, incense or herb
          Mint
          4 candles, your choice of colours
When: Preferably a Tuesday or a Thursday on a Full Moon. If neither of those days is possible, then a Friday or Sunday would be fine, too.

Charms

A charm differs from an amulet in that it's something created specifically for you. You make it for yourself, or someone who knows and cares about you makes it for you with your consent. The charm usually consists of a bag that holds special objects. The bag should be fabric, preferably cotton because it's porous. Silk is also good, but it isn't as porous as cotton, so it should remain open just a bit at the top. This allows the power of the charm to move out into the world.

The bag should contain objects that are personally meaningful, yet related to your purpose. And there should be only one purpose per charm. Don't, for instance, make a charm to win the lottery *and* to find the love of your life. Look through the list of herbs in this book and select one or two herbs that fit your purpose. If you're into crystals, then select one whose colour is aligned with what you're trying to accomplish. The other objects you include in the bag should be personally significant.

Limit your objects to four or five. As you close the bag, state your purpose, then carry the charm bag with you. Once you get what you want, throw the bag away, expressing your gratitude for its help.

As a herb, rue strengthens willpower, sage is excellent for mental clarity and protection and a general cleansing of negative energy, and mint speeds up the results of a spell. You can also consult the lists of herbs in this book and add any others that you feel are appropriate. Tuesday is ruled by Mars, which governs sexual energy. Jupiter, as Thursday's ruler, means expansion, luck.

If you're casting this spell in the hopes of seducing someone, then one of the candle colours should be red. Allow your intuition to guide you on the other three colours.

Light your herbs first, so their scent permeates the air where you're working. Next, light the candles. As you light each one, imagine your sexuality and your charisma burning brightly during the time that you need it to do whatever you're going to do!

The Flow

The flow is one of the millennial buzzwords and usually has 'go with' preceding it, as in *Go with the flow*.

The biggest problem with this phrase is that it implies passivity. It seems to be saying that if we don't do anything, if we just wait for things to unfold, we're going with the flow. In actuality, the flow is like a current made up of synchronicities. It's up to us to figure out what these often odd connections mean, what their deeper significance is, and in doing so, we're able to determine the direction and purpose of the flow. This in itself is empowering. We feel as if we're hooked into something larger than ourselves, that the *bigger picture* is vastly more complex than we dared imagine.

While I was working on this chapter, my friend Vicki called to relate a string of synchronicities that had happened to her in the last several days. These events involved the words *bowling, a blown electrical transformer* and *adoption*. In each instance, the word or phrases recurred at least three times. Vicki sensed it was significant, and as we talked about it we started tying the threads together.

Something was coming up that would 'bowl' her over. It would happen suddenly and unexpectedly and, in some way, would 'transform' (the blown electrical transformer) her life. We both suspected it was connected to Vicki's daughter, whom she had

Brainstorming: Into the Flow

Describe a recent synchronicity you have experienced. Circle the key words and try to connect them to repetitive themes or events in your own life.

What does this synchronicity tell you about the flow in your life?

given up for adoption thirty years ago. She felt that her daughter was looking for her.

Vicki wasn't content to just sit back and wait. She acted on the pattern by doing an Internet search. She logged onto a genealogy site maintained by the Mormon church – Ancestry.com – and typed in her maiden name in the search engine. On the message board for her maiden name was a request for information on a woman with her full name (first, middle, last) and her birthdate (wrong by ten years, but the right day). The birthplace was wrong, but the city was where Vicki had been living when she'd given up her daughter.

She contacted the individual who had posted the message. They exchanged e-mails for a couple of days, each one trying to find out as much as possible about the other without saying too much. A week to the day when the pattern had started, Vicki and her daughter finally connected.

This reunion may have happened regardless, but it may not have happened as quickly if Vicki hadn't entered *the flow*.

The flow of a river is altered constantly by the curvature of the land that contains it, weather patterns and a myriad of other environmental details. In the same way, the purpose of *the flow* in our lives changes as our goals and needs change. By developing an awareness of this deeper stratum of our lives, we're better equipped to anticipate opportunities, to deal with challenges and to fulfil our potential. In short, we are empowered.

Spell for Empowerment

This spell requires no tools except for the belief that magic works – and that it can work for you. As you're waking up in the morning, before your eyes open, when you're still in that drowsy state halfway between dreams and full consciousness, visualize whatever it is that you desire. Then say it silently to yourself.

Maybe your desire is to get an A in an exam. Visualize it as vividly as possible, a big red A at the top of your exam sheet. Pour emotion into it. Imagine how excited you'll be when you see the A. Then say 'I get an A in my exam'. Again, put emotion behind the statement.

Animal Totems

Pick an animal with which you feel an affinity and that expresses your goals and needs. A goat, a symbol for the ambitious Capricorn, for instance, might symbolize ambition; a dog, loyalty. A cat might represent grace; a cheetah could symbolize speed. Find a figure of this animal, ask it to aid you in your journey, then carry it with you.

Energy Centres

Chakra	Colour	Function	Location
First	Red	Survival	Genitals
Second	Orange	Sexuality, nurturing	Below navel
Third	Yellow	Emotions, power	Solar plexus
Fourth	Green	Compassion, love	Heart
Fifth	Blue	Communication	Throat
Sixth	Purple	Intuition, intellect	Between eyebrows
Seventh	White	Spirituality, knowledge	Crown of head

When you've done this with great vividness and backed it with emotions, get out of bed and forget about it. Release the desire. Assuming that you've done your part to get an A in the exam (studied or otherwise prepared yourself), you should get an A.

This spell can be done quickly and can be done anywhere – not just as you're waking up in the morning. The most important ingredients are the vividness with which you visualize the end result and the intensity of the emotion behind your desire.

Your Field of Energy

Chinese medical practitioners call it *chi*. Hindu mystics refer to it as *shakti*. Medical intuitives call it an *energy field*. Occultists refer to it as an *aura*. Its existence has been recorded since ancient times, notably in primitive art. In the Sahara desert, for instance, in the rocky massifs of that harsh terrain, paintings that date back to the ninth millennium BCE show human figures surrounded by an envelope of light. In Catholic literature, these luminous orbs are traditionally depicted as halos.

This energy field '... is an intuitive language of the body', writes Judith Orloff, MD, in *Judith Orloff's Guide to Intuitive Healing*. 'It is the essence of who we are, a subtle vibration underlying everything physical, both living and inanimate... some of us may see it more easily... others may feel it.'

The energy field radiates outward from the body, forming a dome of light that can be several inches or several feet wide, depending on the individual's emotional, spiritual and physical state at any given time. It's composed of at least seven energy disks or chakras that run down the centre of the physical body, from the crown of the head to the base of the spine. Each of these chakras has a different colour and function, which are important to medical intuitives. More on the energy field and energy centres is provided in the chapter on health spells (Chapter 13). For the spells in this chapter, however, the colours and the function of each energy centre are the most important elements.

Let's say that you're going to be interviewed for a job that seems absolutely ideal for you. Great hours, great flexibility – the real

McCoy. But you're nervous about the interview, uncertain about what to say or how to say it. A spell to enhance and empower your throat chakra might be just what you need to get through the interview with flying colours.

Perhaps you're having trouble with a boss at work. You're unable to claim your rightful power because the boss intimidates you. In this situation, a spell for the solar plexus chakra may be just the ticket to resolve the problem.

The idea here is that by focusing on the appropriate areas of your energy field, you're delivering a double whammy of empowerment.

Spell for Empowering the Energy Centres

For the first energy centre:

    Tools: 4 red candles
    When: A Friday night on the Full Moon

This spell is quick and simple. It only requires you to bring your intent and your belief to the spell.

Place the four candles at the four cardinal directions. Starting at the north, move clockwise to light the candles. With each candle that you light, imagine your first centre as a swirling orb of strong, pulsating energy that imbues your being with sexual charisma and power.

When you have finished lighting the candles, spend a few minutes in the centre of your candle circle, preferably in the lotus position. Inhale deeply several times, then exhale quickly, expelling all the air from your lungs. Pinch your right nostril shut, inhale through the left and hold to the count of ten. Exhale through the right nostril. Repeat five times and switch sides. As you do this alternate nostril breathing, imagine your first energy centre imbued with power.

This spell can be repeated with each of the centres, using the appropriate colours. When you feel comfortable casting spells, you can create your own rhyme for each of the cardinal directions, to say when you light the candles. Extinguish the candles when you have finished the spell.

Atoms

'Ancient Hindu literature... describes matter as being composed of *anu* or "atoms", and says that the subtle vibratory energies of the human energy field exist *paramanu*, or literally beyond the atom.'

Michael Talbot
The Holographic Universe

Morning Chakra Work

Before you get out of bed in the morning, check your chakras for balance. First, place your palm inches above your solar plexus and try to sense the energy. At first, you may not feel anything. But once your skin becomes attuned to the chakra's energy field, you may feel a sensation or warmth or even detect form. With practice, you'll be able to tell whether the chakra is functioning the way it should be.

If, after several mornings, you don't feel anything at the solar plexus, try another energy centre.

Stretching Your Energy Field

People who have presence, who have personal power, often have an expanded energy field or aura as well. The energy field, in fact, is what we react to when that person walks into our view.

With practice, you can learn to expand your energy field from the usual several inches around your body to several feet. The field is easy to detect through touch. Stand in front of a mirror and open your arms wide, as if you're about to hug someone. Bring your hands slowly towards your head until you feel a slight resistance. This should happen when your hands are several inches away from your head. When your energy field expands, you'll feel the resistance further away from your head.

You can also train yourself to see your energy field. Gaze into a mirror in a twilit room; it's best if a dim light is at your back. If you wear glasses or contact lenses, remove them. If you have 20/20 vision, gaze at your head in the mirror and let your eyes unfocus, so that your reflection seems hazy.

The longer you gaze at your reflection in this way, the more likely you are to see a halo of light surrounding your head. Some people detect colours, others simply see a halo of transparent light. Now think of something that made you happy, buoyant, ecstatically happy – your marriage, the birth of your child, the purchase of your first home, getting the offer for a great job. Conjure the emotions that you felt during this event or experience. Let the emotion fill you completely. As the emotions suffuse your entire being, your energy field will start to expand and the halo will balloon.

As you're feeling your energy field expand, take several deep breaths. Pinch your right nostril shut and breathe in through your left nostril. Hold your breath to the count of ten and exhale through your right nostril. Repeat three times, then switch nostrils. Alternate nostril breathing stimulates both hemispheres of the brain, and as you become accustomed to charging your energy field, the alternate breathing signals your unconscious of your intent.

With practice, you can charge your energy field in ten or fifteen seconds. You can use this technique for just about anything – when you're hoping to attract love, new job opportunities or meet new friends. Your body becomes the tool. Best of all, it can be done anywhere and at any time.

Chapter Eleven

Spells for
Your Home

Our homes are the mirrors of our feelings about where we live and a mirror of whatever we've experienced while living in the house. This sounds like an obvious statement until we're confronted with what it actually means. Nowhere is the significance more apparent than when we see the reflections in other people's homes.

For most of us, our impressions about a house are probably formed the moment we walk in the front door. We immediately sense whether the place is friendly or hostile, chaotic or organized, formal or casual. We immediately like it or dislike it. Usually, our feelings don't have much to do with the furnishings or the colour of the carpets, and may not even be related to the layout of the rooms. We're reacting, instead, to a general overall impression, a *feeling tone*.

Each Home is Unique

In homes that aren't brand new, the feeling tone is something that has built up over a period of months or years. If the people who live in the house are predominately happy, we feel it. If tragedies have happened in the house, we feel that, too. Houses, just like people, carry emotional baggage with them.

Even new houses have a certain feeling tone. It's as if everyone from the architects to the tradespeople has left their imprints on the rooms. Houses, flats, tower blocks: all of them speak to us. Even hotels have voices. The Overlook Hotel in Stephen King's classic *The Shining* has absorbed decades of emotions from the guests who have stayed there, and in a sense that emotional residue has taken on a life of its own. In a sense, that hotel is very much alive.

The same is true in Shirley Jackson's book *The Haunting of Hill House*, in Richard Matheson's novel *Stir of Echoes*, and in every similar story ever written or filmed. The difference between fiction and life, however, is that the energy that imbues a place isn't always bad. Just as often, it's uplifting, buoyant, optimistic, and makes us feel on top of the world as soon as we cross the threshold.

When we started looking for a larger house, we searched all over Florida and must have seen several hundred places. Most are now blurred in my memory, but a few stand out because of their *feeling tone*. I used to keep notes on the various houses we saw in a particular area, and the notes invariably ended with a brief description of how I *felt* when I was inside the house, walking through the rooms. It didn't seem to matter if the place was furnished or not. The walls held secrets. The floors whispered tales. Porches laughed or wept.

There was one house in Jupiter, Florida, that we considered buying, an older home for Florida (as much as twenty years). The layout suited us. The windows were large. The floor was Mexican tiles. There was an acre of land, beautifully landscaped. The rooms had been freshly painted. But I felt something odd in that house, something I couldn't describe until much later.

I think it started in the kitchen, when I noticed a narrow crack that ran through the tile and that the floor seemed to slope downwards slightly. The estate agent blamed it on the settling of the floor and the tiles after the kitchen had been redone several years earlier. No big deal. But for me it became a very big deal. The crack was trying to tell me something. Something had happened in that room, something emotionally strong and unpleasant.

We returned to the house several times. I started becoming obsessed about that crack. Then one afternoon, while I was napping, I dreamed about it, about the crack. In the dream, I stepped on it and dust flew up. A lot of dust. The crack became a chasm, and when I peered down into it I could see a foundation turning to mud.

When we went back the next day to look at the back garden, my daughter and I happened to look behind the fence and discovered a veritable rubbish tip. Discarded appliances, mattresses, doors, windows, frames, probably even a kitchen sink somewhere in the mess. It felt like a cover-up. It felt as if the people who lived in this house had spent their lives hiding who they were, becoming more and more repressed until something had erupted. If they had covered up their junk by stashing it behind the fence, then there was no telling what other flaws or defects in the house they had tried to cover up.

We didn't put in an offer on that house.

On the other hand, the second we walked into the house we finally bought, we loved it. Not just one of us, but all of us. It radiated happiness, expansion and the kind of friendly chaos found in many large families. Nothing was hidden. The sprinkler system had leaks, the

---

The Life of a House

'Houses themselves have a quality, a life, that is picked up by potential buyers....When you live in a house that belongs conspicuously to another age, you are to some extent avoiding the contemporary nature of life...'

Jane Roberts
The Unknown Reality,
Volume 2

garden had ants and scorched patches where nothing grew, the fence had graffiti scrawled on the outside, the top of the stove had a crack through it. But none of that mattered, because the feeling tone was exactly right.

What is the feeling tone of the place where you live? Use the 'Brainstorming' exercise opposite to find out.

Analyzing Your Home

Question 7 is especially important because it helps to identify possible challenges and problems in your life right now. Look at the various listings as a metaphor. Let's say your garage door is stuck: it won't go up. If we look at the metaphor for what a garage door represents, perhaps you have trouble admitting new people and experiences into your life. Maybe you feel trapped. Maybe you don't know how to *open a door* to opportunity.

The answers to 8 and 12 may be similar. If your experiences in your home are predominately positive, that is probably what other people will feel. The reverse is also true. This doesn't mean that the *feeling tones* of a place are confined to either/or, good or bad, black or white. Quite often, we live in shades of grey. We take the middle path. We don't experience extremes. Our homes also absorb that.

With spells, we can protect, energize and calm our homes. We can cleanse them of negative energy, boost their positive energy, ward off potential enemies or problems and create atmospheres of success and happiness within their walls. We can make our homes easier to sell, and we can cast spells to find the home of our dreams. In short, we can do for our homes and living spaces what we do for ourselves. The same rules apply. It's all about belief, intent and desire.

Spell to Get Rid of Negative Energy

Tools: Sage, the herb
When: The waning moon

This ritual originates with Native Americans and is a popular method for cleansing just about anything.

Brainstorming: Your Home

1. Describe your home. _____
    _____

2. Describe how you feel about your home. _____
    _____

3. What would you change about where you live? Why? _____
    _____

4. Describe how you feel most of the time when you're at home. _____
    _____

5. Is your home spacious enough to comfortably accommodate everyone who lives in it?
    _____

6. Are the rooms cluttered? _____
    _____

7. Circle the items in your home that don't work or the spaces that need attention:

Attic	Electrical Items	Floors	Plumbing
Basement	Taps	Locks	Roof
Carpet	Fixtures	Walls	Sinks
Doors	_____	_____	_____

8. How do most people react to visiting your home? _____
    _____

9. Do you like your neighbourhood? If so, why? If not, why not? _____
    _____

10. Describe your dream house. _____
    _____

11. Why did you rent/buy this place? _____
    _____

12. Overall, how would you describe your experiences in this house? Have you been
    predominately happy? Sad? Indifferent? What? _____
    _____

Healing a House

Quite often, we instinctively know what to do when our homes need an infusion of energy. Most of it is common sense. We paint the exterior of the house or paint the inside of the rooms a different colour. We clear clutter, toss out that stuff in the attic that we haven't missed for the last ten years, repair what doesn't work. Maybe we rearrange or buy new furniture. All of these measures shift energy.

You can also smudge the rooms, then burn a white scented candle in each room. Follow this with a brief meditation in which you request that harmony and happiness now enter the house. Extinguish the candle when you have finished, and do not leave a burning candle unattended.

When burned, sage is a sweet-smelling herb. Some types smell acrid and bitter; others smell of summer in the great outdoors. But the scent of the sage is less important than the cleansing properties of the sage itself.

To cleanse a room, have ready a saucer or other fireproof receptacle, then light the smudge stick, holding the saucer under it to catch any falling embers. Waft the smoke of the burning sage over the walls, into the corners, the cupboards, any nooks and crannies where shadows – and energy – gather. Pass the smoke along the frames of the doors and windows. Let it eddy across the floor. This simple process is vital whenever something tragic, negative or emotionally wrenching has happened. It's beneficial if someone in your home is physically ill or feeling out of sorts. You don't have to say anything, you don't have to engage in any ritual. Simply hold the intent in your mind that you are cleaning the area of negative energy.

A sage wand is ideal for smudging. It doesn't have to be relit, it's easy to carry, and when you've finished, you simply extinguish the burning end so that it can be used again. Basil can be used instead of sage.

The waning moon is the ideal time for this spell because you're *getting rid of something* – you're cleansing.

Spell to Invite Greater Happiness into Your Home

Tools: Several round-leaf house plants
        Lavender-scented incense or lavender essential oil
        Vase of freshly cut flowers
When: Any time

Inviting happiness into your home shouldn't be confined to a particular time of day or night, or even to any phase of the moon. Before you run out for plants and oils, however, you should smudge your home to clear out any negative energy.

Select your house plants with care. Round-leafed plants are friendlier symbolically than, say, cacti or plants with pointed leaves. Jade plants are excellent choices – they do well indoors, especially if near a window, have gently rounded leaves and represent wealth, prosperity and happiness.

Position your house plants with the same care with which you selected them. Usually, every room has several 'power spots' where plants seem to flourish. Quite often, the family pet will snooze in or near power spots; or you may sense them on your own. As you position your house plants, request that they bring happiness into your home.

Freshly cut flowers enhance the energy in any home. Select flowers that are brilliantly coloured or that seize your attention.

You don't have to have incense or oils burning constantly in your home to invite happiness inside. You might simply light one or the other as you're placing the plants in your house and arranging the fresh flowers.

Making these small gestures towards inviting happiness into your home – and thus into your life – may inspire you to go even farther. Do any of the rooms need to be painted? Are blinds broken or curtains torn? Maybe it's time for a general facelift.

The People and Pets at Home

The people and pets who share your living space contribute to the overall feeling texture of your home. If you have a flatmate or someone else in your home with whom you don't get along or who is mostly negative, then you need to take measures to rid the rooms of that negativity. This may call for a sage smudging at regular intervals and for other remedial adjustments. These adjustments could include a piece of onyx in or near the person's room to absorb the negative energy; burning a black candle in or near the person's room to absorb the negative energy; smudging the area once a week for a month, then once a month after that.

If you burn a black candle to absorb negativity, let it burn all the way down, then throw it away. You don't have to throw out the onyx; just bathe it in sea water (or water with some sea salt in it if you don't live near the sea) and then set it in the sun for a few minutes to charge it.

If you have a pet that is hostile towards you or other people, you might try a little feng shui magic. Locate the family area of your home. This area lies in the eastern part of the house or, in Black Hat sect feng shui, the furthest left-hand side of your house when you stand inside

Books for Your Feng Shui Library

Feng shui has been one of the hottest home topics of the last several years. Here are some reading suggestions to get you started:

George Birdsall: *The Feng Shui Companion*

Lillian Too: *The Complete Illustrated Guide to Feng Shui*

Simon Brown: *Practical Feng Shui*

Denise Lynn: *Creating Sacred Space with Feng Shui*

Stephen Skinner: *The Living Earth Manual of Feng Shui: Chinese Geomancy*

your front door. Add a tabletop fountain to the family area, a couple of jade plants and something black. And, of course, don't forget to give your pet plenty of love.

If you have children, the best area in feng shui for them lies in the western part of the house or, if you're standing in the front door, directly opposite the family area. If your kids are hostile or angry, use anything yellow in that area – flowers (with round leaves), curtains, linen, quilts, whatever feels right. Symbols for children and creativity are also good here, as are music, bells and lights.

Once the negativity in the children area is purged, put a white crystal or white flowers somewhere in the room. It helps to balance the emotions.

Selling Your Home Quickly

Few things are more frustrating than putting your house on the market and then having it sit there, month after excruciating month, with nothing happening. There are always dozens of rational excuses for why the house hasn't sold – the wrong time of year, rising interest rates, the house needs work, the neighbourhood isn't close enough to schools. But it only takes one person to buy your home, and a little help from the universe doesn't hurt!

Several years ago, the parents of a friend of mine had put their house up for sale and moved to another part of the country to be closer to one of their children. The house languished for months on the market, and prospective buyers found all sorts of things to criticize about the house. My friend finally asked me what she could do to get the house sold.

Her parents had lived in the house for more than thirty years. Even though their marriage had been predominately happy, three decades is a lot of emotional baggage for a house to absorb. For the last several years they had lived in the house, both of my friends' parents had been infirm, and I suspected that people might be picking up on the sadness of those last few years.

I suggested to my friend that, for starters, she should smudge the house with sage, starting in the room that was visible when you walked in through the front door. I told her to smudge in each of the

Feng Shui Tips for Your Home

A little bit of feng shui magic in your home will go a long way towards making the rest of your magic more powerful.

1. Get rid of clutter. This is one of the core principles of feng shui. The idea here is that clutter blocks the movement of energy or *chi*. If energy can't move freely in your home, then it isn't going to move freely in your life, either.

2. Instead of trying to apply feng shui principles to your entire house, start with one room.

3. In a house with two floors, feng shui principles should be applied to each floor separately.

4. Feng shui principles can be applied to a desk.

5. Don't procrastinate with repairs around your house. Paint walls, repair leaking taps and faulty electrical connections, repair roofs and basements. Change light bulbs as soon as they go out.

6. Allow your intuition to speak when you're applying feng shui principles to anything.

7. When you use a mirror as a feng shui cure, make sure you keep it clean.

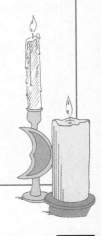

Releasing

Why did your neighbour's house sell two days after the 'For sale' went up, and why has your home languished on the market for six months? The answer may have less to do with the desirability of the individual houses and properties than it does with your willingness to release your house.

If you're serious about moving, then you must release your own place first. Walk through your home and express your gratitude towards it for having sheltered you and protected you. If you have good memories of a particular room, express it. Smudge each room with sage as you walk through the dwelling.

four directions first, then smudge the doorways, the skirting board, the windows, the whole lot. She was to repeat this in each room. I also reminded her to smudge the cupboards, the garage and even the attic if she could. Several weeks later, her parents' home was sold.

So if you're trying to sell your home, begin with a smudging as described above. Then proceed to the next spell.

A Spell to Sell a Property

Tools: 1 gold candle
             1 red candle
             Your favourite oil
When: During a waning moon

Before you even place your home with an estate agent or put out that 'For sale' sign, add a few drops of oil to the water bowl of your favourite oil burner. Place a red candle on one side of the burner and a gold one on the right. As you light each one, say:

My house sells quickly
For at least (state the price you want).
Make it so.

Repeat it throughout the waning moon period. Allow the candles to burn down.

Spell to Honour Your Home

To sell your home, you must be ready to release it. You have to be ready to let go emotionally. You have to be able to vividly imagine yourself living elsewhere and doing so without regrets, otherwise no spell in the universe is going to get your home to sell.

Once you make that emotional transition, make your peace with the home where you've been living. Express your gratitude. You may feel odd talking to inanimate objects like walls and floors, but do it anyway. Spend a few minutes in each room, remembering good experiences you have had inside it. Express your gratitude. Then get out of the way and let events unfold.

Spell to Find a Home

Tools: Paper, pen, glue, scissors, cardboard
When: The Full Moon

You can either sketch the home you're looking for or find pictures or photographs that depict the home. Glue these illustrations to a piece of cardboard and hang the poster where you'll see it often. The idea here is to create a visual tool for what you desire. Make it vivid and detailed. Get the rest of the family involved: children love doing this sort of thing and often come up with things you didn't think of. The more energy that is poured into the desire, the quicker it will materialize.

Wish Boards

A wish board consists of a piece of cardboard covered with photos, pictures, sayings and affirmations that relate to one or more different goals and desires. It's a powerful visualization device, especially when the wish board is put somewhere so visible that you can't help but see it.

One woman I know not only did a wish board of the house she wanted, she actually picked out the exact location – the town and the exact spot on a beach. She had an aerial photograph of the area where she wanted to live, and a red X marked the exact spot. Because her specifications were so specific, it took her over a year to find the house and slice of beach, but the location was within a mile or two of where she had stipulated.

A wish board can be used for any goal or desire, but is especially potent when you're looking for a new home.

Spell to Protect Your House

A word of caution about this spell. In one sense, it implies a belief in victimization, which is why I almost didn't include it. However, there are times when we feel better knowing that the odds are stacked in our favour, so if you use the spell in that spirit, it can be applied to any number of situations.

A Wish Board for Your Home

If you're house-hunting, make a list of exactly what you're looking for – from the square footage to the numbers of rooms and bathrooms to the size of the property. If you can sketch, draw a blueprint of the house on cardboard. You don't have to draw it to scale, but the more specific you can make it, the better.

Leave some space along the borders for photographs or pictures from magazines and other sources that illustrate various aspects of the house you want.

Post your wish board where you'll see it regularly.

Tools: Cedar oil
       Animal totem, such as a figurine or picture
When: Whenever you feel the need

The totem you select should be that of an animal with which you feel a kinship and which, to you, represents protective power. Light your burner and when the scent begins to billow from it, pass the totem through it and say:

Protect this home,
High to low,
Fence to fence,
Door to door,
Light to dense,
Roof to floor.

Moving into a New Home

Any kind of move entails a monumental shift in energy. You are shifting gears not only in the physical world, but on a metaphysical level as well. Quite often, moves coincide with other major life events and experiences – births, marriages, divorces, death, work transfers or new jobs. Not only do you have to contend with the physical logistics, but the psychological adjustments as well. Whether the move is a few miles away or across the country, it can be stressful for everyone involved. Even when a move goes smoothly, you're faced with the daunting task of unpacking your belongings at the other end. Spells can help ease the stress.

Spell to Ensure a Smooth Move

Every Friday night for the month before you move, burn some basil oil or chamomile essential oil. The first promotes harmony and the second blesses a person, place or thing. As you light both, vividly imagine your move going smoothly, seamlessly, everything clicking into place and unfolding according to plan.

If at all possible, it's wisest not to move when Mercury is retrograde. Since Mercury rules communication and travel, glitches

Retrograde Mercury and Contracts

When we say that a planet is going retrograde, it means that it's moving backwards through the zodiac. It isn't actually moving backwards, of course, but when observed from our viewpoint here on Earth, it appears to be moving that way. Every planet except the moon and the sun goes retrograde.

When Mercury goes retrograde, which it does every several months, it stays that way for about three and a half weeks. Since Mercury rules, among other things, communication and contracts, it's best not to sign a contract when the planet is retrograde. This means any kind of legal, binding contract – such as to buy or sell a house.

When Mercury is retrograde, there are communication problems. Faxes don't come through, your e-mail server goes down, your hard drive crashes, travel plans are messed up, flights are cancelled and legal documents that you sign may have to be drawn up again.

If you've never heard of Mercury retrograde, however, and your life has worked out well enough so far, then don't pay too much attention to it. As one wise astrologer says, 'Mercury retrograde became an issue only after I learned what it was.'

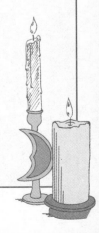

usually show up when the planet is retrograde. Check with an astrologer or on any of the astrology sites on the Internet for the periods when Mercury is retrograde.

Blessings for a New Home

The first things you should bring into your new home are a loaf of freshly baked bread, a bottle of wine and a new broom. The bread and wine ensure that you will always have enough to eat and drink in your new home. The broom represents the hearth – and the sweeping away of negative energy that the former tenants may have left behind.

Parting Thoughts about Home

Become more aware of how you enter and leave your home. Do you arrive or depart in anger, slamming doors and muttering to yourself? Or do you arrive and depart with respect for the space itself? Do you take off your shoes when you enter your house? In Japan, the removal of shoes is considered respectful.

Whether arriving or departing, you are imbuing the home with your energy. If the energy is angry or hostile or sad, then over a period of time that becomes the dominant energy in the home. If, on the other hand, the energy is upbeat and happy, *that* becomes the dominant energy. If you live with other people, of course, you can't control how they feel within the home, but you can at least make them more aware of how they enter and leave.

If you have children, pets and live plants, the energy is apt to be more lively and upbeat. The chi also flows better. Live plants are also telling about the general mood in the home – if they flourish, the dominant energy is probably upbeat and positive.

If you work from home, then it's even more important to keep the dominant mood in your home upbeat and positive. If you develop awareness about and respect for the place where you live, then it's more likely that you will 'Live long and prosper'.

Wise Words

'The land that is nowhere, that is the true home.'

Richard Wilhelm
*The Secret of
the Golden Flower*

Chapter Twelve
Spells to Enhance Creativity

In its broadest definition, 'creativity' is the act of coming up with something new, rather than producing an imitation. We tend to think of creativity as belonging to the arts or to inventions or some other *area*, but in actuality it belongs to all life.

If you doubt this, walk outside on any given day and simply take in the variety of plant and animal life. Things may be similar, but not *identical*. A saguaro cactus and an aloe plant share certain attributes, but they are not identical. Even though identical twins look exactly the same, their inner experiences are varied and different – and so are their personalities.

All of us are inherently creative. Every day, we come up with new ways of doing something, new ideas, new approaches, new perspectives and insights. Our right brains are tireless workers. They churn out ideas twenty-four hours a day, every day, every year of our lives. Part of our problem, however, is that we're creatures of habit. If something has worked in the past, we tend to keep following that groove because it requires less effort – and besides, who wants to interfere with success? We begin to approach living from some sort of internal formula: if we do A, then we do B and C all the way to Z, even though it may feel old and tired and used up. Then we sit up one day and realize with a certain creeping horror that we are mired in a rut.

The 'Your Creative Life' brainstorming activity opposite will provide insight into your own creative process, what you need to alter to become more creative and what your ultimate creative goals are.

Getting Out of the Rut

Let's say that your rut is work. You detest your job but at the moment, you don't have any other prospects on the horizon. However, you're preparing a CV, you have put out feelers and have set things in motion. In the meantime, you can do some simple magic, and this starts with nothing more than taking a different route to and from work.

On the first morning that you take the new route, give yourself some extra time. Leave ten or fifteen minutes earlier than usual. Notice how this route to work differs from the one you usually take.

Brainstorming: Your Creative Life

1. If you could do anything with your life, what would it be? _____
   _____
   _____

2. What are your hobbies? Why are these things your hobbies? _____
   _____
   _____

3. Do you consider your hobbies creative? If so, why? If not, why not? _____
   _____
   _____

4. Do you consider yourself creative? _____
   _____
   _____

5. What do you consider the most creative part of your life, and why? _____
   _____
   _____

6. Do you feel you have hit a rut in any area of your life? If so, are you willing to change it?
   _____
   _____

7. Describe the rut you're in. _____
   _____
   _____

8. What do you think you can do to change it? If it's a job, are you willing to change jobs?
   If it's a relationship, are you willing to revise it or get out of it? _____
   _____
   _____

9. What is the first step you would take to get out of the rut? _____
   _____
   _____

10. How can you apply your creative talents in another area of your life to getting out of
    the rut? _____
    _____
    _____

Is it more scenic? More hectic? Is it longer or shorter? Make a note of any feelings you have during the drive, any thoughts and insights that come to the surface.

Throughout your day at work, notice if you feel any differently about your job. Are you more committed to finding something else to do? Are your thoughts any clearer? Does your boss still rub you up the wrong way?

By changing your habitual way of doing things, you're making a symbolic gesture to the universe that you're ready for change.

Years ago, when I was teaching Spanish to schoolchildren, I used to dread getting up in the morning. I had got to the point where I detested teaching and spent most of my free time working on a novel and writing freelance articles. I had become caught in a rut and I knew it. I just wanted to get out of the job so that I could write full-time.

I didn't know much about magic then, but I was accustomed to following my hunches. One morning, my hunch said to take a different way to work, so I did. It was a longer route, past emerald-green pastures where cows and horses grazed peacefully in the morning light, past long stretches of open land. I was late for work, but I felt lighter, more buoyant, more optimistic. My resolve was so strong, I simply knew that one way or another, I was going to get out of teaching and do what I loved.

I began changing other, smaller routines in my work. My fears about not having a regular paycheck receded. My writing output increased dramatically. I sold my first short story for £180.

When I came up for contract renewal that spring, I turned it down. And that June, I walked out of the teaching field and into a new life.

My husband and I got married in July, with £3,000 in the bank and our heads filled with dreams. He had also left his job as a reporter that June. He had also climbed out of the rut into which he'd fallen. We had big plans. We also had setbacks. In the autumn, we ran out of money and took part-time jobs. In September the following year, my first novel sold and a few months later, we were given a ghostwriting project.

We created new lives, with new dreams. But none of it would have happened if we hadn't changed our *habitual thinking* and our *old patterns*.

Spell to Change Outmoded Patterns

Once you've identified the patterns you want to change in your life, make one small gesture that expresses your intent. Then do the following: on the first night of the Full Moon, jot down your desire on a sheet of paper in ink of a colour that seems appropriate for what you want. In other words, if your wish is to be more creative with your financial investments, use green ink. If you want to be more creative in your professional life, use gold ink. Then light two candles of a close or matching colour and read your wish out loud three times. Back the words with emotion – say them as if you mean them. Tuck your written desire under a power object and let the candles burn out naturally.

On the second night of the full moon, light two more candles of the same colour. Repeat your wish three times. Then touch the paper to one of the flames and say:

> *As this paper is burning,*
> *I release my wish, my need,*
> *My deepest yearnings,*
> *A new life's seed.*

When the second pair of candles have burned out on their own, throw them away.

Spell to Enhance Creativity

Choose something that represents the area of your life where you would like to enhance or increase your creativity. Just about any object or symbol will do. Keep it in a place where you'll see it daily. Every time you see it, say 'Make it so'.

Feel the words as you think them. Feel your changing beliefs. Make a gesture that's connected to your creativity at least once a day for a month.

Creativity and Dreams

Books on dreaming are filled with stories about how a dream provided the missing piece of an invention, vital scenes in a novel, the finishing touches of a film or some unique image in a painting. Dreams are so intimately connected to creativity and to the creative process that to ignore them or to write them off as merely pleasant interludes is to cheat yourself.

The fodder that dreams provide comes in ways that are unique to each of us. Some dreams are symbolic, others are literal. Some are ordinary, others are bizarre. Some are fun, some are terrifying. Regardless of the terms in which a particular dream is couched, it is *your* dream, intimately connected to a process that churns along inside you twenty-four hours a day, every day of your life. That process is creativity.

In *Writers Dreaming*, Naomi Epel quotes Stephen King, who writes movingly of the roles that dreams have played in his creative life. In some instances, he has taken a scene from a dream and written it as it happened, right into a book. 'Creative imaging and dreaming are just so similar that they've got to be related', he says.

Dreams are the conduit through which we connect to each other and to the deeper, oceanic parts of ourselves. Within that vast inner ocean are buried creative seeds that may never sprout unless we bring them into the light of day. Dreams, by their fundamental nature, are magic.

Here are a few guidelines on how to recall your dreams and work with them to enhance your creativity:

- **Voice what you need or want.** Before you fall asleep at night, say aloud that you would like to remember the most important dreams of the night. If you're trying to find a particular solution to something, then request that an answer comes to you in a dream and that you'll remember the dream in detail.
- **Back up your request with a gesture.** Put a tape recorder by your bedside or slide a notebook under your pillow so that

you can immediately record what you remember when you wake up. You might even jot your request on a page in your journal. Date it. Make notes the next day about whether you remembered any dreams. Sometimes the act of trying to write about your dreams when you're sure you haven't remembered any is enough to trigger recall.

· **Pay attention.** Any dream fragment that you remember may relate to your request, even if it doesn't appear to do so. Don't judge it. Forget your left-brain censor. Just write down the fragment. Record it.

· **If you don't succeed at first, keep trying.** Yes, it's a cliché. It also happens to be true. If you've spent thirty or forty years forgetting the bulk of what goes on while you sleep, then you can bet that your remembering wheels are rusty. Oil them and keep making your requests. Sooner or later, you'll have one memorable dream, in which you'll remember the characters, the texture and the nuances.

· **Experiment.** If you don't seem to be remembering any dreams or your requests don't appear to be working, try to sleep elsewhere for a couple of nights. On the sofa. In a sleeping bag. At your mother's home. When we break the rut we're in by changing a habit, new things unfold.

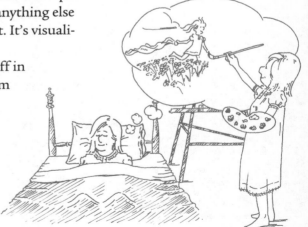

What I am talking about in these guidelines is nothing less than spell work. You are bringing your intent, will, emotions and anything else you can muster to get a creative solution to your request. It's visualization in another form.

'My safest place is in my dreams', writes Judith Orloff in *Intuitive Healing*. 'There I become centred. I inhabit a form that feels more fluid, and I effortlessly replenish myself with images, energy, tones that are a bigger stretch to accommodate otherwise.'

Maybe that's the key. Each of us must befriend our dreams, must approach them as though they are old friends who will listen to us and offer a fresh perspective on whatever we're looking for or need.

Spell to Bring About Vivid Dreams

Create a ritual about going to bed. Have a cup of chamomile tea beforehand, or a glass of milk or a bowl of ice cream. Treat yourself to a food or drink from which you derive comfort, the kind of comfort that your parents gave you when you were a child preparing to go to bed.

Place a sprig of vervain under your pillow, next to your dream journal or recorder. Vervain promotes vivid dreams. So do the colour blue, the scent of cedar (incense or oil), a warm bath and the sound of water. A small fountain will do the trick, and so will the gentle caress of ocean surf against a beach. Sometimes the whisper of wind is invaluable. Do something that soothes each of your senses.

As you get into bed, state your request. Spend a few minutes reading or doing whatever relaxes you. As you turn out the light, state your request again. Trust that your request will be answered.

Practical Creativity

This sounds like an oxymoron. But first and foremost, creativity is always practical. It's the perfect blend of right and left brain. What the right brain can conceive, the left brain can put into action.

However, when your creative impetus feel sluggish, when you can't seem to get anywhere with spells or dreams or anything else, maybe it's time to go through the back door. Maybe it's time to do some left-brain defining.

When I first started out as a fiction writer, I was totally opposed to doing outlines for a novel. To me, the creative process was partially about facing a blank computer screen and letting the right brain do its magic. All too often, though, that blank screen stayed blank for days or, worse, it filled with 300 pages of stuff before I found page 1. There it was, PAGE 1, the actual first page of the novel on page 341.

So 340 pages would go into the Trash and I would start with page 341. Months gone, months wasted, I invariably thought.

Nothing in the creative process, of course, is ever lost. Those 340 pages are still there, down in the ocean depths with other stuff, with

other discarded pages and experiences and events, just waiting for the right instant to put in an appearance. But in *practical* terms, this type of creativity cost me dearly.

Then I got an agent who insisted on a proposal for fiction. I rebelled, my right brain rebelled – how could anyone insist on such a thing? *I became creatively indignant.* Nonetheless, I did it. I wrote many fiction proposals for the same book and, eventually, one of them worked and I was able to write my novel. The finished product deviated quite a bit from that proposal: the ending was vastly different. But I realized that without the left-brain structure, the creative process would have kept spewing out another 340 pages that didn't fit into the plot.

The creative process begs for a structure. *Give me a goal*, it pleads. *Give me a backbone. And if you can't do that, then give me a deadline.*

A deadline often provides the badly needed backbone for creativity. The advertising executive needs three spots for tomorrow's slot at 8 AM. The reporter needs to have her story in at noon. The gallery needs two paintings for this week's exhibition. Forget dreams. Forget visualizatons. Forget the tools that have worked before. You need a product – and you need it *now*.

At such times, the creativity god slams into overdrive. It plucks up this remnant from schooldays and that vague memory from the day your mother died and tosses in the colour purple and a scent of pine. It squeezes all these seemingly disparate pieces into the backbone your left brain created, and suddenly you have a product. You have an answer. You have a solution.

Left brain, right brain. The difference, on the surface, is nothing more than hemispheres and directions. The left brain, the experts tell us, is good at maths and reasoning, good at minutiae and connecting the dots. The right brain excels at seeing the whole picture. Neither is better than the other. We need both. We can't survive if the signal from one is very weak or very strong. *We need a balance between the two, and it doesn't matter which one takes the lead.* Creativity rises from a perfect blend between the left brain and the right brain.

> ## The Muse in Action
>
> 'I know when my writing is going well because I feel like I'm plugged into something larger than myself. The words just flow. It's as if I have become a conduit, a channel.'
>
> Anonymous

Spell to Balance the Hemispheres

Before you dive into a creative project, find a comfortable spot anywhere, shut the door and sit on the floor with your back against a wall. Hold your left nostril shut and breathe through the right. Hold it to the count of ten and exhale forcefully through your mouth. Repeat this three times, then switch sides and repeat three times.

This breathing exercise, used in certain yoga traditions, balances both hemispheres of the brain, allowing them to work smoothly together. It allows them to talk to each other. And that talk, that private conversation they have, is essential to any creative process.

Once you get the hang of it, you can do this breathing exercise anywhere at any time.

Creativity and Nature

You're stuck. The alternate breathing stuff doesn't work. You haven't received anything from dreams. You're so ingrained in the rut that you can feel its walls collapsing around you, over you.

Time for a break.

Time to put on your walking shoes and head for the great outdoors. If you live in a large city, the outdoors is probably a few square feet of green or a park. In the suburbs you may have a few more choices, and any of these will do the trick, but what I'm talking about here is the *real outdoors*. No convenience shops within fifteen or twenty miles. No MacDonalds, no petrol stations, no shopping centres, no cinemas. That's the best scenario. In place of that, find a green place that is moderately private.

In South Florida, where I live, the real outdoors no longer exists. Oh, there are patches of it here and there – a pasture, a wide-open field where the grass smells of summer, a stretch of highway with nothing on either side. But if you go inland for a while, you hit the Everglades. If you go north and inland, you hit the Ocala National Forest. If I'm not in the mood for either of those, I am able to head for the beach.

Use what's available where you live. The idea here is to get out, walk, trek, ride a horse, *break your routine in a major way.*

Observe the wildlife. Enjoy the smell of the air, the hardness of the ground under your feet. And take note of how your thought processes start to change. You'll hear some grumbling and moaning at first, the usual body complaints about *it's too far, I'm hot, I'm thirsty, I'm hungry, where's the toilet*. But when you get past all that – and you will – something magical happens. You can almost feel the inner shift.

Your thoughts begin to flow rather than to splutter. Your rhythm changes. Your pace quickens or slows. You feel lighter, happier, more optimistic. And this is exactly the right atmosphere for your creativity to percolate in.

Julia Cameron, author of *The Artist's Way* and *The Right to Write*, recommends walking every day to get the creative juices going. Mystery writer Sue Grafton runs three miles a day. My husband, a novelist, landscapes the garden when he needs inspiration. He always has an ongoing project that involves digging, planting, beautifying the landscape. It's as if when he digs into the earth, he is actually digging deep into himself to extract what he needs. As he plants, he is seeding ideas.

Annie Dillard, in her Pulitzer-prize winning book *Pilgrim at Tinker Creek*, took creativity and nature to a whole new level. Nature's rhythms became *her* rhythms, and nature's wonders became the fodder for her book. Loren Eisley, a naturalist who wrote a number of books, discovered universal truths during his treks through nature.

Quite often, when you venture into nature simply to see what you'll discover, your creativity is stimulated in unusual and, sometimes, enduring ways. When biologist and author Rupert Sheldrake was a young boy, his father used to take him to see the freeing of homing pigeons that had come from all over Britain. 'When the appointed time came, the porters opened the flaps and out burst hundreds of pigeons, batch after batch, in a great commotion of wind and feathers', he writes in *Seven Experiments That Could Change the World*. His fascination with homing pigeons as a boy eventually led to the first experiment in his book many decades later.

Getting in Touch with Your Muse

The creative muse is nearly always spoken of as 'she'. But a muse can also be a 'he' or have no gender at all. It can simply be energy that you name, as you might a beloved pet.

To get in touch with your muse, simply put out the request. You can write it; you can suggest to yourself as you're falling asleep that you're going to communicate with your muse in a dream; or you can meditate on it. One woman I know wrote her muse a note:

Dear Muse,
I really could use some help right now. I need your input. I need your advice. Please respond ASAP.

Your pal,
Katherine

Creativity and Animals

At the age of thirty-seven, Susan Chernak McElroy found herself in the middle of a cancer crisis. 'Staring death in the face, I made some spiritual decisions. And the animals became the bellwether of my search', she writes in *Animals as Guides for the Soul*. She threw herself into her soul's work, her cancer retreated and she went on to write two bestselling books about animals and our relationship with them.

Anyone who has pets realizes their roles in our creativity. They are part of the natural world that we bring indoors, into our lives. Once we invite them into our lives and they accept the invitation, our lives invariably change. If we're lucky, our cats teach us how to laze in the sun with our bellies to the sky, so totally immersed *in the moment* that the rest of the world goes away. We may not be able to smell what our dogs smell in the summer grass, but we can learn that same focus by watching them. From our pet birds, we learn how to be true to ourselves.

Wild Animals

When we run across an animal in the wild, we are seized by an archetypal energy of freedom and instinct. Depending on the circumstances and the type of animal, we may be seized by fear as well. But even fear can galvanize our creativity.

Years ago, while I was driving to work one morning, a Florida panther, a big cat, ran across the road less than thirty yards in front of my car. I was so astonished that I stopped and gaped as it streaked into the trees on my left. It was gone in seconds, but the vividness of that brief impression is still with me. I can still see the panther's magnificent sleekness and speed, the colour of its fur in the morning light, and I can still feel the hammering of my heart.

At the time, the official count of panthers in the wild was less than a hundred; but here was one that probably hadn't been counted, that had been living on the border between suburbia and the Everglades in the wild thickets of pine that shrank daily. I felt both awed and humbled by the experience. Years later, when I began

The Wondrous Dolphin

'Among Native Americans, the dolphin is a symbol of "the breath of life..." and breaks the limits and dimensions of physical reality so that we may enter the Dreamtime.'

Jamie Sams and David Carson
Medicine Cards: The Discovery of Power Through the Ways of Animals

writing fiction, at any time I wrote about a character's experience with wildlife, that panther was my barometer.

The Magical Powers of Dolphins

Olivia De Bergerac was born with a hole in her heart. When she was fifteen, she went through surgery to have the hole sewn up. But as she describes it in her book, *The Dolphin Within*, her heart wasn't fully healed until she swam with a pod of Monkey Mia dolphins that continually zapped her with their sonar. 'Such sound therapy, such high-tech surgery was absolutely revolutionary for me... I realized I had a new heart.'

She and a partner went on to form the Dolphin Society, an Australian-based non-profit research foundation. It is 'dedicated to exploring the effects on humans of interaction with dolphins, facilitating a process of discovering the "Dolphin Within".' In addition to the healing aspects of interaction with dolphins, De Bergerac writes movingly of how interaction with dolphins allows people to access their full creative potential and cites stories to back up her claim.

The Dolphin Society emphasizes interaction between humans and wild dolphins, rather than those in theme parks and dolphin centres. However, there is considerable anecdotal evidence that even interaction between humans and dolphins in centres can have a beneficial impact on healing, creativity and spiritual insight. Dolphins Plus, a research centre in Key Largo, Florida, is one such facility.

Dolphins Plus is primarily a research centre with eleven bottle-nose dolphins and two sea lions. Until recently, the dolphins were allowed to come and go pretty much as they pleased. But boat traffic along the canal behind the facility has grown so heavy in recent years that a fence was erected primarily as a safety device.

The facility has several programmes for human and dolphin interaction. Their therapy programme is for children with disabilities and draws people from all over the world. Their structured swim programme guarantees contact with dolphins and is the only one I know of in Florida where children of ten and older are welcome; in other facilities, they must be twelve and older. The non-structured

> ### The Magical Dolphin
>
> 'Perhaps the most magical animal in the sea and the one closest to humans, at least in a spiritual sense, is the dolphin. It was so sacred to the Greeks that to kill one was a capital offence.'
>
> Frank Joseph
> *Synchronicity and You*

programme provides an atmosphere where humans can swim in the same water as the dolphins, but the dolphins determine the contact.

My daughter has wanted to swim with dolphins since she was old enough to know what a dolphin was. A friend who's an animal activist recommended Dolphins Plus. So on a hot August day, Megan and I knelt on a dock with a marine biologist and trainer who instructed us in hand gestures and body language and explained what was going to happen.

Groups in the structured swims usually run from two to six. But we were fortunate – it was just the two of us. The dolphin, a female, was already scanning us when she came up under our palms, which were flat against the surface of the water. That first touch seemed electric to me, as visceral and intimate as sex. But this was just a prelude to an experience that remains essentially indescribable because so much of it is internal. The language of this kind of inter-action is symbolic, almost mythic. Strange and beautiful images float to the surface of the mind. The ancient seas whisper into the humid air. And for brief periods of time, there is complete immer-sion in the dolphin's watery world, so very similar, I suspect, to the embryonic world that spawned us.

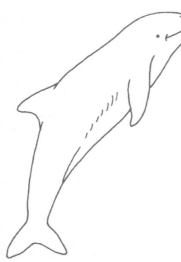

Afterwards, I kept thinking about a dolphin named Alpha. I imagined she had been in the government's mammal defence programme, trained to plant explosives on the hulls of ships in enemy waters. Maybe one day while she is out on manoeuvres, she displays intelligence, forethought, the capacity for strategy and planning, and turns the tables on the government. Perhaps she is some sort of dolphin high priestess, an evolved being who commands legions of dolphins. Too over the top? Too bad, I thought, and began writing a novel called *Vanished*.

It's set in the Florida keys, at a dolphin research centre, and the dolphins know something we don't: how to move almost instanta-neously through space. It was as if that single swim with dolphins opened a whole new creative world for me. Even though *Vanished* has been published, the creativity that spun away from the experience is just getting started.

De Bergerac notes that people who swim with dolphins experi-ence alpha and theta wave brain patterns after their swim. Alpha is a brain wave pattern that hums along at nine to thirteen cycles per second and is the state of consciousness associated with the early stages of sleep and dreaming, and with meditation. Theta waves are only four to eight cycles per second, the same as deep sleep, and are also present in meditation. 'If the brain can't slow down and produce more alpha and theta wave frequencies, individuals suffer from stress, anxiety, and a lack of creativity in the long run', De Bergerac writes.

Alpha and theta waves are the frequencies at which we are the most creative. When we are 'plugged in' to something we're creating, we are fully immersed in the moment. We are *in the flow*.

Practical Spells

So let's take this stuff about creativity and animals, creativity and dreams, creativity and nature, and make it practical. Do you have a screenplay to sell? A painting or photographs that deserve to be exhibited? Have you written a great thriller that deserves to be published?

Spell to Sell

Tools: Pen and paper
Something that represents what you want to sell
Aromatherapy burner and any oil or incense whose scent makes you feel happy and optimistic
3 candles – red, gold and violet
When: Three consecutive nights, beginning with the Full Moon

The item you choose to represent what you want to sell is especially important in this spell. If, for instance, you're an estate agent and are trying to sell a particular house or property, then you might choose a little house or a hotel from a Monopoly game to represent the property. If you want to sell a manuscript or screenplay, a book or a video can serve as a symbol. On a piece of paper, write your desire in the present tense: *My screenplay sells quickly* or *The Smiths' house sells quickly*. Slip this under the item that symbolizes your desire.

> **Embrace Your Creative Energy**
>
> 'Creative energy is a constant and we can *always* tap into it... It is our resistance to our creativity that causes us to equate it with suffering. It is important to remember that "effort" and "suffering" are two different things.'
>
> Julia Cameron
> *The Vein of Gold*

Creativity as a Spiritual Process

'All of us,' writes Julia Cameron, 'are richer than we imagine. None of us possesses a life devoid of magic, barren of grace, divorced from power. Our inner resources, often unmined and even unknown or unacknowledged, are the treasures we carry, what I call our spiritual DNA.'

Cameron is perhaps best known as the author of *The Artist's Way, Vein of Gold* and *The Right to Write*. All three books deal with creativity as a spiritual path that isn't restricted to a select few, but is open to anyone willing to do the work. And the work, as she explains in *Vein of Gold*, lies in recognizing that we are all rich. 'Once we know our own worth, then we will be able to know the worth of what we create and can therefore create more freely.'

Light the oil or incense. As you light the red candle, say your desire out loud three times. The red brings energy into your desire. Let the candle and the incense burn down. Leave the vestiges of the red candle on your altar or wherever you do the spell.

On the second night, repeat this ritual, but light the gold candle, which represents your desire for success. Again, let the candle and the incense burn down and leave the spent gold candle next to the red one. On the third night, light the purple candle; this symbolizes your highest good. When it has burned down, toss all three candles out, releasing your desire.

Chapter Thirteen

Health Spells

A health spell is no different from any other spell. Its effect is dependent on your intent, your passion and beliefs, and your ability to focus. If you're doing a spell for your own health, *you* are the one who makes things happen. If you're doing a spell for someone else's health, the effects depend on the other person's willingness to be healed.

Health spells involve many of the same components that other spells do – herbs and incantations, visualizations and affirmations, colours and sounds. They also involve prayer, meditation and touch. None of these things, however, is a substitute for treatment by a qualified doctor or homeopath.

Take special note of your answers to questions concerning your beliefs about health and illness. It may be that the three colds or the flu you get every year is directly related to your belief that getting three colds a year or coming down with the flu during the winter is normal. Read your answers several times. If you find that you hold negative or limiting beliefs concerning health, then changing these beliefs will do more for you than any spell.

The Human Energy Field

'Your body is designed to heal itself', writes Donna Eden in her book *Energy Medicine.*

In fact, we have all the tools we need to heal ourselves, and this process begins with an awareness of the subtle energies that give our bodies life. In China, these energies are called *chi* or *qi*. In India and Tibet, the energy is known as *prana*. The Sufis call it *baraka*. It runs through meridians in our bodies and is contained in seven major centres, or chakras, that extend from the base of the spine to the crown of the head.

Chakra literally means a disk or vortex. Imagine a swirling centre of energy of various colours, and you'll have a pretty good idea of what it looks like. When our energy is balanced, we are healthy. When our energy centres are unbalanced or blocked, we may fall ill. Each energy centre has a particular function and governs certain organs and physical systems within its domain. When a chakra is

Individual Intuition

'Intuition is more like passion. Everybody's experience of it is singular, not quite like anyone else's.'

Mona Lisa Schulz
Awakening Intuition

Brainstorming: Your Health Inventory

By taking an inventory of your health, you'll have a clearer idea about which spells will work best for you.

1. Most of the time, is your energy level high or low? _____

2. When was your last visit to a doctor? Why did you go?_____

3. Do you have regular check-ups? **Yes No**

4. Do you have any chronic health problems? If so, what are they? _____

5. Do you get several colds a year? **Yes No**

6. How much sleep do you need a night? _____

7. When do you feel happiest and healthiest? _____

8. Are there certain times of the year when your health is better or worse? **Yes No**

9. Do you worry a lot about your health? **Yes No**

10. Do you worry about death? **Yes No**

11. Do you experience fluctuations in your moods? **Yes No**

12. Do you consider yourself a basically optimistic person? **Yes No**

13. Do you have a particular spiritual belief system? **Yes No**

14. In general, how would you describe your health? _____

15. Have you noticed any particular patterns related to your health? If so, what are they?

16. What are your beliefs about illness and health? Do you, for instance, see illness as something that happens to you or do you see it as a disease in your emotional or spiritual make-up?_____

17. Have you ever sought alternative treatment for an illness or disease? If so, what sort of alternative treatment? _____

18. Describe your beliefs about health and illness. _____

19. Do you meditate? **Yes No**

20. Have you ever consulted a medical intuitive? **Yes No**

21. Does anyone in your family or close circle of friends have a chronic illness? If so, what kind of chronic illness? _____

22. Do you consider yourself an open-minded individual? **Yes No**
    Give specific examples. _____

blocked or unbalanced or not functioning properly, the organs and systems within its domain may suffer the effects.

The energy centres are said to contain everything we have ever felt, thought and experienced. They are our body's data banks in this life and are imprinted with our soul's history throughout many lives. Illness manifests first in the body's energy field, where it can be seen by an individual who can perceive the field.

When a medical intuitive, for instance, looks at an energy field, he or she is able to perceive a number of details. As Caroline Myss writes in *Anatomy of the Spirit*, 'In addition to reading specific dramatic childhood experiences, sometimes an intuitive can pick up on superstitions, personal habits, behaviour patterns, moral beliefs and preferences in music and literature. At other times the energy impressions are more symbolic.'

Donna Eden says basically the same thing: 'If I know your chakras, I know your history, the obstacles to your growth, your vulnerabilities to illness and your soul's longings.' In other words, to a medical intuitive, your chakras make you an open book.

You don't have to be a medical intuitive, however, to pick up information about your health or the health of someone else. One night I was a guest on a radio show to talk about *Your Cosmic Kids*, a book I wrote on understanding your children through astrology. After the show was over, the host asked if he could call me later to take a look at his chart to see if I could spot health problems. He was facing a health crisis, he said, and needed input from another source.

Medical astrology is a very specific branch of astrology, where the astrologer looks for specific health issues in a person's horoscope. I told the man I'm not a medical astrologer, but that I would look at his chart. Later that evening, I told my husband about it and without knowing anything at all about the chat show host, not even his name, Rob said, 'Oh, it's his heart.'

'How do you know that?' I exclaimed.

He shrugged. 'I don't know. I just do.'

I looked at the man's chart the next day, and although I saw some health issues for the year, I didn't see anything specific. Medical astrology is a precise science, and my knowledge of the field is sparse. When the man called to talk about his chart, he explained that a few years previously, he'd caught some sort of virus that had affected his heart and was facing heart surgery. So my husband was right after all.

How did he do it?

He went with his first impression. He didn't filter that impression through his left-brain, rational self. He didn't pause to argue with himself or even to ask himself how he could know such a thing. He simply went with his intuitive impression. He went 'from the gut', using the solar plexus energy centre. Medical intuitives basically do the same thing.

Intuitives use different methods to perceive information contained within the chakras. Some use their hands, passing them over the energy centres or even touching the physical areas where the chakras are located. Other intuitives 'see' the information in mental images or as impressions or as symbols. Others 'sense' the information in a way unique to them.

In addition to the major energy centres and the meridians, there are dozens of smaller chakras – in the palms of the hand, for instance, the fingertips, even on the soles of your feet. The sidebar on energy centres on page 146 defines the function of each of the major energy centres, its associated colours and its location in the physical body.

Intuitive Methods

Intuitives usually agree that illness and disease are intuitive signals that are telling us we need to address certain issues in our lives. But every intuitive has a different method and sees different aspects of an energy field.

Donna Eden, for instance, claims that each energy field has seven distinct layers. The deeper she penetrates into an individual chakra, the more information she is able to access. Barbara Brennan, a renowned healer and author of *Hands of Light*, also sees layers, but not in the same way. She sees the chakras with several distinct functions. The front of the throat chakra, for example, 'is associated with

> ### Love the Self
>
> 'No matter what the problem, the main issue to work on is LOVING THE SELF. This is the "magic wand" that dissolves problems.'
>
> Louise Hay
> *You Can Heal Your Life*

Diagnosis at a Distance

In the early days of her intuitive training, Caroline Myss worked with Harvard-trained MD Norman Shealy, founder of the Holistic Medical Association, to diagnose patients. They worked out an arrangement where Shealy would phone Myss, who was 1,200 miles away, when he had a patient in his office. Initially, Shealy merely gave Myss the patient's name and birth date and Myss would provide her impressions of the patient's medical problems.

As their partnership evolved, Shealy encouraged Myss to be more specific, to go through each organ systematically to 'check' it. He says that Myss's accuracy is 93 per cent.

taking responsibility for one's personal needs'. But the back of the throat chakra 'is associated with the person's sense of self within the society, his profession and with his peers'. Caroline Myss classifies energy fields according to three spiritual traditions: the symbolic meaning of the seven Christian sacraments, the Hindu teachings concerning chakras, and according to the Tree of Life in the Kabbala, the mystical teachings of Judaism.

Mona Lisa Schulz, MD, intuitive and author of *Awakening Intuition*, calls the energy centres 'emotional centres'. Her correlations between the chakras and the physical areas they cover differ from Myss's. Whereas Myss, for instance, sees the skeletal system governed by the seventh chakra, Schulz says it's governed by the first energy centre. Schulz perceives the seventh centre as governing the muscles, connective tissues and genes. Myss puts the circulatory system in the fourth centre area and the hips in the second; Schulz puts blood and hips in the first.

Medical intuitive and author Louise Hay rarely mentions chakras or energy centres. She gets right down to the parts of the body and equates them with emotions. In Hay's system, the throat (fifth energy centre) 'represents our ability to "speak" up for ourselves, to "ask for what we want", to say "I am" etc. When we have throat problems, it usually means we do not feel we have the right to do these things. We feel inadequate to stand up for ourselves.'

For Hay, all the body has meaning. 'If you cut your index finger, there is probably anger and fear that has to do with your ego in some current situation', she writes in *You Can Heal Your Life*.

As you work with your own energy centres, either through spells or some other method, your system will be unique to you. The more you learn about the human energy system, the better equipped you are to maintain your health.

Emotional Patterns and the Energy Centres

The **first energy centre** is what Myss calls 'tribal power'. It relates to our families, our framework in life and where our basic needs are met as children. It's where we learn to trust and to help ourselves. When this centre isn't working the way it should, we may experience chronic lower back pain, sciatica, rectal problems, depression and immune-related disorders.

Myss calls the **second centre** 'power and relationships'. The issues governed by this chakra have to do with individuating ourselves from our tribe – our family. Power issues are invariably involved over our autonomy, money and sex, blame and guilt, creativity. Money worries often manifest in this area. When this chakra doesn't function correctly, we may have trouble with our reproductive organs, bladder, urinary tract, hips and pelvis.

The **third energy centre** is what Myss calls 'personal power'. It is dominant when we're in puberty and are attempting to establish who we are, our 'ego self'. Issues involved are trust, responsibility for making our own decisions, our self-esteem. Schulz says this energy centre is about 'me against the world'. When the centre is off-balance, we have problems such as ulcers, Crohn's disease, anorexia or bulimia, addictions, liver trouble, obesity and adrenal dysfunction.

This centre is where many of us experience intuitive insight. A 'gut feeling', for example, originates here.

The lower three centres, says Myss, are where most people spend their energy. 'Most illnesses result from a loss of energy from these three chakras.' Both Myss and Schulz note that even when someone develops a disease related to the upper chakras – heart or neurological problems, for example – the energy origins of the illnesses often come from the bottom three chakras. 'Emotions such as rage and anger hit us physically below the belt, while an emotion like unexpressed sadness is associated with diseases above the belt,' she writes.

The **fourth centre** is known as the heart chakra. This is all about our emotions – how we feel or block them, how we express them and to whom we express them. It's about identifying what we feel at any given moment. Once we know what we feel, we can take steps to change what needs to be changed in our lives. When this chakra isn't functioning correctly, the physical problems that can result include asthma and allergies, lung cancer, heart attack, bronchial pneumonia and breast cancer.

Miracle, Magic or Something Else?

The patient has a malignant tumour on his left hip and the doctors send him home without treatment.

The patient goes to Lourdes to bathe. As he enters the spring, a sensation of heat suffuses his body. In a few months, he feels so revitalized he insists that his doctors X-ray his hip again. The tumour has shrunk and the doctors are so surprised, they begin documenting the changes. Soon, he is walking again. Over the course of several years, his hip bone has regenerated itself.

The patient is Vittoria Michelli. His medical file was sent to the Vatican's Medical Commission, a panel that examines evidence in cases of so-called miracles. They determined that Michelli had experienced a miracle.

Is it possible that through faith in the healing powers of Lourdes's spring Michelli somehow effected his own cure?

'Feeling and expressing *all* emotions, in a balanced way, is essential to health in the fourth emotional centre', writes Schulz.

The **fifth centre**, the throat chakra, has to do with personal will and expression. This is the area that's engaged in spell work. It also involves issues such as pursuing and living our dreams, timing, the way we express what we want and our capacity to make decisions. 'Health in this centre', writes Schulz, 'calls for a balance between expressing ourselves and listening to others; between pushing ourselves forward to fulfil our needs or waiting, when necessary, for things to come to us; and between imposing our will on others or allowing others to impose their will upon us.'

When the chakra isn't functioning the way it should, we may experience problems with our throats, gums or mouths. We may develop swollen glands or have thyroid problems. Quite often the smooth functioning of this chakra depends on expressing what's in our fourth centre, in our hearts.

The **sixth energy centre** concerns thought and perception. Its issues concern our intellectual abilities, openness to new ideas, our ability to learn from experience. When this chakra doesn't function correctly, the physical problems that may crop up are brain tumours and stroke, neurological problems, such as Parkinson's, seizures, spinal difficulties and problems with the ears, eyes and nose.

The **seventh energy centre** concerns our spirituality and being able to integrate it into our daily lives. As Schulz notes, the fundamental question that we all ask is 'Why am I here?'

'All of us, as we go through life, need a sense of our own life's purpose. The failure to connect with our purpose affects us profoundly in the seventh emotional centre.' In some instances, the failure to connect with our life purpose can prove fatal. After all, if you don't have a reason to live, your body simply shuts down. This energy centre is about taking responsibility to create our own lives.

Some of the physical problems that can occur when this centre doesn't function properly are chronic exhaustion, Lou Gehrig's disease, multiple sclerosis and what Myss calls 'energetic disorders'.

This is by no means a complete list of emotional patterns related to the various chakras. But it should provide enough information to do the spells in this chapter.

Energy Centres and Health
(Based on Caroline Myss's system)

Chakra	Where	Organs and Systems
1	Base of spine	Immune system Rectum Feet, legs, bones
2	Below navel	Sexual organs Large intestines Appendix, hips, bladder
3	Solar plexus	Abdomen and stomach Upper intestines Liver, kidneys, gallbladder, pancreas Middle vertebrae Adrenal glands
4	Between nipples	Heart and lungs Shoulders and arms Circulatory system Diaphragm Ribs, breasts, thymus gland
5	Throat	Throat Neck Thyroid, parathyroid Trachea, oesophagus, Mouth, teeth, gums Hypothalamus
6	Middle of forehead	Eyes, ears, nose Brain Nervous system Pineal and pituitary glands
7	Crown Skin and muscular system	Skeletal system

Training Yourself to See the Energy Field

The human energy field extends from a few inches to several feet around the physical body. It's like our personal ozone layer, a buffer. When it's healthy, the colours are brilliant and smooth. When it has dark or white splotches in it, has tiny rips or tears or is discoloured in some way, illness and disease may be the cause.

With practice, anyone can train themselves to detect the aura. Some people may see it, others may feel it, and still others may do both. For the activity that follows, you'll need a partner.

Seeing the Aura

Ask your partner to stand against a white, blank wall. Dim the lights in the room. Stand about six feet away from your partner and ask her to think of something that made her happy and to hold on to that feeling, bolstering it if she can. Stare at a point just above her head or to either side of it. Let your vision unfocus.

After a few moments, you should be able to see a pale nimbus of light around her head. At first, it may resemble a heat wave, the kind of shimmering effect you see radiating from the pavement on a hot summer day. The wave may grow as your partner holds on to her happy feelings.

If you don't see any colours, ask your partner to turn up the happiness feeling. You may see sparks of coloured light now – yellow, gold, brilliant blues, violets. If you still don't see colours, ask your partner to think of something that enraged her. Ask her to hold that emotion for a few minutes. Do you see any perceptible change in her aura? Does the wave shrink or get larger? Do the colours change?

With practice, this activity usually enables you to see someone else's aura.

If you would rather work alone, do the same thing in front of a mirror, with a pale, blank wall behind you.

Testing Your Chakras

Intuitive and healer Barbara Brennan recommends the use of a pendulum to diagnose the chakras. You'll need a partner and a pendulum of some sort on a string or chain about six inches long. Either you or your partner should lie flat on your back on the floor.

The pendulum should be as close to the body as possible without touching it. Hold it still over the chakra that you're checking, then remove your hand and let the pendulum begin to swing on its own. A healthy chakra will cause the pendulum to spin easily and steadily in a clockwise or anticlockwise direction. Chakras spin both clockwise and anticlockwise, alternating direction up the body – in addition, the chakra spin direction of a woman is the opposite to that of a man.

If the pendulum doesn't move when it's over a particular chakra, this usually means that chakra is blocked. If the pendulum swings more strongly to one side of the body or the other, then one side of the body is stronger than the other.

The right side symbolizes the male, yang, or active side; the left represents the female, yin, or receptive side. In instances like this, Brennan says, if the right swing is the strongest, then the individual is probably being too active or aggressive in situations where receptivity would be the better response.

A strong swing to the left indicates the individual is being too passive in situations where aggressiveness or decisive action would be more appropriate. The situation is directly linked to the psychological and emotional areas governed by the particular chakra.

The chakras along the back can also be checked in his fashion, with the person lying on his stomach.

Spell to Bolster the First Chakra

Tools: Object that represents your 'tribe'
        1 red candle
        Pen and paper
When: Whenever you feel the need

> ### The Power of Positive Thinking
>
> 'Learn to think in positive affirmations. Affirmations can be any statement you make. Too often we think in negative affirmations. Negative affirmations only create more of what you say you don't want.'
>
> Louise Hay
> *You Can Heal Your Life*

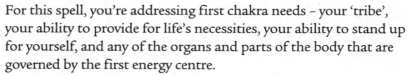

Books, Anyone?

In a number of bookshops, general books on alternative health take up entire walls. Here are some suggestions for your personal bookshelf:

Deepak Chopra: *Quantum Healing; Ageless Body, Timeless Mind*

Norman Cousins: *Anatomy of an Illness; Head First*

Larry Dossey: *Space, Time & Medicine*

Donna Eden: *Energy Medicine*

Marcia Emery: *The Intuitive Healer*

W. Brugh Joy: *Joy's Way; Avalanche*

Louise Hay: *You Can Heal Your Life*

Caroline Myss: *Anatomy of the Spirit; Why Some People Don't Heal and How They Can*

Judith Orloff: *Second Sight; Intuitive Healing*

Mona Lisa Schulz: *Awakening Intuition*

For this spell, you're addressing first chakra needs – your 'tribe', your ability to provide for life's necessities, your ability to stand up for yourself, and any of the organs and parts of the body that are governed by the first energy centre.

The object that represents your support system can be anything – a family photo, a photo of colleagues, a figurine of an animal, something you bought on a holiday or trip. It doesn't matter, as long as it symbolizes your tribe.

Jot down what you're trying to accomplish. If you're mired in depression, write an affirmation: 'I am happy' or 'My mood is great'. If you feel insecure within your tribe, then write 'I am safe and secure' or some other variation of the idea that feels right to you.

Slip the paper under the symbol, light your red candle and say your affirmation aloud. Visualize the end result. As always, back it with emotion. Then burn the paper, releasing your desire, let the candle burn down, and throw it away.

You can do variations of this spell for each of the seven energy centres. Take the second chakra, for instance. Let's say your problem right now is a blockage of creativity or not having enough money. Or maybe you have lower back pain. First, refer to Chapter 10 and find the appropriate colour for the second chakra (orange). Then write out your affirmation and follow the instructions for the first chakra spell.

Spell for a Specific Ailment

First, try to locate the ailment in terms of the energy centres. If the ailment isn't listed in this chapter, then use what you do know. If, for instance, you have a sinus infection, then you would focus on the sixth chakra, which governs, among other things, the nose.

Ask yourself questions couched in terms of the sixth chakra's themes. Are you closed to new ideas? Are you feeling inadequate? You might also want to look at the themes for the third and fourth chakra to see if these fit you.

Once you've decided which chakra or chakras to work with, write an affirmation that states what you want. For a sinus condition, your affirmation might be: 'I am at peace' or: 'I am well'. Next, light the appropriate coloured candle for the chakra you're working on. Focus your full attention on that chakra and vividly imagine the energy in that area in a spinning motion, either clockwise or anticlockwise.

Do the visualization as long as you can maintain the energy. Then say the affirmation aloud, burn the piece of paper on which you wrote it, extinguish the candle and throw it away.

Spell to Get Rid of a Headache

If paracetamol doesn't work, then maybe this will. Rinse a quartz crystal with salt water, then 'charge' it by placing it in sunlight for a while. Hold it to your forehead for several moments and imagine the quartz absorbing the pain. When you're finished, cleanse and charge the crystal again. This is a good method to use for another person's headache, too.

Casting a Health Spell for Another Person

Before you do a health spell for someone else, always ask that person's permission to do so. It may be that the illness or disease the person has serves some function in his or her life. The individual may not see it this way, of course, but on some level, in fact, it may be true.

Schulz relates a story about a woman who had Guillain-Barre syndrome. She had been in a wheelchair for much of her adult life. The woman's husband called Schulz when his wife suddenly began walking again, using crutches. The woman had been having sleeping problems and was more concerned with her inability to get a good night's sleep than she was about the fact that she'd started walking.

When Schulz suggested therapy to strengthen her legs, the woman demurred. 'I'm an invalid', she declared. 'I need a wheelchair and I deserve twenty-four-hour care.'

Schulz realized the woman had not only accepted her limitations but also defended them. She 'chose illness as her life's path and she chose it in the belief that she... needed complete care from the outside'. In other words, her illness gave her life a purpose.

So before you cast a spell for someone else's physical condition, ask their permission to do so. Even then, it's probably a good idea to stick to a general spell to bolster the individual's overall physical health rather than work on any specific area or complaint.

Spell for Another's Health

Tools: Something that represents the other person
Sprig of sage
Aromatherapy burner and eucalyptus essential oil
1 gold candle
1 purple or violet candle
When: As needed

You can use a photograph of the person or an object the individual has lent or given you. Set it in the middle of your work area or altar, with a candle on either side of it, and the oil burner behind it.

Smudge your work area first and also smudge the object that represents the other person by burning the sage and wafting the smoke (see page vi). Add several drops of eucalyptus oil to the water bowl of your burner. Light it, then light the candles. After a moment of reflection in which you fix the person's face and being in your mind, say:

As the oil and candles burn,
Illness gone and health return,
For my (state relationship and name)
Who is yearning,
And so deserving.

Extinguish the candle in the aromatherapy burner. Let the other two candles burn down naturally, then throw them away.

Everyday Health Spells

Sometimes, we feel just *depleted.* We need a day off from work to simply laze around and read, go swimming, take a long walk in the

Essential Oil and Health

Essential oils can be helpful in the health area. Some common uses:

1. Citronella oil on the melted wax of a candle or hot charcoal briquette can dispel mosquitoes and other picnic pests.

2. Rosemary promotes alertness and stimulates memory, so is helpful for reading and studying. Inhale by adding a few drops to a tissue, hold at chin level and smell during long car trips or while reading and studying.

3. For restful sleep, add one or two drops of chamomile or lavender essential oils to an aromatherapy burner (adding the oils to water in the water bowl), light the candle and allow to burn for five to ten minutes, then extinguish the burner.

4. For burns, apply a little undiluted lavender oil onto the affected area, using a cotton bud or Q-tip.

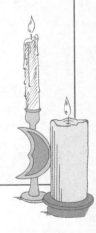

Essential Oils as Mood Enhancers

1. A blend of lavender and grapefruit oil creates a tranquil atmosphere and stimulates the senses.
2. To improve your mood, add a few drops of geranium, lavender and bergamot to the water bowl in an aromatherapy burner, or add to water in a mister bottle, shake and spray all around the room.
3. An essential oil dropped onto a radiator ring or light bulb will fill the room with a wonderful fragrance and also set a calm or uplifting mood.

countryside. We aren't sick, we aren't recovering from any illness – we just need to refuel ourselves.

Spell to Boost Your Energy

Tools:　Your favourite music
　　　　Rose quartz crystal
　　　　Sprig of vervain
When:　As needed

This spell is probably best done when you're alone because you're going to turn the music up very loud. The music you select should be something that boosts your spirits and makes you want to move around, dance, swing your hips and arms.

The rose quartz is intended to amplify the surge in your mood. The vervain, when burned, provides a general boost to the spirit and cleanses negative vibes, among other things.

Light the vervain, put the quartz next to it on a heatproof surface, then put on your music and turn the volume up. Let the music suffuse the room and permeate your senses. Then get up and dance to it. Continue as long as needed.

Chapter Fourteen
Spells for Business

My Goals

First time frame: _____

_____

_____

_____

_____

_____

_____

_____

_____

Second time frame: _____

_____

_____

_____

_____

_____

_____

_____

Third time frame: _____

_____

_____

_____

_____

_____

_____

_____

_____

The quality of your professional life is intimately connected with your beliefs about prosperity and success. If you feel unworthy, this will be reflected in your wallet or purse and in your work. If, on the other hand, you believe you're deserving – of a raise, of a promotion, of better working conditions – this will also be reflected in your life.

In the brainstorming activity opposite, you're going to take inventory of your professional life – the work you do, your bosses and the people who have power over you, your colleagues or employees, or your personal circumstances if you're self-employed.

Spells and Goals

Setting goals is intrinsic to professional achievement. The goals don't have to be set in stone, but it's important to have a picture in mind of what you would like to accomplish professionally.

When my husband and I were starting out as freelance writers, we used to sit down every New Year's Eve and make up a list of goals for the year. We would review our goals quarterly, to get some sense of how far along we had come – or had yet to go – to achieve the goals for that year and revise our goals as necessary. Whether you want to change professions or jobs or to simply move ahead in the profession or job you presently have, setting goals helps you clarify what you want. Once you can clarify what you want, it's easier to do spells because you know what you're after.

Write down your goals for three specific periods of time (see the sidebar on the left). You select the time divisions. If you're an impatient person, you may want to make the increments small – a few days, six weeks – so that you can see what progress you're making. If you've got the patience of a saint, then make the increments cover a large chunk of time.

When I'm working on a book, I set daily and weekly goals. These, in turn, become monthly goals. Usually, the goals are related to the number of words or pages that I want to get done in a given time frame. Since I'm an impatient person, I find that daily goals work well for me. I can push myself away from my computer at the end of a day and feel good that I've accomplished the goal I set.

Brainstorming: Your Business World

If You Work for Someone Else:
1. Describe the work that you do. Give specific details. _____
2. Is your work satisfying? Why or why not? _____
3. Do you get along with your boss? _____
4. Do you get along with your colleagues? _____
5. Are you passionate about your work?_____
6. What would you change about your work if you could? _____
7. Do you have moral or ethical objections to the work you do? _____
8. Do you feel you're paid fairly for what you do?_____
9. What are your professional goals for the next year? The next five years? _____
10. Do you have any regrets about the professional path you've chosen? _____
11. Have you had regular promotions and raises? If not, why not? _____
12. Is your work life filled with power struggles of one kind or another? If so, explain.

_____

If You Are Self-Employed:
1. What type of service do you provide?_____
2. Do you have employees? If so, how many? _____
3. Do you like most of your employees? Do they do good job for you? If not, explain.

_____
4. What would you like to change about your business and why? _____
5. Do you consider yourself a fair boss? _____
6. Are you earning enough for what you do? _____
7. What are your professional goals for the next year? The next five years? _____

_____
8. If you could choose to do anything you wanted, what would it be? Why? _____

_____
9. Are you passionate about what you do? _____
10. If your passions lie elsewhere, can you imagine earning your living at them? _____

If your answers to the above questions are primarily positive, then you're probably exactly where you want to be in life right now. If the answers are predominately negative, keep them in mind as you read the chapter.

Spell for Clarification

This spell is intended to clarify a goal that you have. Quite often we think we want one thing and later on find that what we wanted was something else entirely. So before you get to the 'later on' point, do this simple spell for clarification.

Tools: Aromatherapy burner and cedar essential oil
Pen and paper
When: As you feel the need

Put a couple of drops of cedar essential oil in your burner and light it. As the scent suffuses the air, write down your goal. Keep it simple. Now shut your eyes and sit quietly for a few moments with your goal in mind. Imagine that you have achieved this goal. How does it feel? Are you comfortable with it? How do your family and friends act towards you? What is your life like now that you have attained what you wanted?

The more vivid and detailed your imaginings, the greater benefit you derive from this visualization. Do this as long as you can keep imagining vividly, then stop. Now read your goal again. Is it what you really want? If not, rewrite it. You may find that you merely need to fine-tune what you've written.

If you rewrite your goal, let it sit for a day or two before you look at it again. Then ask yourself if it feels right. Chances are that it will.

New Ventures

A new job, a new profession, a new lease on your professional life: all those things fall in this category.

Nothing can be as frightening as the prospect of starting something new. We worry about whether we should give it a whirl. We worry about if we're young or old enough, experienced enough, talented enough to make a go of it. We worry because we've been conditioned to worry, to berate ourselves, to naturally assume we don't have what it takes to make it.

Make It So

'I became aware that a gloom which had been haunting me for days could be drastically altered by willing the change.'

Carlos Castaneda
The Art of Dreaming

A young writer wrote a book, didn't think it was good enough to be published, and threw it in the rubbish. His wife retrieved the manuscript and it was not only published, but became a bestseller and a film. The author? Stephen King. The book? *Carrie*.

Back in the early 1980s, a young woman had an idea about colour and skin tones. But she didn't know how to put it together. On a plane trip, she happened to sit next to a young man and told him her idea. He became second-in-command, she became the boss, and the company was called Color Me Beautiful.

Sometimes it takes another person to recognize our genius and to organize it.

Recognizing Your Genius

This spell is intended to attract the individual who recognizes your genius and helps you pull together your vision of what might be, whatever that vision is.

Tools: Seeds for a plant that has round leaves or purple flowers
           Ceramic pot
           Potting soil
When: Thursday during a waxing moon

Fill your ceramic pot with potting soil and place nine seeds at various points in the soil. As you plant the seeds, say aloud:

> *As I plant these seeds*
> *I draw to me*
> *The one who sees*
> *What I can be.*
> *So mote it be.*

Once the seeds begin to sprout, the person who recognizes your genius should appear in your life. Until that happens, keep the plant in the northern part of your home – the place for career. However, if this isn't possible for one reason or another, locate the wall or section of your home that is directly opposite your front door. If you have a particular room in your home where you do most of your work, the pot could also go in here, along the wall opposite the door or along the northern wall.

Spell to Enhance Magnetism

This spell helps on that first day in a new job, with a new boss, new colleagues, new ventures and professional situations.

> Tools: 1 red candle
> 1 violet candle
> 1 quartz crystal
> Aromatherapy burner and your favourite oil
> When: Waxing moon

What you're doing with this spell is enhancing your aura, filling it with magnetism that attracts what you need – and yet protects you from what you don't need. The quartz crystal amplifies the magnetism.

Light your burner and as the scent suffuses the air, inhale deeply and light the red candle. Say aloud:

> *The magnetism of this red flame*
> *Enters me by name,*
> *(say your name)*
> *So mote it be.*

Light the violet candle and say:

> *The protection of this violet flame*
> *Enters me by name*
> *(say your name)*
> *So mote it be.*

Let the candles burn down. Bury them in your garden or in a flower pot, so the power stays with you always.

Amulets and Charms for Business

In Chapter 10, we talked about amulets and charms for personal power. The objects you selected and made for that purpose will also work for business power, but you may want to have separate objects for business purpose.

You may feel a bit strange the next time you walk into a business meeting with an amulet or charm in your pocket. But who needs to know besides you? And if it imbues you with power or magnetism or whatever else you need, what difference does it make?

An amulet for business power is merely an object imbued with power through your intent and desire. A four-leafed clover, for example, is traditionally recognized as an amulet for luck. But if you weed clover out of your garden, then your business power object should be something else. It could be a stone that resonates for you. Or an animal figure. Or even a piece of fabric. The actual object matters less than the sentiment you attach to it.

One day my daughter and I were browsing in a shop and came across tiny animal figures carved of a shiny metal. I selected a frog; she chose a ladybird. I carry my frog in my purse when I'm in need of professional clarity and creative inspiration. She keeps her ladybird tucked into the parade of miniature horses on her dresser where she can see it when she's doing homework or school projects. My friend Vicki carries 'the bear', a little totem carved of some mysterious stone that hangs from a chain. She uses it as a pendulum, a business and personal amulet.

An amulet doesn't seem to be something you can look for. It comes to you, it appears, it falls off a shelf at your feet. It's something that speaks to you, only to you, and when you first see it, you know it's yours. You *know*.

You can have an amulet for business and an amulet for love, an amulet for travel and an amulet for protection. You can have one for every occasion. Just make sure you know which is which!

A charm is the Western equivalent of a shaman's medicine bundle. It should be made of cotton or silk. When you're making it for personal power, the colour of the cloth should be purple. When you're making it for business power, the colour should represent the chakra you use most frequently in business. If you

Power and Scents

If you're a woman who enjoys perfume, experiment with different types of perfume and pay attention to their effects on people. Which perfumes do others comment on?

How do certain scents make you feel? Calm? Sexy? Powerful? Businesslike? Romantic? Which scent(s) make you feel best?

Once you begin to take notice of how different perfumes affect your emotions, you'll have a better idea of what scent to wear to your next business meeting.

do a lot of talking in your job, then blue might be the best colour for the bag because blue represents the throat chakra, the centre of your expression. If your job entails counselling or therapy, then the cloth might be a mixture of blue for expression and green to represent the compassion of the heart chakra. If the chakra's colours don't seem to fit your work, then consult the colour list in Chapter 10.

You want the bundle to be small enough to carry with you, yet large enough to accommodate the objects you put inside it. Keep the number of objects to a minimum, and preferably not too large. Be sure you select items that symbolize something significant and important to you.

From time to time, you should remove the items in your charm bag and cleanse them. Either wash them in sea salt and charge them in the sun, or if they can't be washed, simply set them outside in the sun for a few minutes. As your charm works its magic on particular projects or with particular issues, consider replacing the items with other objects. A bundle can also contain slips of paper on which you've written your desire or need.

If you do a lot of business travelling, you may want to make a business charm that relates specifically to travel. This charm would entail not just safe travel, but smooth travel – no problems with your reservation, no cancelled flights, no long waits in airport lobbies, no irate passengers or lost baggage; in short, what you require is a charm that gets you from point A to point B with a minimum of hassle.

Be imaginative with your business charms, and by all means have fun making them.

Mitigating Negative Situations

Most of us have bad days now and then at work. Occasionally, however, a bad day collapses into a really negative situation. Then it's more difficult to get back on the right track because it seems we're surrounded by negativity, mired in it.

In situations like this, the longer you dwell on what went wrong, the worse it looks and the more negative and bleak you

Patience Is a Virtue

'There are people who live in a state of perpetual hurry without ever attaining inner composure. Restlessness not only prevents all thoroughness but actually becomes a danger if it is dominant in places of authority.'

The I Ching
(Wilhem edition)
Hexagram 32, Duration

become. It's one of those self-perpetuating cycles. To break the cycle and mitigate a potentially negative situation, the first thing you have to do is step back and detach yourself emotionally from whatever has happened.

Remember that your point of power resides *in the moment*. You can't change what has happened, but you can alter your perspective about it, and that in turn can soften the impact.

Spell to Release Negativity

Tools: 1 white candle
           1 bay leaf
           White flowers, preferably carnations
When: The waning moon

If the situation is immediate or pressing, you can do this spell at any time. But any spell to release or cleanse is most powerful during the waning moon.

Place the bay leaf next to your vase of flowers and light your candle. Say aloud:

> *I now release (name the situation)*
> *and create new, positive energy to carry me forward.*
> *I trust this is for my highest good*
> *and affirm my commitment to this new path.*
> *I say so be it.*

Let the candle burn down. Throw away the bay leaf with the flowers when they die.

Point of Power Spell

With this spell, you're affirming that your point of power is in the present. The moment is your launching pad for the rest of your life. You can do this spell in conjunction with the previous spell, or you can do it alone, for virtually any situation or issue.

Recognizing Opportunities

Sincere intent, deep passion, profound need: these traits are needed in casting spells. But regardless of how many spells you cast, they won't change anything if you're unable to recognize or make your own opportunities.

When we don't recognize an opportunity, it's usually because we can't connect it to what we think we want. But such opportunities may serve as stepping stones to something else, which becomes another stepping stone... and so on until the string of opportunities brings us to where we wanted to be in the first place.

When opportunities come to us in this way, synchronicities are usually involved. If you recognize a synchronicity – or a cluster of seeming coincidences – then take notice. It may be opportunity staring you in the face.

Tools: Piece of root ginger
Potted plant with yellow flowers
1 green candle
1 purple candle
Business amulet (se page 201)

When: Thursday or Friday during a waxing moon

With this spell, you're affirming in your own mind that your point of power is, indeed, in the present. Put the piece of ginger between each of the candles and the vase of flowers behind the ginger. As you light the candles, say aloud:

> *My point of power,*
> *like this plant that flowers,*
> *some way, somehow*
> *lies in the now.*

Extinguish the candles when you've finished and throw away the ginger. Put the potted plant into the soil where you can see it. If it's not possible to plant it outside, then transplant it to a larger pot and put it in a window where you can see it.

Spell to Get a Raise or Promotion

Do this spell only if you're convinced that you're worthy of a raise or a promotion. Otherwise, you're just saying words.

Tools: 2 gold candles
£20 note that represents your raise
Sprig of sage
Pen and paper

When: During the waxing moon, preferably on a Thursday night

The banknote you use to represent your raise can be of any denomination. It's merely a symbol.

Jot down what you would like your raise to be. Phrase it in the present tense and add 'or better' at the end of it. Your statement

might read: 'I get a £2,000 raise or better'. If you're doing this for a job promotion, jot it down in the same format.

Set the piece of paper and the bill between the gold candles. As you light the candles, say aloud:

> *Element of fire,*
> *Hear my desire,*
> *A raise (promotion) is due to me,*
> *(state what you want) or better,*
> *Make it so to the letter.*

Once you feel the rightness of what you're saying, once it *resonates* inside you, then burn the piece of paper on which you wrote what you wanted, thus releasing the desire. Extinguish the flames and safely dispose of the candles and the ashes of the sage.

Spell for the Frequent Business Flyer

If you travel frequently on business, this spell can save you time, aggravation and stress. Do this spell several hours before you leave for the airport.

Tools: Aromatherapy burner and sandalwood
essential oil
1 violet or purple candle
Sprig of sage
Pen and paper
When: As needed

On a sheet of paper, write: *My trip unfolds smoothly. I arrive safely and on time at my destination.* Set the paper next to the candle. Light the burner for the sandalwood, then light the sage on a heatproof surface. Light your candle and read what you've written out loud. Read it again silently and see yourself at your destination, on time, with your baggage, refreshed and at peace.

Read what you've written aloud once more, then burn it, releasing your desire. Extinguish the candles and throw them away with the sage. Extinguish the candle in the burner and give thanks that you are in a position to travel.

Power Symbols in Business

Some years ago, a book packager arranged for me to work on a book with Dionne Warwick. I flew out to Los Angeles and, through her agent and the book packager, had the opportunity to meet her.

The meeting took place at her home in Beverly Hills. I was incredibly nervous. This was the woman whose music I had grown up with during the 1960s, who sang from the heart. I wore pale green, a colour to instill calmness in myself and to communicate that I was coming from the heart with this project. I also wore a tiny emerald necklace that I had bought for myself when my first novel sold. Before her agent and I went into the house, I grounded myself with some deep breathing.

A housekeeper answered the door and ushered us into the living room. I just stood there for a few moments, absorbing everything. And there was plenty to absorb. The walls were tastefully decorated with African art. Grand wooden sculptures stood like sentries at strategic points in the room. The colours were bold and dramatic. But the focal point was the piano, a gorgeous black Steinway, with a surface so shiny it reflected the ceiling directly above it. Right then and there, I felt so intimidated that I nearly turned and fled.

Then she entered the room, a stunning woman who radiated such warmth that I felt immediately at ease. We settled, the three of us, some distance from that ubiquitous piano, and spent several hours talking about the strange, the mystical and the psychic. Dionne was always completely *in the moment*, attentive, fully present.

Every now and then, the objects around me would drift into my awareness, each object perfect in its simplicity and beauty, and in its message. *This is part of who I am*, these objects seemed to say, as if they were extensions of Warwick herself. Only later did I realize these objects were powerful precisely because they were imbued with her spirit. If I had seen any single item in a shop, separate from Warwick,

Colours in Your Professional Life

Don't confine your use of colours to spells. Use them consciously in the way you dress, in your office, even in your car. The meanings of the colours provided in Chapter 2 don't differ all that much from the meanings of colours you use professionally. But certain situations may call for some thought and imagination.

Red. Use or wear it when you want to be noticed

Beige. Use or wear it when you want to blend in or to create a sense of peace and security for yourself or others

Pink. A calming effect

Green. Pastels work best – calm, soothing, earthy; belongs to the heart, the fourth chakra

Blue. Pastels are peaceful, turquoise is vibrant, navy is sombre; in general, blue promotes trust and clarity

White. Innocent, perfect, the ideal, understanding

Black. Mysterious, a shield – others project what they want to see; can come across as emotionally distant

Yellow. A boost in energy for yourself and others; alive and happy

Orange. Too flashy, calls too much attention to the self – confine it to accessories or in small bits elsewhere

Purple. Makes a statement, especially when you're wearing it; avoid in clothing unless you look stunning – use in your office or in other ways; triggers spirituality and creativity

they would have caught my interest – especially that Steinway piano. But they wouldn't have seemed particularly powerful.

This is an important distinction. An object is merely an object until it has, for lack of a better word, *soul*. And that soul comes from the person who owns it, touches it, takes care of it, and in doing so, imbues that thing with the uniqueness of who he or she is.

When we go to museums and see the original works of van Gogh, Rembrandt, Matisse, Picasso, we *react* to the artistry, yes, but we also feel what the artist felt as the painting was being painted. We feel the artist's soul.

Objects absorb and reflect our energy, just by virtue of being in the same space that we inhabit. If we're passionate about a particular thing, that energy is heightened. It lingers. This happens without any great effort on our part. But when we consciously imbue an object with our passion, intent and desires, then the object becomes extremely powerful.

Look around your work area. What do you see? With what objects have you surrounded yourself? What do they mean to you? Do the objects have a story attached to how you got them? Do they have a history? If you need the upper hand in a situation, if you need a bit of power on your side, make sure that the objects around you are there for a purpose and not just for decoration.

Chapter Fifteen
Spells for Lean Times

Lean times happen to all of us, and they aren't just financial. They can happen in any area of your life or several areas at once. Your partner loses a job. One of your parents dies. Your novel doesn't sell, your marriage falls apart, you develop a health problem. No matter where you turn, bad stuff happens.

Why the Lean Times?

Well, the facile answer is that that's life. Life happens. Life isn't always a great and magnificent adventure. Sometimes it hurts. Sometimes it's so painful we just want to curl up and sleep until the bad part is over and done with. Most of the time, in lean cycles, what's happening is so far beyond our immediate comprehension that we just have to get through it.

Lean times seem to be cyclic for many people, but with awareness and applied intent, the pattern can be broken. Do your lean times seem to happen during a particular time of the month or year? Do the cycles seem to be connected to the phases of the moon or to the summer or winter solstice? Do things usually pick up for the better around or right after your birthday?

Using your birthday as a starting point, it's possible to plot your personal cycles by dividing the year into quarters. The first three months after your birthday tend to be a productive, busy time. You're actively involved in the outer world, there are many demands on your time and energy, but things get done.

The second three months are still productive, but less active. This is a good time to assess what you've been doing in the last three months and to fine-tune.

The third quarter, beginning six months from your birthday, is usually a time of harvest. You're reaping the benefits of that first three months. You feel prosperous.

The fourth quarter – beginning about three months before your birthday – can be stressful. You may find that you tire more easily, that you're more irritable. If little things that go wrong during this period aren't fixed, they tend to become bigger problems.

You should be able to recognize a pattern in your quarterly cycles. As you work with them, other patterns may emerge.

Listen to Your Soul

'Belief consists in accepting the affirmations of the soul; unbelief, in denying them.'

Ralph Waldo Emerson

Yearly Cycles

The example here uses an arbitrary birthdate to illustrate the range of the yearly cycles.

Cycle	Dates	Energy	Things to Do
1	7/6–7/9	Productive, energetic Demands on your time Growth	Get out into world Launch new ventures and projects Move Find new job/career Sign up new clients
2	7/9–7/12	Slower pace Productive but less active	Organize, get rid of clutter Fine-tune projects/ventures Brainstorm for new ideas Conserve your energy Take a holiday
3	7/12–7/3	Reaping benefits of first cycle More prosperous period Achievement, attainment Energetic, buoyant time	Projects are completed Closure to what was begun in first cycle Actively seek new projects, interests Network, establish new contacts
4	7/3–7/6	Energy is lower Can be stressful Sudden, unexpected events Demands on your time increase	Take up meditation Learn to relax Reassess Set new goals

Brainstorming: Plotting Your Cycles

To plot your yearly cycles, jot notes about major events that happened during each quarterly period. Include details about how you felt. If you can't remember that far back, then begin with your most recent birthday and carry it through the year to your next birthday.

Date of my birthday:

_____

First Cycle
Dates: _____
Events: _____
Emotions: _____

Second Cycle
Dates: _____
Events: _____
Emotions: _____

Third Cycle
Dates: _____
Events: _____
Emotions:_____

Fourth Cycle
Dates: _____
Events: _____
Emotions: _____

Spells to Initiate Each Cycle

The Birthday Spell: Cycle 1

On or close to your birthday, set aside a few minutes to write down what you would like to happen in the next three months. Be specific, read it aloud, then post it where you would see it frequently – on the door of the fridge, your bathroom mirror, next to your computer.

Every time you read what you've written, feel that reality around you. You can also create a charm or find a power totem that represents your desire and carry it with you. After you feel comfortable with what you've written – several days, a few weeks, whatever it takes – burn the paper, thus releasing your desire.

On your birthday, do something special for yourself to celebrate the beginning of a new annual cycle.

Spell for Cycle 2

On or around the date that marks the beginning of the second cycle, do what you did in the birthday spell. Since your energy during this period may be lower, light two red candles before you read aloud what you've written, then extinguish them. After several days or weeks, burn the sheet of paper.

Spell for Cycle 3

On or around the date that the third cycle begins, write down, as before, what you want for this period. This is your harvest period, so light a gold candle to represent continued prosperity and a violet candle to represent your gratitude for all the good things that have come your way, then extinguish the candles.

Spell for Cycle 4

On or around the date that marks the beginning of the fourth cycle, follow what you did at the beginning of the three previous cycles. Light a red, gold and violet candle, then read aloud what you've written before extinguishing the flames.

On the day when this period begins, do something special for yourself and extend yourself to someone else – i.e. do a good deed.

Fear

One of the biggest challenges we face during lean times is that old devil, fear. Fear can cripple the best intentions, squash the most buoyant spirit and make a lean cycle a permanent condition.

It's difficult to imagine that you're prosperous or successful when you're unemployed and have £10 left in the bank. It's difficult to imagine yourself in a happy relationship when you're alone and feeling miserable. Difficult, but not impossible. Several breathing techniques can override fear, at least temporarily, and while the fear is at a low ebb, imagination can be employed to work through the fear and move beyond it.

Another way to break through the barrier of fear is as you're waking up in the morning. When you're still in that in-between state, not quite awake and not quite asleep, state your fear in a simple sentence. Draw an imaginary box around it. Light a match and set the imaginary box on fire. Sweep the imaginary ashes out the imaginary front door of your house.

As soon as you've done this, replace the statement about your fear with a positive affirmation. If, for instance, your fear is about debt or not having enough money, then some possibilities for positive affirmations might be:

· I have plenty of money.
· Money flows into my life from expected and unexpected sources.
· My life fills with abundance.
· I am rich.

As always, state your affirmation in the present tense and back it with emotion.

The place between sleep and wakefulness is an especially powerful state of consciousness for doing belief work. If you do it in the morning before you get out of bed, you're setting the tone for the

Birthday Affirmation

As your birthday approaches, post this affirmation where you see it frequently. The day after your birthday, throw the affirmation away, thus releasing it.

I trust that I am on a path of abundance and happiness, of gratitude and prosperity. I am peaceful, calm, filled with the certainty that all my days, from this day forward, are rich and splendid.

day. If you do it at night as you're falling asleep, your unconscious works on it. If you cling to your fear – or it clings to you – your lean times may linger because like attracts like.

Fear of Flying

Years ago, I had a deep fear of flying. I wouldn't sleep well the night before a trip; I would sit rigidly throughout the flight, unable to even get up and use the toilet. I finally confronted the fear by taking flying lessons. I found that once I understood why a plane flies and learned how to fly it myself, my fear began to abate – but only as long as my instructor was in the plane with me.

One afternoon, we practised a couple of landings and take-offs, then he asked me to pull over to the tarmac. I did and he got out. 'You're ready for your solo. Happy flying.'

A terrible paralysis crept over me. I sat there for a few minutes, trying to work my way through it, then I mustered the courage to taxi down the runway. As soon as the plane was airborne, an incredible euphoria swept through me. I had conquered the fear! My solo went well, and for several weeks afterward, I practised touch-and-go landings on my own. Then it was time for my first solo cross country.

About thirty minutes into my flight, I noticed *stuff* on the windscreen. It oozed across the glass in long, dark ribbons. I wondered if I had hit a bird and leaned more closely to the windshield examine the liquid. It didn't look like blood, I didn't see any feathers, and I reasoned that I would have heard or felt the impact.

My fear was now threatening to run amok inside me, and I quickly radioed the tower and explained my problem. They recommended that I land at the nearest airport.

The nearest airport back then was barely more than a spot on the landscape below me. I kept peering below, trying to locate the landmarks on my map. I finally spotted the airport. The stuff on the windscreen was so thick I couldn't see anything in front of me. My fear now approached full-blown panic.

I radioed the airport and they gave me a heading for my landing. I kept reminding myself that I had done dozens of landings, I knew

---

What's the Lesson, Anyway?

During lean times, it can be helpful to try to identify what you're supposed to be learning from the experience. If you're in debt, what are you learning about how to manage money? Or about the monetary value of your skills and talents? If you're lonely, what is your loneliness teaching you?

Quite often, if you understand the lesson, whatever it is, the problem begins to ease.

how to do this, I **would** do this. My landing was far from perfect, but I was so grateful and relieved to be on the ground that anything short of crashing would have been just fine with me.

The stuff on the windscreen turned out to be oil. The plane had recently gone in for its 100-hour check and a valve apparently hadn't been tightened sufficiently.

I never did get my licence. I like to think it's because the lessons were too expensive at the time, but I suspect the truth is simpler: I was afraid. In the years since, I have flown in other small planes, I fly in commercial airliners, and other than the usual travel hassles, I enjoy it. But I've never put myself in the pilot's seat again. I'm getting to the point, though, where I might like to try it again soon. I've realized that my fear wasn't the plane or even flying it alone. My fear was simply of my own mortality.

This story aptly illustrates how like attracts like. Other people had flown that plane since it had its 100-hour check and nothing had happened. But because I had so much residual fear when I embarked on that solo cross country, my fear attracted the circumstances in which I had to confront the very thing I dreaded.

Other Methods for Breaking the Fear Barrier

The next time fear is staring you in the face, don't turn around and run. Stare back. Confront it by asking yourself: *What is the absolute worst that can happen? What is this fear really saying to me?*

Edie, a massage therapist, went into business with her husband when they got married and gradually let go of her clients and therapy practice. She got pregnant before her first anniversary. By the time she was four or five months into the pregnancy, her husband had overextended himself by trying to maintain two restaurants that literally ate up all of his time. Problems developed in the marriage. She was unable to sleep, her insides were continually knotted up with anxiety, and her fears surfaced fully grown.

Before she could even begin to think clearly, she had to confront those fears. What, she asked herself, was the worst that could

Getting Rid of Fear

Sit in a comfortable spot, with your back against a wall. Shut your eyes and breathe normally for a few moments. Gradually deepen your breathing until you can feel it deep in your stomach.

Pinch your right nostril shut and breathe in deeply through the left. Hold to the count of ten and exhale through the right nostril. Repeat three times, then switch nostrils.

When you've done that, you should be feeling calm, grounded and not afraid. Imagine as vividly as possible what you desire. Feel what it would be like.

In this calm, centred state of mind, state your wish silently to yourself three times. Then repeat the alternate nostril breathing. Each time you exhale, imagine your wish rushing out into the world, where it will manifest.

happen? Once she had grappled with a worst-case scenario, the absolute bottom line, she was able to deal more lucidly with the situation and took the necessary steps to straighten out her life.

She also realized that her fears were telling her to deal with the situation now instead of procrastinating in the hopes that things would improve on their own.

Identify your fear: that sounds pretty basic, but it isn't as easy to do as you might think. For Edie, her fear about problems in her marriage was actually a fear about not being able to provide for her daughter and the new baby when it arrived. *Her bottom line fear was of her finances.*

Another method to break through the fear barrier is to *release it.* I have a friend who, when confronted with a fear, finds an object to represent the fear, then takes a hammer to it, shattering it. Physical exercise sometimes serves the same purpose. When you find yourself in the grip of fear, head for the outdoors, if you can, and walk fast.

Occasionally, nothing seems to work to break the hold a particular fear has on you. In that case, you simply have to keep working with it and live through it.

Getting Through Lean Times

In lean times, draw on every tool and resource that you have – spells, affirmations and visualization; dreams and oracles, power totems, colours, everything discussed so far in this book. In addition, you have to take action in the ordinary world – network with friends and accept emotional support from friends and family and any groups to which you belong. Recognize that it's OK to depend on others when you have to, especially when that support is offered.

In lean times, it's helpful to take stock of what is working in your life, rather than focusing on what you don't have or what isn't working. Instead of bemoaning what's happened, try to look at it as an opportunity.

If you've lost your job, consider it as an opportunity to redirect your life towards work that is more satisfying. If your marriage has fallen apart, consider it an opportunity to get to know yourself as an

Nothing to Fear But Fear Itself

'You cannot be hounded from one level of reality to another by a fear that you do not understand. You cannot be threatened in this life by fears from your early childhood, or by so-called past existences, unless you so thoroughly believe in the nature of fear that you allow yourselves to be conquered by it.'

Seth
Seth Speaks

individual rather than as half of a pair. If you didn't get the job you wanted, didn't sell your screenplay or novel, didn't land an account you went after, there may be reasons for it that you can't see yet. At times, we may glimpse the bigger picture of our lives, but usually we don't live in that big picture. We live in the connect-the-dots scenario, the daily minutiae.

Years ago, I was sacked from a job as a children's librarian. At the time, I was devastated. But in retrospect, it was the best thing that ever happened to me. I didn't like the job, my boss or the city in which I lived. I dreaded going to work in the morning, I used to hide out in the basement during my lunch hour just to avoid my boss, and when I went home in the evening I was so tired I could barely muster the energy to cook dinner and have a shower. I had convinced myself I couldn't leave the job, so the universe took care of it for me and I got fired.

I was unemployed for about seven months, but eventually found a job in social work in another town. In that town, I met a man who eventually became my first agent. By resisting the change I knew I had to make (leaving the job as a children's librarian), I made things more difficult for myself. It's easier to go with the flow than it is to resist. Try to look at adversity as opportunity. If you can't do it, then pretend. If you pretend long enough, you'll eventually trick yourself into believing it's true. If you live with the trick long enough, it eventually becomes your belief.

These five 'attitude adjustments' will help you navigate lean times more easily:

· Use all your resources
· Focus on what is working in your life
· Use adversity as opportunity
· Don't resist change; try to go with the flow
· Trust the process – we rarely have the full picture

Lean Times Affirmations

During lean times, try these affirmations. Write or type them out and post them where you see them frequently.

1. I am now pulling in abundance and happiness.
2. My life is filled with great experiences.
3. I am grateful for all that I have.
4. I heal daily.
5. I give love freely.
6. I forgive and release.
7. I am moving forward with trust and love.

Recapitulation

During Carlos Castaneda's relationship with Don Juan (see chapter 5), he reached a point where he needed to remember everything that had happened to him in order to increase his personal power. *Everything.* Every experience, every nuance, every detail. In essence, the process of remembering – of recapitulation – allowed him to take back the power he had invested in these experiences so that the power would be at his disposal *now*.

You aren't going to try to remember everything that's ever happened to you. You're only going to try to remember the major events of your life that have been great. Maybe you had a fantastic childhood. Maybe you have a wonderful marriage or a terrific career. Perhaps you have loyal, compassionate friends or close relationships with your siblings. Without giving it too much thought, list five things in your life, past or present, that have been or are about as near perfect as possible:

1. _____
2. _____
3. _____
4. _____
5. _____

Allow yourself to sink into the feeling of these experiences, regardless of how far back in time they happened. Fill yourself with the euphoria and warmth of these experiences. If you have old photo albums with pictures that remind you of these experiences, then by all means get out the pictures, mull them over, create a collage of the good things in your life.

In a sense, this activity allows you to recapture the power of those moments. You feel grateful for everything you have in your life and less bitter about what has gone wrong. In fact, if you do this at least once a day during lean times, you won't be in a blue funk for very long. And once your mood lifts, so do your thoughts and beliefs, and pretty soon your reality also shifts.

That's the true meaning of magic.

Psychic Change, Personal Power

'Any time we are moving up to or through a major psychic change, we do so best by drawing our energy into our own core and beginning to keep our own counsel.'

Julia Cameron
Vein of Gold

Bibliomancy

I considered putting this section in the chapter that includes oracles, but decided it fits better here because it can illuminate your path through lean times.

Bibliomancy is simply asking a question, then opening a book and pointing your finger at a particular line or word, which will be your answer. Sometimes, the response is precise, other times it leaves you with even more questions. But it's fast, you can do it anywhere, and I believe that when you do it with sincerity, it works well.

My husband is especially good at this, particularly when he uses a dictionary. You may prefer using a Bible, a novel or some other kind of book. Whatever you use, it should be a book that has some personal significance for you.

Sometimes, bibliomancy gives you a silly answer, something that doesn't fit even if you really stretch the metaphor. When that happens, just leave it alone and come back to the book later, with the same question, but reworded. If you still don't get a sensible answer, then give it up. Apparently you aren't supposed to know the answer. Or maybe the energy that governs your question is still in flux, still forming.

Visualizations for Lean Times

Create a visualization for each of your energy centres. Use the colour and emotional correspondence lists in Chapter 13 on health spells to aid you in creating an appropriate visualization.

First, for each chakra, define your purpose for the visualization. Do you want to bolster the chakra's energy? To heighten your awareness of the energy? To use the energy in some specific way?

Next, select images for each chakra that are familiar to you. It makes them more powerful.

Don't work with all the chakras at once. Work with one a day, for a week. As you become more practised, you can do your chakra visualizations anywhere, at any time.

Chapter Sixteen
Travel Spells

Foreign Travel

To stack the deck in your favour during travel, follow these simple guidelines:

1. Try not to travel when Mercury is retrograde.
2. Prepare your travel charm bag three nights before you leave. That way, if you change your mind about what to include, you still have time to reorganize.
3. The night before you leave, do the spell for a smooth journey.
4. Pack a journal.
5. Before you fall asleep the night before your trip, vividly imagine your arrival at your destination – on time, refreshed, and ready to explore.
6. Get a copy of Michael Crichton's book *Travels* for your trip.

If you fly regularly at all, you're no doubt familiar with this scenario. You arrive at the airport an hour or more ahead of your flight, check your bags, and half an hour later find out the flight is going to be delayed two hours or has been cancelled.

Maybe you're fortunate and your flight leaves on time, but every seat is filled and you're crammed in a window seat next to someone who sneezes constantly during the flight or has a crying baby. To make things worse, the person in front of you lowers the back of his or her seat all the way down, so that your knees are nearly crammed under your chin.

Welcome to air travel in the twenty-first century. Even if you arrive at your destination on time, the physical discomforts of air travel are often considerable and they, in turn, create emotional turmoil. Is there any way to mitigate the effects?

The Physical Factors

To counter space constraints on a flight, your best bet is to extend your aura. People generally sense each other's boundaries, and if your energy extends several feet from your body, it's less likely that someone will violate your personal space.

Extending Your Energy Field for Travel

Ten or fifteen minutes before you board your flight, sit with your feet flat on the floor and focus on the tips of your shoes. Stare until your vision begins to blur, then imagine yourself in a cocoon of white light.

The cocoon should encompass all of you, from the tips of your toes to the top of your head. At first the cocoon may be small, extending a few inches from your body. Imagine the cocoon expanding, filling with even more light. Colour the light if you want – just about any colour except black will work. Imagine the cocoon of light expanding until it stretches several feet from your body in all directions.

When you feel the energy has expanded to where you want it, silently repeat: *I am safe, protected, and comfortable throughout my flight.* Repeat this several times. Then give yourself the suggestions that every time you repeat this phrase, your energy field will automatically expand so that it stretches at least two or three feet from your body.

During your flight, repeat the phrase whenever you feel the need. If you do this when you're jammed in a window or middle seat, the person next to you is going to feel it. The person may shift his body away from yours. If you maintain the cocoon at several feet, the person may even get up and move to another seat – if there are any.

Dealing with the Person in Front of You

This activity is specifically targeted at the person directly in front of you who, ten minutes into the flight, drops his or her seat back so that your tray is now jammed into your kneecaps.

First, calm yourself. Resist the urge to jackknife your legs against the seat. Maintain your extended aura. Shut your eyes and focus on your heart. Visualize waves of soft, pale light pouring from your heart's energy centre. Extend the waves until they spill over the seat in front of you. Imagine the waves of light surrounding the person in front of you. When you feel reasonably sure that the light surrounds the person, silently request that the person puts the seat up.

Repeat your request several times. If this doesn't work, extend the light even farther. Your success is dependent on how vividly you can imagine the light.

How to Calm a Crying Baby

Infants are sensitive to the change in atmospheric pressure on a plane, and it's likely that crying may help them clear their ears. If you're seated next to or near a crying infant, the surest way to ease the child's misery – and by extension, your own – is to work from the heart energy centre.

Once again, imagine light pouring from your heart centre; this can be any pastel colour. Let the light surround the child, cradling it.

Your Travel Charm

The charm bag you use when you travel should contain fewer items than charm bags you use at home. It's a good idea to carry it close to your body. There should be at least one item inside which, when you touch it, communicates a strong sense of safety and protection.

When you feel the child within the light, rock the light gently, as though you were holding the child in your arms. Whisper to the child in your mind. Keep this up for several moments, even after the child stops crying.

Waxing Moon Travel

Tools: 1 white candle
Rosemary, essential oil or herb
Rose quartz

When: As needed, within twenty-four hours before your departure

If you're going to be travelling when the moon is waxing, this spell should be done the day before you leave. It's more powerful if you do it at night, but it can be done during the day as well.

Light the rosemary essential oil or herb. As you light the white candle, say aloud:

In the light of the growing moon,
I am protected and blessed in my journey,
And arrive at my destination soon.

Now extinguish the candle.

Waning Moon Travel

Tools: 1 white candle
1 gold candle
1 white flower in a bowl of water

When: As needed, or twenty-four hours before your departure

The waning moon is a time of decrease, so you need a bit of a boost when travelling under this moon phase. The white flower you use in this spell should be broken off just below the bud, so the petals float on the surface of the water. Any kind of white flower can be used.

As you light the candles, imagine that any negativity associated with your trip is absorbed by the flower. Then say aloud:

As time does tell,
My journey goes well.
So mote it be.

Now extinguish the candles.

Staying Centred

The flight was barely two hours long, but this flight was jammed to the hilt, every seat taken. Her window seat was in the next to the last row, and the other two seats were taken. Before the plane had even taxied to the runway, the woman in front of Jan decided to flop back her seat for a quick snooze. Jan abruptly found herself staring at the crown of the woman's head, unable to even bend forward for her bag, which held a bottle of water she desperately wanted just then.

Before she could ask her to put her seat upright, a terrible tightness spread through Jan's chest. 'I could barely breathe. A wave of intense heat flooded through me and I broke out in a cold sweat. I knew I was in the grips of an attack of claustrophobia and that if I didn't create space for myself – and very quickly – I was going to leap up and race, screaming, for the nearest door.'

She squeezed her eyes shut and forced herself to take deep breaths. She used a visualization technique to create space in her mind. She made the visualization vivid enough so that her body believed the image in her mind. By the time the plane took off, she was relatively calm, no longer sweating, and the woman in front of her had put up her seat.

Once during the flight, the woman in front of Jan put her seat back again and Jan was able to maintain the space in her mind and didn't panic. But she did ask the woman to put her seat up because it was simply too crowded, and the woman complied.

So what was the technique?

Before You Leave Home

Before you pull out of your drive or away from the kerb, take sixty seconds to surround your car with light. White light is probably the best because it's a symbol for protection, but pastels work, too. Avoid black and brilliant colours.

Imagine the light as a rubbery cocoon. Trust that you will glide along inside your cocoon through traffic both thick and sparse.

Creating Space in Your Head

This visualization technique works for claustrophobia, but also mitigates fear, near-panic, anxiety and high emotions.

Centre yourself with a couple of deep breaths, then create a mental image of a wide-open space. Jan conjured an image of the beach and the ocean. But any type of open space will do the same thing – a field, a park, an open country road.

The more personal the image, the better it works. Jan imagined a particular beach that she goes to, and she made it vivid: the hot sand against her bare feet, the scent of salt in the air, the blue perfection of the water, gulls screeching through the sunlight.

The tricky part is holding the image long enough to convince your body and emotions that the crisis has passed. But with practice, nearly anyone can do it.

Other Types of Travel

So far, we've concentrated on air travel. But, depending on where you're going and who you're with, travel by car can also be stressful. Any parent who travels by car with young children knows that it can be difficult. *Are we there yet? I have to go to the toilet. I'm bored.* Writer Nancy Pickard, however, had a more specific challenge. When her son was very young, he used to get car-sick.

She was reading Louise Hay at the time, and Hay said that the probable emotional cause of motion sickness was a fear of being trapped, of not being in control. Instead of trying to reason with her son about why he shouldn't feel trapped or afraid in the car, she came up with another solution. Every time her son started to feel sick in the car, she would start singing, 'I am in control'. Her son would start singing it, too, and pretty soon the motion sickness passed without problems.

A playful approach to fear or problems often dissolves the underlying emotion before it can take root and grow.

A sceptic might say that singing *I am in control* while a child is about to vomit in your back seat doesn't change anything. And that

---

It's in the Seeing

'The real voyage of discovery consists not in seeking new landscapes, but in having new eyes.'

Marcel Proust

same sceptic would probably say that affirmations, visualizations and spells are just so much hot air. My response to sceptics is that doubt is easy. It may be one of the easiest things any of us do. It's much harder to try something that contradicts your beliefs about what is possible just to see what happens.

Remember Castaneda's leap into the void? That's the sort of curiosity and trust we should cultivate. Quite often the best time to take the leap is when you travel by car. A long road trip or a trip to the supermarket or ballet lessons: the where is less important than the trying. So start small. The next time you're circling a car park in search of a parking space, *create the space in your head*. See the parking space, see yourself pulling into it, trust that it'll happen.

This type of manifestation is probably one of the simplest to do if your desire is strong enough. Try it yourself.

Spell for Smooth Sailing

This spell is great for travel in general, but is especially good for long distance air travel, foreign or domestic.

> Tools: 1 white candle
> Your favourite herb or aromatherapy burner and favourite essential oil
> Object that represents your trip
> When: Twenty-four hours before your departure

The day before your departure, light your herb or burner. As the scent permeates the air, light the candle and say aloud:

> *By this flame's bright light*
> *My trip to (name destination)*
> *Unfolds smoothly, on time, without blight.*
> *Make it so.*

Pass the object through the smoke of the herb or oil, then extinguish the burner and candle, and throw away the candle.

Compressing Time

This visualization technique comes in handy when you want to get where you're going very fast.

Wherever you are, shut your eyes, empty your mind and focus just on your breathing. When you're calm and centred, imagine your trip as a giant beach ball. Make it a vivid colour – red, purple, bright gold. The ball bounces across the sky or the road or the train track, however you're travelling. As you watch it bounce, make it shrink. Keep at it until the beach ball is hardly any larger than an ant. Keep focusing on that little shape and make it so small that it vanishes away altogether.

This is a way to compress time for any situation.

A Different Kind of Travel Experience

With a little practice, you can project your consciousness into the future. For starters, sit quietly and try to tune in on tomorrow's headlines or whether a favourite share will go up or down tomorrow. Record your impressions.

If you have more misses than hits in the beginning, don't worry about it. You're merely stretching muscles you may not have used for a while. Keep at it. With practice, you'll have more hits than misses. Once you get the hang of how to project your consciousness into the future, you'll be able to do it at any time for virtually anything.

Your Travelling Magic Kit

Kids operate under the wisdom of taking a blanket or toy with them when they travel. These objects help them acclimatize to a new place because they're familiar and comforting. Your travelling magic kit is intended to fulfill the same function.

Here are some suggestions about what to include in your kit.

1. Your favourite stone
2. A couple of sticks of your favourite incense
3. A perfume whose scent puts you in a calm, meditative state
4. A small candle
5. Cards, runes, even a pocket-sized dictionary for a quick check with the oracles
6. A travel-size, unopened container of sea salt
7. A journal to record dreams, experiences, random thoughts

My travel kit also includes a tiny frog for luck. If I'm stuck in traffic or in a travel situation where my anxiety level is rising, just touching the little frog calms me down. I also use it to create visualizations where I need to 'leap' ahead of something.

Your magic tools may vary from trip to trip. But you should probably have at least one object that's a staple.

Part III

Magic in Many Forms

Chapter Seventeen

Manifestation

The purest form of manifestation lies in the realm of the miraculous – the yogi who materializes a rose out of thin air, the cancer patient who goes suddenly and inexplicably into remission. For most of us, though, manifestation lies in creating a positive ambience for attracting what we desire. In this sense, a spell helps to focus our attention, clarify our intent and bring forth the full power of our emotions.

Most of us manifest things daily and don't even realize it. This happens at such a subtle level that we simply take it for granted or, in many instances, don't notice it at all. But in order to attract what we want, it's necessary to become aware of how we manifest the smaller things in our lives. And to do that, we need to pay attention to the thoughts and feelings that move through us daily.

In the brainstorming activity opposite, chart your emotions and moods for three consecutive mornings as you wake up. Keep a pencil and paper by your bed and jot down any dreams you can remember or thoughts and concerns you have upon awakening.

If your approach to each day is positive, upbeat and eager, then the chances are very good that the rest of your day will move along in the same way. If you get up in a bad or grumpy mood, angry at everything and everyone, then it's probable that the rest of your day will follow in that same vein.

As simplistic as this may sound, the bottom line here is that *like attracts like.* When your energy is positive, then you attract energy that is positive. When your emotions are running high and buoyant, you attract experiences and people that are also buoyant and upbeat. But don't take my word for it – try it for size. Pick a Monday, which is usually the blue day for most people, the beginning of the work week, the end of the weekend. As you wake, make a conscious choice to feel positive. It's not enough to merely think positive; in this experiment, you have to *feel* it. If you don't feel it, then somehow create a positive feeling before you even get out of bed.

One friend of mine creates this upbeat feeling tone by thinking of a pleasant experience she has had recently and then consciously conjuring the emotions she felt at the time. You will develop your own method for doing this. Once you have that warm, pleasant buzz

Dead or Alive?

'Everything is alive. What we call dead is an abstraction.'

David Bohm

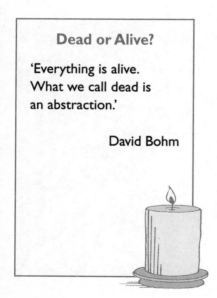

Brainstorming: How You Start Your Day

When you wake, are your first thoughts busy thoughts? Happy thoughts? Depressing? Do you anticipate starting your day or do you dread getting out of bed? Or are you indifferent? What is your general mood? If you recall any dreams, what is their general tone? Upbeat? Dark? Were the dreams in black and white or in colour?

What you're striving for in this section is detail about how you feel when you wake up.

Day 1

Your thoughts upon waking:_____

Your mood upon waking: _____

What dreams do you recall? Give details._____

How would you rate your overall mood and disposition? _____

_____

Day 2

Your thoughts upon waking:_____

Your mood upon waking: _____

What dreams do you recall? Give details._____

How would you rate your overall mood and disposition? _____

_____

Day 3

Your thoughts upon waking:_____

Your mood upon waking: _____

What dreams do you recall? Give details._____

How would you rate your overall mood and disposition? _____

_____

The Banner in the Wind

One windy day two monks were arguing about a flapping banner. The first said, 'I say the banner is moving, not the wind.' The second said, 'I say the wind is moving, not the banner.' A third monk passed by and said, 'The wind is not moving. The banner is not moving. Your minds are moving.'

Zen parable

humming along, keep it going while you get ready for your day. Smile at the first person you see. When you get to work, strive to keep the upbeat emotions buzzing along even if you feel yourself getting irritated by a boss or colleague's demands. This doesn't mean that you should deny the irritation or anger you might feel. Simply acknowledge it – then release it and go about your business.

The challenge, of course, is to maintain your upbeat mood even when things seem to be collapsing around you. This can require a tremendous leap of faith that everything will come out all right in the end, despite all the evidence to the contrary.

Putting This to Practical Use

Recently, our family moved. We thought we had planned everything well, down to the last detail. The day before the move, we planned to hire a van to move boxes of books into the garage of the home we were buying. On the morning of the move, the removals men were supposed to arrive at 7 AM, the completion on the home we were selling was supposed to take place at 11 AM, with completion on the new home to follow at 1 that afternoon.

We had worked out an arrangement with the owners of the home we were buying that we could be able to move our boxes of books into their garage the day before the move – we have a lot of books, and thought this would speed things along.

But the day before the move, the owners of the house we were buying had problems of their own and hadn't moved out yet. We had to move our boxes of books into their living room instead of the garage. I told myself this was a minor glitch and maintained my belief that everything would go smoothly the next day.

Only the Beginning

Yet, when I woke at 6 AM, I felt strangely apprehensive, on edge, and it was more than just moving day jitters. I ignored the feeling. By 8:10, the removals firm still hadn't arrived and I realized I had packed my moving file and didn't have the company's phone number handy.

Our phone service had already been disconnected, so I dug out my mobile phone to call directory enquiries – only to find that the mobile phone was dead. *What does that mean?* I wondered. But it was obvious what it meant on several levels – no communication.

I had to plug the phone into the lighter in our van to power it up and finally located the removals firm. It turned out that the day before, the company had called the house to confirm the move and my husband, believing the caller was a telemarketer, hung up on him. The removals company couldn't get a van to our home before 10 AM. Even then, I told myself this obstacle wasn't insurmountable. But my mood, *my feelings* were rapidly taking a downhill plunge. I ignored that, too.

At 11, the estate agent who represented the buyer arrived for the final walk-through of our house. He refused to sign off because our belongings weren't out of the house and because a spring in one of the windows had popped out and the window wouldn't close. Even this simple symbolism – the window not closing and, therefore, our not completing the house – eluded me.

The estate agent said he would return at 4:30 that afternoon and we could complete at 5. But what about the completion on our new home? I asked. 'Not my problem,' he replied.

The removals people then informed us that their lorry wouldn't accommodate all our things and they would have to make two trips, which would cost us more money. So we hired another van. I notified the other estate agents about what had happened, said that we wouldn't be able to close at 1, and things at that end began to fall apart as well. It suddenly looked as if we were going to be homeless, our belongings crammed into two lorries, which would have to go into storage until the next day, when we would be able to close on our new home.

The Mishaps Continue

The estate agents who sold us the new home arranged for a 'dry completion', where the papers are signed but the funds don't come in until the next day. My husband, she said, should 'plead his case' to the sellers of our new home so we could, at the very least, put our belongings in their garage. And could we move into the house tonight? I asked.

No, she replied. Until the funds came in, she said, we would have to stay in a bed and breakfast. My mood hit rock bottom. I couldn't conceive of the chaos this would create. Besides my husband, daughter and I, we had my father, three cats, a dog and a bird to contend with.

At this point, I fled the property with my daughter, one of her friends and our dog, and headed out in search of lunch and a reprieve. I realized I had been feeding into the negative energy of what had gone wrong and that energy was actually making things far worse. I asked Megan and her friend to help me reverse the situation by seeing us in our new house by that evening. We made it a game. We had some fun with it. I felt the energy begin to shift.

While we were out, we had to stop at the post office so I could get a money order that would cover the repair to the window that wouldn't close. I was feeling pretty awful by then, but I also sensed the energy could shift even farther to our advantage, so I smiled at the post office counter attendant, a woman who was usually rather sour and uncommunicative. To my complete astonishment, she smiled back and I thought: *this is going to work out. It has to work out. It will work out.*

The Happy Ending

A few minutes later, my mobile phone rang. The estate agent for our new house said the sellers had consented to let us move our things into their garage and that her husband would drive down to our completion at 5 PM, pick up the cheque, and run it over to the other estate agent so that we would complete on our new home. Eleven hours after the moving van had pulled up in front of our old home, we were in our new home, exhausted but grateful. And in retrospect, I know exactly when the energy shifted: in the car with two children who played along with my request and then again with that smile in the post office.

Fortunately, crisis isn't the emotional degree where most of us live out our daily lives. But this moving day example illustrates what happens when we feed into negative energy: it merely perpetuates itself. By the same token, positive energy also perpetuates itself. And it begins with the moment you open your eyes in the morning. So if you're hoping to manifest good things in your life, the next spell increases your chances of doing it.

Spell to Perpetuate Positive Energy

Tools: Music that lifts your mood
Aromatherapy burner
Eucalyptus essential oil (healing)
Frankincense resin (psychic awareness)
Geranium oil (love spells)
Jasmine essential oil (to sweeten the pot)
1 amber-coloured candle
1 pink candle
1 orange candle
1 red candle
When: New Moon

The New Moon is best for this spell because you're planting new seeds in your life. But you can do this spell on any night, whenever you need a boost of positive energy. When you have done it once, you can cast the spell in an abbreviated form during the day simply through the power of fragrance.

The music you select can be virtually anything that lifts you out of your own skin, music that transports you.

With your intent firmly in mind, put on your favourite uplifting music and add a drop of each oils to the water bowl of your burner. Light the frankincense resin candle in your burner so the fragrance of the oils and resin thickens in the air. Select a candle that feels right to you and place it to the north. Then, moving in a clockwise

The Inner Blueprint

'... reality is produced by a mixture of thoughts or information coming into contact with conscious but unformed material, what the physicist calls "quantum-stuff". The blueprints for reality construction exist within the mind; the patterns are in the implicate order. If the inner blueprint is strong enough, it moulds the inactive conscious material into object reality.'

Norman Friedman
Bridging Science and Spirit:
Common Elements in
David Bohm's Physics, the
Perennial Philosophy and Seth

direction, put the remaining candles at each of the cardinal points. Now move around the circle, lighting each candle and saying:

> *I enter the flow of All That Is.*
> *I am filling with loving kindness.*
> *I forgive and I release*
> *And I draw*
> *The best to me,*
> *So mote it be.*

As you work with this spell, change the wording to fit your needs. Don't get locked into a rigid way of doing this. All spells are merely a way to focus, and what works for me may not work for you.

While you're doing this spell, 'fold' your wish or desire into your thoughts and feelings. This is similar to what my daughter, her friend and I did in the car in the middle of our crisis. We visualized the end result and thrust ourselves into the feeling space of that desire.

The thought and the feeling are two parts of a whole. One without the other will work, but will probably take longer and may not work as well as the two together. Experiment. Have fun with it. When you find what works best for you, don't be afraid to use it whenever you feel the need.

Reality Shifts

In her book, *Excuse Me, Your Life Is Waiting*, author Lynn Grabhorn advocates that we 'create by feeling, not thought'. In her philosophy, 'Every car accident, job promotion, great or lousy lover, full or empty bank account, comes to us by the most elemental law of physics: like attracts like. And since most of us haven't felt too hot about what we've had for most of our lives, we've become highly gifted masters at attracting an overabundance of circumstances we'd rather not have.'

Grabhorn's premise is that we can all improve our lives if we learn how to *feel* our way into what we want. Robert Scheinfeld, in his book *The Invisible Path to Success*, advocates clarity and preciseness in stating what we want. Shakti Gawain, in her bestselling classic

---

Playing with Time

To test your inner sense of time, you need a partner. Sit quietly in a room that has no clocks or any visible way to tell time. Your partner should be in another room with a watch. Agree on a period of time – no less than five minutes, no more than fifteen. When you think the agreed upon time is up, signal to your partner.

You may surprise yourself.

Creative Visualization, says that if you can visualize it happening, something will happen.

These various ideas are actually united in a common thread that is reflected among such diverse writers as physicians Larry Dossey, Deepak Chopra, Mona Lisa Schulz and Judith Orloff; scientists Fritjof Capra, Norman Friedman, Karl Pribram, David Bohm and Rupert Sheldrake; and writers Gary Zukav, Jane Roberts, Caroline Myss and Michael Talbot. And this is just a very small list. The idea that has prevailed in our culture for hundreds of years – that reality is something that 'happens to us' – is rapidly being replaced by an emerging paradigm that says we 'create our reality' – every aspect of it – through our thoughts, feelings and beliefs.

And if we create our reality, then we can certainly change the parts of it that we're not crazy about. Spells, visualization, affirmations, prayer or any other type of focused intent all amount to basically the same thing: they are tools to shift reality.

The end result of any spell for manifestation occurs when your reality shifts. You find your soulmate, meet the love of your life, land a dream job, buy the perfect home: whatever you desire is attained. But our realities constantly eddy and shift, usually in ways so subtle that we barely notice or in ways so strange that we fail to process the importance of what has happened.

A recent e-mail from my friend June, a practitioner of Wicca, listed the top five ways in which reality shifts. You will probably recognize some of these examples as things that have happened to you or to someone you know. Psychologist Carl Jung called them synchronicities, and they tend to happen when we're feeling energized and flowing with the feeling of love.

On days when we're feeling high-strung and discordant, we tend to notice more chaotic shifts in reality. In this category would fall that missing sock that never comes out of the dryer or those car keys that we swear we left on the table last night and that seem to have walked off on their own into another room.

In reality shifts, we discover a wonderful buffet of changes that we can create in and around ourselves. Don't worry if you read through these examples and feel that none of these things have happened to you – if you want to experience them and start paying

The Power of the Mystical

'The most beautiful emotion we can experience is the mystical. It is the power of all true art and science.'

—Albert Einstein

Stretching Time

You know how some days seem to drag and other days seem to fly by? In this exercise, you're going to consciously stretch time. This is a useful tool for when you're on a deadline or having such a good time that you want the time to stretch out indefinitely.

Imagine a brightly coloured beach ball. This represents time. In your mind, you're going to stretch that beach ball as far as you possibly can in every direction until it looks flat. Hold the image and fold in your wish that time will stretch, that you'll be able to do everything you need to do and enjoy whatever you want to enjoy.

attention to the possibility that these things can happen, you'll be more likely to notice them in the future.

The five top reality shifts are:

1. **Appearances.** Groceries in the cupboard and fridge that we swear we didn't buy; letters in the post or post arriving more than once on a given day; a book, record, clothing, toy or anything else that arrives in a shop where the item was out of stock only minutes before; friends who show up, write or phone just as you were thinking of them.

2. **Disappearances.** A car that vanishes in the road ahead of you or in the spot where you need to park; traffic that clears up ahead of you when only moments earlier a traffic jam was imminent; household or personal items that vanish without a trace for no apparent reason.

3. **Transportations.** Things thought to be lost years ago arrive unexpectedly and in mysterious ways; something needed from a distant location arrives without explanation or any apparent means of delivery; objects move back and forth between friends' houses without anyone carrying them there; keys and coats, glasses and wallets move around inside our homes without anyone moving them.

4. **Transformations.** Cuts, bruises and burns vanish; hair that was straight becomes curly; facial features change; traffic lights suddenly turn green when they were about to turn yellow.

5. **Changes in time.** Time slows down, stops altogether or speeds up.

Once you begin to notice these types of shifts in your own life, it means that you are learning to manifest. By becoming aware of these smaller manifestations, you empower yourself to consciously create the reality that you desire.

Chapter Eighteen
Unseen Worlds

The unseen world is very much a part of magical tradition. Everyone has his or her own experiences of this invisible world and of how it works. If you're truly committed to your exploration of the unseen, there are other facets of it about which you should be aware.

Spiritual Guidance

At some point, your magical practice is bound to entail spiritual guidance. Many practitioners have guides whom they call upon for help, illumination, intervention and just general advice and wisdom. There are many ways to connect with your guides – meditation, guided imagery, visualization, dreams, relaxation techniques, even a simple request.

One of the first questions that arises when 'spiritual guidance' is mentioned is the identity of the guide: who is it? In theory, your guide is an entity or personality essence that accompanies you through your life. You may think of this entity as a guardian angel. If you don't believe in angels, then think of this guide as part of your higher self, or as an evolved spirit who has your best interests at heart, or even as someone you love who has passed on. A guide may even be the soul of someone you have known in a past life.

Brian Weiss, a psychiatrist and author of *Many Lives, Many Masters* and several other bestselling books, refers numerous times to the 'masters'. He defines them as evolved beings and first became aware of them when he was working with a patient whom he calls Katherine, a patient whose hypnotic treatment for other problems resulted in her regressing to former lives, where her problems actually originated.

At one point in her therapy, while Katherine was under hypnosis, she began to speak in a slightly different voice. The voice explained that the reason Weiss's young son had died twenty days after birth was because his soul was highly evolved and that he was 'paying off' karma for Weiss and his wife. Weiss doesn't mention what the 'karma' was. But karma of any kind is a debt we bring in with us from other lives. Weiss was shocked; Katherine knew nothing about his young son, who had died in 1974 from a congenital heart defect.

Over the years, Weiss has had other communications with the masters, which he writes about in his book.

Judith Orloff says that one of her guides is Kuan Yin, a Chinese goddess of compassion. For years, she has worn a green jade pendant of Kuan Yin 'for protection and to open my heart'.

She recommends burning sage during the meditative session when you're trying to contact your guides. If you have another favourite herb or essential oil, burn that as well. You can also light different coloured candles. In other words, do anything that helps you relax and that puts you in the right frame of mind.

Caroline Myss refers to 'receiving guidance' and relates it specifically to health and illness. 'In every situation, no matter how challenging, you have the option to pursue the meaning behind the event', she writes in *Why People Don't Heal and How They Can*. According to Myss in the same book, we react to crisis by using 'three powers in the same order we have developed them... Tribal, Individual and Symbolic'.

Of the three, Symbolic is the most meaningful in terms of guidance. Instead of making crisis personal by asking, *Why me?* Myss advises that we ask, *Why is this happening? How can I best respond to it?* 'Think of your crisis as happening to someone you don't even know, and ask yourself how you would advise them. From this position, you will be receptive to guidance and the clearest level of insight.'

Sun Signs and Contacting Your Guide

Suppose you're not a particularly meditative person? Suppose you're too restless and impatient to sit in a dark room, waiting for your guide to appear? I sympathize. I'm not very good at meditation for exactly that reason. But that doesn't automatically deny us the ability to meet our guides.

The differences in our individual temperaments mean, among other things, that what works for one person in contacting his or her

Taurus and Spiritual Guidance

Your spiritual guidance, Taurus, comes through most clearly during intense, transformative experiences. The experiences don't have to be unpleasant – there's nothing to be gained by suffering – but the experiences will definitely be profound. Sex can serve this purpose for you. So can marriage, birth, death, divorce and illness.

Once you discover your guidance, you can tap it at any time, anywhere. You merely have to make a silent request, shut your eyes or put yourself in a light, meditative state and trust that inner voices come through loud and clear. The challenge for you is following the advice you get from spirit. As a fixed earth sign, you're the most stubborn in the zodiac. It takes a lot to convince you to change your mind.

Gemini and Spiritual Guidance

There always comes a point for you, Gemini, when the books you read or the information you cull simply doesn't answer all your questions. That's when you need to strike out on your quest for spiritual guidance. You do it out of some burning need to *know, to experience.*

You, like Aries, are too impatient and restless to meditate, unless it's for seconds at a time. A creative pursuit, however, frees your busy mind and allows spirit to flow through you. When you travel, your spiritual guidance also comes through easily, almost effortlessly, perhaps because you're taken out of your familiar environment. You also receive guidance through listening to other people – listening not with your mind, but with your heart.

guide probably won't work for someone else. Locate your sun sign in the list and discover a technique that might work for you.

How to Get Started

Here are the basics:

1. **Desire is imperative.** You have to really want to embark on this particular journey. It has to matter to you. Otherwise, you're just going through the motions.
2. **Make a gesture.** Decide what type of method best suits your temperament. Then commit to doing it a few minutes each day. Five minutes. Ten. It doesn't have to be a three-hour meditative session.
3. **Keep notes.** A notebook will do. If you aren't the writing type, then talk into a tape recorder. This not only gives you a record of what your guide advises, but builds confidence in the impressions you receive.
4. **Trust the process.** This is an area where many of us fall short. Maybe it's simply part of Western culture, maybe it's just habit. But to be open to and receive spiritual guidance, trust is vital.
5. **Have fun.** When it comes to spiritual issues, we have trouble having fun because we've got the notion, somehow, that spirituality must be, well, *serious.* But if you don't enjoy it, don't do it.
6. **Put your spiritual guidance to use.** It's meant to be pragmatic. It's meant to help you create a better life.

Things That Go Bump in the Night

In *Energy Medicine*, Donna Eden tells a disturbing story about how negative entities can attach themselves to people. 'When entering deeply into another's being, you sometimes open to forces you never invited, wanted or expected', she writes.

A patient, Jim, kept losing control of his car and had come to Eden for help. When she tried to work with him, it seemed that she couldn't get her hands closer than four inches from his body. It was as if an invisible wall were there. A barrier. She finally forced her hands through the barrier and described the sensation as 'ominous'. Quite soon, she started to feel ill.

She worked on him for forty-five minutes, couldn't 'connect with his energy', and suggested that he make another appointment. The rest of her day and night were terrible. In addition to a general sense of malaise, she felt acute discomfort in her lower back. 'Looking back, it felt like I was possessed, though I wasn't thinking in those terms at the time. It was as if something had me in its grip.'

After a sleepless night, she rose early, uncertain about what to do. She had clients to see, things to do, but the discomfort continued. Her husband suggested that she ask her guides what she should do. 'What I heard was that by breaking through Jim's energy barrier, I had taken on the spirit that had been in him. It had left him completely and was now in me. Evil spirits were a foreign concept to me, but I couldn't deny that something real and painful seemed to be slamming against my [lower back].'

When she told her husband what she'd received from her guidance, he performed an exorcism. Eden saw a greyish mass lift up from her body and rise through the ceiling. Then she fell asleep. When she finally woke, her husband was very agitated. He wanted to know where 'it' had gone. When Eden told him, she realized that her husband's work room was above the ceiling, in the attic, where the mass had gone. He told her that the file where he kept the novel he'd been working on – and which he hadn't backed up – had crashed.

Her patient, Jim, reported that their session together had been a complete success.

When we open ourselves to this shadowy inner world, we may also be opening ourselves to energy that doesn't necessarily have our best interests at heart. Even if you don't believe in evil spirits, it's wise to visualize some type of protection around yourself before doing inner work. Say a prayer that holds special meaning for you. Imagine

Cancer and Spiritual Guidance

You don't have any problem communicating with your spiritual guidance. In fact, this inner voice has been a part of your life for so long, you nearly take it for granted. Your challenge is to put your spiritual guidance to practical use.

To do this, you should lay down a strategy and a plan. In what areas of your life can spiritual guidance be most helpful? How can it be helpful? You may have problems initially at putting spiritual matters into such a pragmatic context. But by doing so, you ground yourself more firmly in the physical world and learn how to use your spiritual guidance to improve your life in the here and now.

Leo and Spiritual Guidance

You know more than you tell about spiritual guidance, perhaps out of fear that you will be ridiculed. You need to put that fear aside because it's going to hold you back from tapping into one of your greatest resources.

It behoves you to take a couple of workshops about spiritual guidance or communication with guides, whatever term you want to call it. This would enable you to learn about the process, to talk about your own experiences without fear of ridicule. You would see that spiritual guidance doesn't detract from your individuality at all; it enhances it. You would learn that what benefits one, benefits all.

a white light of protection around yourself. Don't become obsessed about it – but don't ignore some basic precautions.

Ghosts and the Buildings They Haunt

Poltergeist, The Sixth Sense, The Haunting, The Shining: these stories are all about ghosts. But, strictly speaking, a ghost is simply an entity that doesn't realize it is dead. It's become stuck wherever it is.

I never had any problem with the intellectual concept of a ghost. But one night in central Florida, I discovered that I had a very big problem with the emotional impact of ghosts. My husband, daughter and I had gone to Cassadaga, a Spiritualist community just north of Disney World, to visit Hazel West, a friend who is one of Cassadaga's mediums. She suggested that we stay at the Cassadaga Hotel. Our daughter was about a year old at the time, and the proprietor was kind enough to give us two rooms on the top floor.

We noticed that the hotel didn't have many patrons. In fact, we never saw another guest during our twenty-four hours there. The hotel was undergoing renovations. After a pleasant dinner and evening with Hazel and her husband, we returned to our room.

About 1 AM, both Rob and I were woken by a thundering echo that seemed to shake the entire hotel. We turned on the bedroom light and glanced around the room, then looked out the window. Quiet on both fronts. We hurried over to the door and pressed our ears to the wood. The echo sounded like footsteps on the stairs. The footsteps of a giant.

We remained like that for several moments, listening. The footsteps were coming up the stairs. Getting closer. I leaped away from the door and started pushing the dressers towards the door. Rob just stared at me for a moment, obviously certain that I had lost my mind.

'What the hell are you doing?' he whispered.

'They're coming,' I whispered back. 'I'm blocking the doors.'

At the next echoing footstep, he leaped forward and we got the dressers pushed against the doors, blocking them. Then we ran back to the beds, grabbed our daughter and huddled near the window for what seemed a very long time, but probably wasn't.

The footsteps got closer. Our hearts beat faster, harder. I remember it was winter, quite cold out, by the standards for central Florida, and I pressed my face to the cold glass of the window, frantically searching for a fire escape or some other way to get out and down to the pavement. I was in the middle of a full-blown panic, no doubt about it.

If memory serves me, the footsteps reached the top floor, where we were. Then they stopped. For the longest time, we heard nothing but silence. Then there was one final thundering noise, like a punctuation mark, then nothing.

We eventually crawled back into bed and, somehow, managed to go back to sleep. The next day, I asked the woman at the desk if anyone else was staying on the third floor of the hotel. No, she said. We were the only guests in the entire place. When we mentioned our experience to Hazel and her husband, Art, they exchanged a glance, then Hazel replied, 'There are stories that the hotel is haunted. But I hear it's a friendly ghost.'

Even if you don't do energy work, like Eden, that requires you to have physical contact with another person, these types of experiences can happen because you are opening yourself to the unseen. I would like very much to be glib about this and say that if something similar happens to you, just turn over and shut your eyes and pull the blankets over your head. Actually, this probably isn't such bad advice. But if you do that, you'll miss the evidence of your perceptions. You'll miss the first-hand encounter.

E.T. Phone Home

It happens. You open yourself up to spiritual guidance and suddenly little grey beings are running around in your bedroom at night. Whitley Strieber knows about it. So does Budd Hopkins. And Betty Hill.

Strieber, author of *Communion* and other bestsellers, has spent much of his adult life trying to work out the alien and the

Virgo and Spiritual Guidance

You don't have any trouble believing in spiritual guidance. But you want the details. How does it work? Who or what is this energy that whispers to you? You want it to be practical. Ultimately, though, logic and reason may get in your way. Your best bet is to let yourself sink into the depths of your own being, in whatever way is most comfortable for you.

Your dreams, for instance, may be a source of spiritual guidance. Your guide may also speak to you through daydreams, fantasies and any sort of creative work you do. Keeping a journal will satisfy that part of you that needs details and will provide you with a running record of your spiritual work.

Libra and Spiritual Guidance

Someone you care about believing in spiritual guidance makes it easier for you to believe. But the bottom line is that you won't really *believe* until you strike out on your own, free of people's approval or disapproval.

Once you head into this adventure alone, you may sample every venue that exists for getting in touch with and communicating with your guide.

• • •

Pisces and Spiritual Guidance

This area is really your domain. You may be the kind of Pisces who has seen *things* since you were very small. You are comfortable in this netherworld, and it doesn't make much difference to you whether other people believe in spiritual guidance. However, to use your spiritual guidance to its fullest, you need to help other people connect as well.

alien abduction experience. Even after all these years, he hasn't arrived at any definite conclusion about what the aliens are or what they're doing, or what the deeper significance is about their appearance. But he has theories. That they're interdimensional. That they are us, in the future. That we have created them out of our collective unconscious. That they are none of the above.

Budd Hopkins, an artist by profession, identified one important pattern in the abduction scenario – missing time – and wrote about it in his book of the same name.

Betty Hill, who once called herself the original abductee, was the subject of at least two books after she claimed that she and her husband, Barney, were abducted in the early 1960s by aliens who performed horrendous experiments on them.

At this point, you're probably wondering what extra terrestrials have to do with spells. On the surface, they certainly don't seem to be connected. But as Michael Talbot notes in *The Holographic Universe*, '… their actual appearance may be so beyond our comprehension that it may be our own holographically organized minds that give them these shapes… our minds may also be sculpting the outward appearance of the UFO phenomenon'. If this is the case, he says, then perhaps the physical probings and experimentation reported by abductees may be symbolic: '… these nonphysical intelligences actually may be probing some portion of us for which we currently have no labels, perhaps the subtle anatomy of our energy selves or even our very souls. When our collective beliefs and emotions become high-pitched enough to create a psychic projection, perhaps what we are really doing is opening a doorway between this world and the next'.

This doesn't mean that if you begin casting spells or trying to connect with your spiritual guidance that you're going to be confronted with little grey beings with black, spooky eyes and terrifying powers. It does mean, however, that you may discover reality isn't at all what you thought it was.

Spells, Charms and Charlatans

If you consult psychics, you may run across one who will tell you that for *X* amount of money – usually an exorbitant amount – he or she will concoct a spell or create a charm that will win you your heart's desire. This is exactly the moment when you should run in the opposite direction.

In our quest for answers, wisdom and what tomorrow is going to bring, we are often vulnerable to charlatans. It doesn't happen just to naive people, either. When a friend and I went to another city on a business trip, we wandered into a district of bookshops and cafés and saw a sign for a psychic. At my suggestion, we went into the building for readings.

As we climbed the dark, dingy stairs, I began to feel immensely uncomfortable. The air smelled of mould, of places where the sun didn't reach, and I regretted suggesting that we get readings. My feeling intensified once we were in the psychic's flat, a place as dingy as the stairwell. The stink of cooking oil hung in the air, the rug was stained, the walls screamed for a fresh paint job.

The psychic was a perfect reflection of where she lived, and all I wanted was to get out of there. I signalled to my friend that my idea had been a bad one, but she wanted a reading. The two of them vanished into another room and I waited, my unease deepening by the second.

Later, as we were leaving the building, my friend said that the psychic had told her that for a certain amount of money, she would do a spell so that the man my friend was involved with would love her in return.

'I hope you told her to get lost', I replied.

'I paid her half the money up front.'

'How much money?'

'She told me not to tell you.'

Did the woman's relationship work out the way she'd hoped? No. Was she taken to the cleaners? Absolutely. She learned an invaluable lesson from the experience – and so did I. The best spells are the ones you do for yourself, and the best charms are those you create for yourself. To do otherwise is to surrender your power to another.

Scorpio and Spiritual Guidance

You connect with your spiritual guidance in the solitude of your own soul, within the vastness of nature. It's here that you hear inner voices most clearly, here that you feel guidance whispering to you from dense forests, here where the noise of a running stream may be the voice of your deepest connections with your spiritual universe.

In the beginning, you may share your experiences with only one other person, a partner whom you trust, or an old friend. But as you become more confident about your guide, it's likely that you'll reach out to others, perhaps to teach them what you have discovered – that spiritual guidance can't be controlled. It must unfold.

Sagittarius and Spiritual Guidance

You already feel that you're protected by higher powers. You may even be eager to share what you know with other people. But when it comes to spiritual guidance, keep your own counsel in the beginning. Check the facts of your experiences. Read books on the topic. Network with other people about it. Educate yourself. Let your left brain step in so it can organize the right-brain picture.

Once you're committed to this path of discovery, nothing can deter you. But remember: you can't change anyone else's beliefs. Your arguments, regardless of how persuasive they might be, are merely words to someone who isn't ready to embrace the idea of spiritual guidance. Know when to speak — and when to keep silent.

For every charlatan, however, there are honest, gifted psychics. The best way to find them is upon recommendation from other people who have gone to them.

Parting Thoughts

Regardless of the types of spells you do, they work only when your intent is focused and specific and when you don't attempt to hurt others. If you've done a spell, have given it a reasonable amount of time to work and nothing seems to be happening, then you need to do some fine-tuning.

First, re-evaluate your goal. Since you first did the spell, has your goal changed? If so, then revise your spell to reflect your needs and desires now.

If your goal has remained the same, then perhaps you should do the spell again, but with renewed passion and greater clarity about what you want. The more passion and emotion you put behind a spell, the greater the chances are that it will work quickly.

The other element about spells that we sometimes overlook is that they should be done in a spirit of fun and adventure. This isn't the same as doing a spell frivolously, just to see what happens. The difference lies in your attitude and in your intent.

When casting any spell, it's always wise to open with a prayer for protection for yourself and others. This prayer can be from a traditional religion or one that you create yourself. Make such a prayer your opening ritual.

Happy casting!

Capricorn and Spiritual Guidance

You see a hill and think, *I'll never reach the top.* But that doesn't stop you from trying. Your relationship with your spiritual guide is much the same. At first, you see it as an obstacle, a challenge that you must meet. Then you plot a strategy, come up with a plan for doing it. But the best route for you is the less aggressive one.

At first, approach your spiritual guidance as something that will simply enrich your life – not as a means to further your ambitious goals, although that can certainly be one of the results. Go within to find out what your guide has to say. Once you can do that, the world opens up to you.

Aquarius and Spiritual Guidance

You're no stranger to spiritual guidance. You've read about it, taken workshops about it, belonged to groups where the topic was discussed by people of like mind. You've connected with your guide time and again. But now, Aquarius, you must connect with guidance at the heart.

This can be a real challenge for such an intellectual sign. It means that you must *feel* your guidance, feel it in your body, in your blood. This brings bold, dramatic power to your spiritual guide – it brings the passion and ability to draw this energy into your external life in a way you've never experienced before. Throw yourself fully into wherever your passion lies. That's where your guide will come through most clearly.

The Sabbats in Wicca

The Sabbats are eight holidays in the course of the year that are compared to points on a wheel.

Yule, the winter solstice, December 20–23. Marks the beginning of the Wheel of the Year.

Brigid, Candlemas, February 2. Dedicated to Brigid, the goddess of fire and inspiration.

Spring Equinox, March 20–23. Celebrates the beginning of spring.

Beltane, May Eve. The traditional May Day celebration.

Litha, Summer Solstice, June 20–23. Celebrates the beginning of summer, the longest day of the year, and the beginning of the earth's descent into darkness as the days following grow shorter.

Lughnasad, August 1. Celebration before the harvest. The time of waiting.

Mabon, Autumn Equinox, September 20–23. Celebrates the time of harvest.

Samhain, Halloween, October 31. The ending of the year. The New Year.

Appendix

The Magic
of Flowers

This list is one of the most complete reference tools I've ever seen about the magical properties of flowers, so I've put it in an appendix so you can use it for easy reference.

African Violet

Gender: feminine; planet: Venus; element: water

Used for spirituality and protection. The purple-coloured flowers and plants are grown in the home to promote spirituality within. The plants are slightly protective.

Alyssum

(aka: alison, madwort)

Used for protection and moderating anger. Can be carried as an amulet. It has the power to 'ex-spell' charms. Also has the power to calm anger if placed in the hand or on the body!

Aster

Gender: feminine; planet: Venus; element: water; deity: Venus

This plant is used for love. It was the sacred flower of the Greek gods. Use in sachets; carry blooms to attract love.

Bachelor's Button

Gender: feminine; planet: Venus; element: water

Love, again. Wear it near your heart or carry it in your pocket.

Bluebell

(aka: harebell)

Used for luck and truth. Next time you see a bluebell, pick it up, concentrate, and say, 'Bluebell, bluebell, bring me luck before tomorrow night.' Slip it inside your shoe to seal the spell.

Burdock

(aka: cockleburr, hardock)

Gender: feminine; planet: Venus; element: water

Used for protection and healing. Cast around the home to ward off negativity. Add to protection incenses and use in such spells. Gather burdock root in the waning moon.

Carnation

Gender: masculine; planet: Sun; element: fire; deity: Jupiter

Used for protection, strength and healing. It was worn in Elizabethan times to prevent an untimely death by scaffold. Carnations can be used in all-purpose protection spells. Place in convalescent rooms to enhance strength and energy.

Chrysanthemum

(aka: mums)

Gender: masculine; planet: Sun; element: fire

Used for protection. Wearing the flowers protects against 'the wrath of the gods'. When grown in the garden, it protects the home from evil spirits (negative energies).

Cotton

Gender: feminine; planet: Moon; element: earth

Used for luck, healing, protection, rain and fishing magic. Cotton placed in a sugar bowl will bring luck. Burning cotton brings rain.

Crocus

Gender: feminine; planet: Venus; element: water

Used for love and visions. The plant, when grown, attracts love.

Daffodil

(aka: daffy-down-dilly, narcissus)

Gender: feminine; planet: Venus; element: water

Used for love, fertility and luck. The flower is placed on the altar for love spells, or carried for love. Placed in the bedroom, it aids in fertility. Pluck it and wear it next to the heart, and good luck will come your way.

Daisy

Gender: feminine; planet: Venus; element: water; deities: Freya, Artemis, Thor.

Think love and lust with this one. Sleep with a daisy root under your pillow to bring a lost lover home. When worn, the daisy brings love.

Deerstongue

(aka: vanilla leaf and wild vanilla)

Gender: masculine; planet: Mars; element: fire

Love and lust again. When it's worn or carried, it attracts men and can be sprinkled on the bed for that purpose. It is worn to help with psychic powers.

Elecampane

(aka: elf dock, elfwort, wild sunflower, among others)

Gender: masculine; planet: Mercury; element: air

Used for love, protection, psychic powers. Make a sachet of pink cloth out of the leaves or the flowers and wear it to attract love. It can be carried for protection and the herb can be smouldered on charcoal to enhance psychic ability, particularly when scrying.

Eyebright

Gender: masculine; planet: Sun; element: air

Mental and psychic powers. Brewed into a tea, eyebright clears the mind and aids in memory. Soak a cotton ball in brewed eyebright and place on closed eyes to aid in clairvoyance (this must be persisted with to achieve results).

Fumitory

(aka: earth smoke, fumiterry, vapour, wax dolls)

Gender: feminine; planet: Saturn; element: earth

Used for money and exorcism. An infusion of fumitory sprinkled around your home and rubbed onto your shoes once a week will bring money to you quickly. For centuries, fumitory has been burned to exorcise evil spirits/ negative energy.

Gardenia

Gender: feminine; planet: Moon; element: water

Used for love, peace, healing and spirituality. Fresh blossoms are placed in sickrooms or on healing altars to aid the process. Dried petals are mixed into healing incenses and mixtures. Dried gardenia is also scattered around a room to induce peaceful vibrations. Gardenia is used in love spells and is possessed of very high spiritual vibrations.

Geranium

Gender: feminine; planet: Venus; element: water

Fertility, love, health, protection. Geraniums of all types are protective when grown in the garden or brought into the home freshly cut and placed into water. A plot of red geraniums planted near a witch's cottage told of visitors coming – they were magically charged so the flowers would point in the direction of the approaching visitors. Banks or pots of reds are quite protective and strengthen health; pinks are used in love spells; whites are used to increase fertility.

Ground Ivy

(aka: cat's foot, haymaids, hedgmaids, turnhoofs, among many others)

Used for divination. Use ground ivy to discover who is working negative magic against you. Place the plant (in its herb form) around the base of a yellow candle and burn it on a Tuesday. The person will become known to you.

Heather

(aka: common heather, heath, ling, Scottish heather)

Gender: feminine; planet: Venus; element: water; deity: Isis

Used for protection, rain making and luck. Heather can be charged and carried to protect against rape and other violent crimes, or just to bring good luck. White heather is best for these. Heather, when burned with fern, attracts rain. It has long been used to conjure ghosts.

Honeysuckle

(aka: Dutch honeysuckle, goat's leaf, woodbine)

Gender: masculine; planet: Jupiter; element: earth

Used for money, psychic powers and protection. To bring money, ring a green candle with honeysuckle flowers or place them in a vase in the house. Lightly crush fresh flowers and rub on the forehead to heighten psychic powers. If a honeysuckle plant grows outside near your home, it will bring good luck. If it grows over your door, it will keep fevers at bay for the household.

Hibiscus

Gender: feminine; planet: Venus; element: water; deity: Isis

Used for lust, love and divination. Flowers of the red hibiscus are brewed into a strong tea, which is drunk for its lust-inducing powers. This drink was forbidden to women in ancient Egypt for this very reason.

Hydrangea

(aka: seven barks)

Used for hex breaking. To counter a hex, carry or scatter around the home, or burn.

Iris

Gender: feminine; planet: Venus; element: water; deity: Juno

Used for purification and wisdom. The iris, one of the loveliest flowers, has been used for purification since Roman times. The fresh flowers are placed in the room to cleanse it. The three points of its flowers symbolize faith, wisdom and valour, and so can be used to induce these qualities.

Jasmine

(aka: jessamin, moonlight on the grove)

Gender: feminine; planet: Moon; element: water; deity: Vishnu

Used for love, money and prophetic dreams. Dried jasmine flowers are added to sachets and other love mixtures. They will attract a spiritual (as opposed to a 'physical') love. The flowers will also attract wealth and money if carried, burned or worn. Jasmine will also cause prophetic dreams if burned in the bedroom, and the flowers are smelled to induce sleep.

Jade

In feng shui, this plant, with its small, rounded leaves, symbolizes prosperity and abundance. Put in your prosperity corner to attract wealth or in any room where you want to lift the energy.

Juniper

(aka: geneva, gin berry, gin plant, among others)

Gender: masculine; planet: Sun; element: fire

Used for protection, anti-theft, love, exorcism and health. Juniper is used throughout Europe for protection. It was probably one of the earliest incenses used by Mediterranean witches. Juniper hung at the door protects against evil forces and people and is burned in exorcism rites. If you carry a sprig, it protects against accidents and wild animal attacks. It also guards against ghosts and sickness. When carried or burned, juniper enhances psychic powers and breaks hexes and curses. Also drives off snakes.

Lavender

(aka: elf leaf, nard, nardus, spike)

Gender: masculine; planet: Mercury; element: air

Used for love, protection, sleep, chastity, longevity, purification, happiness and peace. Lavender has long been used in love spells and sachets. Clothing rubbed with the fragrant flowers (or placed in drawers with clothing) attracts love. Paper scented with the flower is used to write love letters. The scent particularly attracts men. Lavender water or oils were worn by prostitutes several centuries ago to attract customers. If worn, lavender protects against a cruel spouse.

The flowers are burned or smouldered to induce sleep and rest, and scattered around the home to maintain peacefulness. The plant is considered to be so powerful that if you gaze upon it, all sorrow will depart. The odour of lavender is conducive to long life and should be smelled as often as possible if this is a concern. Lavender is also used in healing mixtures, carried to make the user see ghosts, worn to protect against the evil eye, and added to purification baths. Despite lavender's love associations, in the Renaissance it was believed that, when mixed with rosemary and worn, it would preserve chastity.

Lilac

(aka: common lilac)

Gender: feminine; planet: Venus; element: water

Lilac is used for exorcism and protection. It drives away evil wherever it's planted or strewn. The New England lilac was originally planted to keep evil from the property. The flowers, when fresh, can be placed in a haunted house to help clear it.

Lily of the Valley

(aka: Jacob's ladder, ladder to heaven, lily constancy, may lily, Our Lady's tears)

Gender: masculine; planet: Mercury; element: air; deity: Apollo, Aesculapius

The lily is used to enhance mental powers and to attract happiness. It improves the memory and the mind. When placed in a room, these flowers cheer the heart and lift the spirits of those present.

Magnolia

(aka: blue magnolia, cucumber tree, swamp sassafras)

Gender: feminine; planet: Venus; element: water

Used for fertility. Place magnolia near or under the bed to ensure faithfulness.

Marigold

(aka: bride of the sun, calendula, drunkard, goldies, holigold, husband-man's dial, marybud, marygold, mary gowles, ruddles, summer's bride)

Gender: masculine; planet: Sun; element: fire

Used for protection, prophetic dreams, legal matters and the development and enhancement of psychic powers. Marigolds, when picked at noon, when the sun is at its hottest and strongest, will strengthen and comfort the heart. Garlands strung on the doorpost will stop evil from entering the house. When scattered under the bed, the petals protect you while you sleep and bring prophetic dreams. Especially effective in discovering a thief who has robbed you. Looking at the bright flowers strengthens your eyesight, and when carried in your pocket they will help justice smile favourably on you in court.

Morning Glory

(aka: bindweed)

Gender: masculine; planet: Saturn; element: water

Used for happiness and peace. Place the seeds beneath the pillow to stop all nightmares. Grown in the garden, blue morning glories bring peace and happiness. The root of the morning glory may be used as a substitute for the root of the herb High John the Conqueror.

Orange, Sweet

(aka: love fruit)
Gender: masculine; planet: Sun;
element: water

The flowers are used to attract love; fragrant orange blossom added to bath water entices a mate. Orange peel can also be added to love amulets.

Pansy

(aka: heart's ease, banewort, garden violet)
Gender: feminine; planet: Saturn; element: water

Associated with mental focus and remembrance, pansy is commonly believed to be a love flower, perhaps due to its heart-shaped petals.

Passion Flower

(aka grandilla, maracoc, maypops, passion vine)
Gender: feminine; planet: Venus; element: water

Passion flower is used in spells to attract love and friendship, and for emotional balance, peace and prosperity. A flower placed under the pillow is thought to encourage relaxation and sleep. Cultivate passion flower inside your home for domestic harmony.

Peace Lily

In feng shui, the peace lily is used to protect against negativity. Place a peace lily near electrical equipment such as televisions and computers to absorb electromagnetic emissions.

Peony

Gender: masculine; planet: Sun; element: fire; deity: Apollo, Paeon

In Japan, peony flowers symbolize happy marriage, fertility and wealth. In feng shui, peonies and peony images are displayed to attract romance. The dried root of the plant may be carried as a protection amulet.

Poppy

Gender: female; planet: Moon; element: water; deity: Hypnos, Ceres, Somnos

The seeds or seed pods are used as amulets to bring prosperity.

Primrose

(aka butter rose, English cowslip)
Gender: feminine; planet: Venus; element; fire; deity: Freya

Primrose is associated with protection. If you grow it in your garden, it is said to give protection to everyone in the home.

Rose

Gender: feminine; planet: Venus; element: water; deity: Venus, Demeter, Isis, Adonis

The flower, a traditional lovers' symbol, is used to attract love – to draw a lover to you, add rose petals to bath water. Rose also brings healing, joy, luck and protection, and may enhance psychic awareness; rose incense may be used in rituals for this purpose.

Rosemary

(aka dew of the sea, guardrobe, incensier)
Gender: masculine; planet: Sun; element; fire

Promoting faithfulness in love, rosemary is also associated with protection and healing. Carry a little sprig with you for a safe journey over water, or hang the herb in your home to protect your property. To improve concentration and memory, use rosemary essential oil in an aromatherapy burner or as a room mist (by adding a few drops to water in a mister bottle) which can be particularly helpful when working or studying at home.

Rue

(aka herbygrass, mother of the herbs)
Gender: masculine; planet: Sun; element: fire; deity: Diana

Used to aid recovery from ill-health and to expel negativity, rue is associated with boosting willpower and helping to banish negative patterns. The herb also brings protection when carried as an amulet or hung above a door. In mythology, it is associated with repentance. Inhaling the fresh herb is thought to clarify matters of the heart.

Saffron

(aka autumn crocus)
Gender: masculine; planet: Sun; element: fire

An infusion of saffron is used for bathing the hands before giving healing. In the East, saffron and water is poured over Buddhist temples as a ritual of purification.

Sage

Gender: masculine; planet: Jupiter; element: earth

In Native American tradition, sage and sweetgrass were key ingredients in herb bundles burned to purify, or 'smudge' a space. To space-clear after an argument, or when moving into a new home, burn a ready-made smudge stick or bundle and tie dried sage leaves with cotton thread, light and, waft the smoke into all corners of the space to be cleansed. Hold a saucer underneath to catch embers as you walk, and extinguish the stick when you have finished. Sage can also be carried as an amulet to promote wisdom, prosperity and healing.

Sunflower

Gender: masculine; planet: Sun; element: fire

Sleeping with a sunflower under the bed is believed to reveal the truth of any situation. The plant brings luck to whoever cultivates it, and in folklore sunflower seeds were eaten by women who wanted to conceive.

Thistle Flower

Gender: masculine; planet: Mars; element: fire

Associated with protection and healing, thistles and thistle flowers may also enhance spirituality and improve finances. The plant can be displayed to symbolize strength, or the flower carried as an amulet for joy and protection.

Thyme

Gender: feminine; planet: Venus; element: water

Thyme bestows courage and focuses energy – a sprig can be carried as an amulet, which some believe may also help you see fairies. A purifying herb, thyme is burned as preparation for magical ritual, and it is thought to enhance psychic powers. Women who wear a sprig of thyme in their hair will attract men.

Tulip

Planet: Venus

The tulip is associated with reconciliation, harmony and beauty.

Valerian

(aka all-heal, St George's herb, garden heliotrope, set well)

Gender: feminine; planet: Mercury; element: water

Valerian is associated with love and peace, and can be used in love spells and purification rituals.

Vanilla

Gender: masculine; planet: Jupiter; element: fire

Vanilla helps in love and seduction, and improving mental power. Carry a vanilla bean as an amulet for extra energy and focus, and particularly to enhance romance.

Vervain

(aka holy herb, herb of enchantment, Juno's tears)

Gender: feminine; planet: Venus; element: water

Vervain may be used to purify negativity, give protection and attract love; hang it in your home to benefit from its magic. The herb is also thought to lift the spirits, encourage creativity and bring prosperity, and aid divination.

Violet

(aka sweet violet)

Gender: feminine; planet: Venue; element: water

Associated with protection, violet can be carried as an amulet for protection and good luck, especially for love relationships. In folklore, picking the first violet of spring means you will have whatever you wish for.

Woodruff

(aka woodrove, herb walter)

Gender: masculine; planet: Mars; element: fire

A herb of purification and springtime, carrying woodruff as an amulet is believed to strengthen resolve during times of change, and bring success.

Yarrow Flower

Gender: feminine; planet: Venus; element: water

Yarrow enhances psychic ability, and is associated with love and protection. To dispel negative influences, carry a little dried yarrow as an amulet. A bunch of dried yarrow hung over the bed or yarrow used in wedding decorations is said to make love last for at least seven years.

FURTHER READING

In addition to the books mentioned in the text, the following are useful.

Abadie, M. J. *The Everything® Candlemaking Book*. Adams Media Corporation, 2002.

Adler, Margot. *Drawing Down the Moon*. Viking Penguin, 1997.

Andrews, Ted. *Animal-Speak*. Llewellyn Publications, 1993.

Ash, Steven. *Sacred Dreaming*. Sterling Publications, 2001.

Beyerl, Rev. Paul.
A Compendium of Herbal Magick. Phoenix Publishing, 1997.
The Master Book of Herbalism. Phoenix Publishing, 1985.

Bonewits, Isaac, and Philip Emmons Bonewits. *Real Magic*. Red Wheel, 1991.

Budapest, Zsuzsanna. *Grandmother of Time*. Harper San Francisco, 1989.

Budge, E.A. Wallis. *Amulets and Superstitions*. Dover Publications, 1978.

Campanelli, Pauline, and Don Campanelli. *Ancient Ways: Reclaiming Pagan Traditions*. Llewellyn Publications, 1991.

Cavendish, Richard. *History of Magick*. Penguin USA, 1991.

Cooper, J. C. *Symbolic and Mythological Animals*. Thorsons, 1992.

Cunningham, Scott.
Cunningham's Encyclopedia of Crystal, Gem and Metal Magic Llewellyn Publications, 1988.
The Magic of Food: Legends, Lore, and Spellwork. Llewellyn Publications, 1996.

Currot, Phyllis. *Book of Shadows*. Broadway Books, 1999.

Drew, A. J. *Wicca for Men*. Carol Publishing Group, 1998.

Frost, Gavin, and Yvonne Frost. *Good Witch's Bible*. Godolphin, 1999.

Gordon, Lesley. *Green Magic: Flowers, Plants, and Herbs in Lore and Legend*. Viking Press, 1977.

Graves, Robert. *The White Goddess*. The Noonday Press, 1997.

Green, Marian. *Natural Witchcraft: The Timeless Arts and Crafts of the Country Witch*. Thorsons Pub., 2002.

Hall, Manly Palmer *Secret Teachings of All Ages*. Philosophical Research Society, 1994.

Hutton, Ronald. *The Triumph of the Moon*. Oxford University Press, 2001.

Knight, Sirona. *Dream Magic*. Harper San Francisco, 2000.

Kunz, George Frederick. *The Curious Lore of Precious Stones*. Dover Publications, 1972.

Leach, Maria, and Jerome Fried, eds. *Funk and Wagnall's Standard Dictionary of Folklore, Mythology, and Legend*. Harper San Francisco, 1984.

McArthur, Margie. *Wisdom of the Elements*. Crossing Press, Inc., 1998.

Matthews, John. *The World Atlas of Divination*. Bulfinch, 1992.

Roche, Lorin. *Meditation Made Easy*. Harper San Francisco, 1998.

Starhawk: *The Spiral Dance*. HarperCollins, 1999.

Telesco, Patricia.
Dancing with Devas. Crossing Press, 1996.
Exploring Candle Magick: Candle Spells, Charms, Rituals, and Divination. New Page Books, 2001.
The Healer's Handbook. Samuel Weiser, Inc., 1997.
A Kitchen Witch's Cookbook. Llewellyn Publications, 1994.
The Language of Dreams. Crossing Press.1997.

Wilson, Colin. *The Atlas of Holy Places and Sacred Sites*. DK Publishing, 1996.

Index